THE GREAT ADVENTURE

America in the First World War

The Great Adventure

AMERICA IN THE FIRST WORLD WAR

BY PIERCE G. FREDERICKS

E. P. DUTTON & CO., INC.
New York   1960

Library of Congress Catalog Card Number: 60–12108

For

J.T.C.

No one ever had a better friend

CONTENTS

ILLUSTRATIONS

A concise history of the American participation in the war in photographic form will be found between pages 126 and 127.

THE MAPS

(By Vaughn Gray and Lucas Manditch)

TO BEGIN WITH . . .

IT is truly remarkable how little has been written about the American participation in the First World War. Stories about the air war had a certain vogue in the twenties and there have been two fine dramatic works—*What Price Glory* on the stage and *The Big Parade* on the screen—but the general neglect is such that Hanson Baldwin, the distinguished military editor of the New York *Times,* once called it "the forgotten war."

It was an important war for us. It made us one whole country as we had not been, perhaps, since the Civil War. It was the beginning of the breakdown of our traditional political isolationism. It began a movement toward France and Paris that profoundly influenced our arts, letters, and mores. As a military matter, it organized us for a national war for the first time and saw the beginning of our Air Force. More important, it saw us emerge—however unwillingly—as a member of the world family of nations. The ideal of the League of Nations that Woodrow Wilson held before us has been reborn as the United Nations, by no means perfect, but still our best hope of peace.

The country came on the world scene grudgingly—as a child grows to maturity—but we did come on. We took our place, a little simple-mindedly perhaps, a great joke to the older, more sophisticated diplomats of France and England. We made our mistakes and we managed to learn enough to correct some of them one war later. We're still learning to correct the remainder. The nation is old enough now to look back with some tolerance on these mistakes and to be proud that in the First World War we did dare to hold the seemingly impossible dream of permanent peace before the world.

PIERCE G. FREDERICKS

New York
May, 5, 1960

THE GREAT ADVENTURE

America in the First World War

Chapter One

"THERE IS ONE CHOICE WE CANNOT MAKE":

HOW THE WAR CAME

MONDAY evening, April 2, 1917, is a good time to start. President Woodrow Wilson has tried to make the hours pass by taking a walk and shooting a round of golf. Now, at twenty minutes past eight, he steps from the White House into his waiting car and sets out through the misty, drizzly evening toward the Capitol. A protective cavalry escort rides alongside; a man with a long memory might recall a similar troop escorting Lincoln to his first inaugural, spurring their horses to make them dance and throw off the aim of any southern hotheads in the crowd. Tonight the suspects are a handful of pacifist demonstrators who have milled through Washington all day, white tulips in their buttonholes. One, a young Princeton athlete, has so far forgotten himself as to take a punch at interventionist Republican Senator Henry Cabot Lodge. Lodge promptly punched him back.

Now in the streets, though, the pacifists are far outnumbered by people waving small American flags or red, white, and blue handkerchiefs, as they watch the cavalcade ride by.

Lit from below, the dome of the Capitol shines in the wet haze. Inside, in the House chamber, are the Senators, the Representatives, the Supreme Court, and the Diplomatic Corps. Mrs. Wilson has one of the seats in the packed galleries. Most of the members of Congress carry the same small flags to be seen in the streets outside.

Speaker Champ Clark announces, "The President of the United States," and there is a thunder of applause from these men and women summoned to receive "a communication concerning grave matters." French Ambassador Jean Jusserand and English Ambassador Sir Cecil Spring-Rice look "expectant and happy." Picking up the proclamation which he has typed himself, Wilson—his voice "husky with feeling"—begins to read.

Everyone knew what was coming. On Sunday, April 1, page one of the New York *Times*—an interventionist paper, to be sure—had carried a headline reading: "Congress Lining Up with Wilson; Patriotic Spirit on Eve of War." A press roundup in the *Literary Digest* had shown feeling summed up in phrases such as "neither virtue nor dignity in a nation which, being warred against for two years, still refuses the gage of battle . . ." ". . . it looks like war for this country of ours, with only one thing left to praise God for: that, if a war comes, it was not of our own making. . . ." Or, simply, "If Germany wants war with us, she shall have it." This last was from the Boston *Globe*, in a city full of anti-English Irish-Americans.[1]

Inside the *Times,* on that day before Wilson spoke, there had been a story on Ford car owners in New York forming a "machine-gun corps," and a society-page head: "Naval Officers Marry in Haste." Buried deep was an ironic little item: "New Drive to End Death Sentence." The rotogravure picture section featured the Officers Reserve Corps drilling, the Women's Self-Defense League simulating a bayonet charge, and the Philadelphia Athletics Baseball team getting close-order drill during spring training.

On the editorial page there was an attack on "Pacifist Sophistry," a tribute to the heroes of the American Revolution, and a box explaining that the editors felt obliged to accept pacifist advertising even though they didn't agree with it. The lead editorial denounced the telegram that German Foreign Secretary Alfred Zimmerman had dispatched to Mexico offering that nation Texas, New Mexico and Arizona if it declared war against the United States.

Wilson spoke on, nervously at first, then with greater assurance, and came to the words, "There is one choice we cannot make, we are incapable of making: We will not choose the path of submission. . . ."

On the instant old Chief Justice Edward White—Confederate veteran—was on his feet cheering, tears streaming down his face. Behind him the Congress and the galleries took up the roar. Only a few refrained. Senator Robert La Follette, the Progressive from Wisconsin, sat grimly, arms folded.

How had we come to it? This was a president whose campaign slogan the year before had been "He Kept Us Out of War." His conduct had caused the militant Teddy Roosevelt to howl that the country "is passing through the thick yellow mud streak of 'safety first.'" The very day before, Wilson's own ambassador to England, author and editor Walter Hines Page, had written, "He has not breathed a spirit into the people: he has encouraged them to supineness. He is *not* a leader, but rather a stubborn phrasemaker."[2]

The very night before this President had said to his friend Frank Cobb of the New York *World*: "Cobb, once lead the American people into war and they will forget there ever was such a thing as tolerance. To fight, you must be brutal and ruthless. The spirit of ruthless brutality will enter into the very fiber of our national life, infecting Congress, the courts, the policeman on the beat, the man in the street. Conformity will be the only virtue. And every man who refuses to conform will have to pay the penalty. If there is any alternative, for God's sake, let's take it!"[3]

Now, he was asking the Congress for war.

It is easy to laugh at the state of American diplomacy when war came to Europe in August of 1914. Our chief foreign preoccupation was a hurly-burly in Mexico where power was bouncing like a football between Carranza, Huerta, and Pancho Villa. Our troops went to Veracruz, but neither Wilson nor Secretary of State William Jennings Bryan was particularly happy about it. They knew what they did not want to do—impose a government on the Mexican people—but while that negative aim was a highly worthy one, they had no very firm positive objective with which to supplement it. We knew what we wanted—a democratic, stable government for Mexico, but the Mexicans stubbornly refused to produce the desired result. We were faced with a choice between evils—the situation in which great power diplomacy finds itself most of the time—but we were new at the game and didn't know quite what to do about it.

It is remarkable that Mr. Bryan was concerned with foreign affairs at all. Certainly nothing in his past experience had fitted him for the work. A lawyer and newspaperman who had removed from Illinois to Nebraska, he had first come to fame as an advocate of free silver as a means of getting the nation's farmers out of hock. Came the Democratic presidential nominating convention of 1896, and the Boy Orator from the Platte arose to deliver his "cross-of-gold" speech and cried, "You shall not press down upon the brow of

labor this crown of thorns, you shall not crucify mankind upon a
cross of gold!" His audience was so carried away that they nominated
him for president although he was only thirty-six years old. In spite
of an incredible 600 more speeches, William McKinley beat him
out in a close race.

During the Spanish-American War Bryan became colonel of a
regiment that never got overseas, and gave some hint of his stand
on foreign affairs by coming out against American acquisition of
the Philippines. In 1900 he ran for president again, and again
McKinley whipped him—this time by a larger margin. By 1904 conservative eastern Democrats were tired of losing with Bryan, and
lost with Judge Alton B. Parker instead. In 1908 it was back to
Bryan, and this time Teddy Roosevelt defeated him.

By 1912 the Republicans were so split between Roosevelt and
Taft that almost any Democrat could have won, but time had run
out on the aging Boy Orator. William Jennings Bryan had to take
what satisfaction he could from using his weight to win the nomination for a progressive Democrat, Wilson. As a reward, Wilson made
him his secretary of state. It was a politically logical but unhappy
choice. Here was a man whose major interests were in domestic,
not foreign matters. He had traveled little and brought to the job
what one would expect of a fundamentalist Presbyterian who before his death in 1925 would make headlines as attorney for the
prosecution in the Scopes Monkey Trial, at which he argued that
Jonah really had been swallowed by the whale.

In office Mr. Bryan ingenuously negotiated treaties with no less
than thirty-one countries whereby they consented to put their problems to arbitration and allow a period of one year for that arbitration
before going to war. The powers signed this ringing denunciation of
the man-eating shark and muttered about Mr. Bryan's sanity. A
little consideration of the Mexican matter might have convinced
Bryan that real life was somewhat more complicated, but he, like
most Americans of the day, regarded the job of secretary of state
as one which, properly conducted, would make itself unnecessary. An
international situation meant not that some genuine conflict of interests had arisen, but that someone had neglected to get the proper
number of anti-shark manifestoes signed. One must not laugh at Mr.
Bryan. As recently as Munich we would have to learn all over again

that peace, as an over-all proposition, is a splendid aim, but by itself no policy.

European war meant things were going to be different. Straight-talking David Houston, who was Wilson's secretary of agriculture, wrote about Sarajevo, "There had been so much fighting and turmoil in the Balkans that I had become accustomed to them. For the moment, it looked like more of the same thing on a larger and more serious scale." Came England's declaration of war, though, and "I had a feeling that the end of things had come. Figuratively speaking, I stopped in my tracks, dazed and horror-stricken."[4]

Sentiment was for neutrality. Wilson announced it after the invasion of Belgium: "We are a true friend of all nations of the world, because we threaten none, covet the possessions of none, desire the overthrow of none. . . . We are champions of peace and of concord." True, "peace and concord" had just gone out the window, but he abjured his country, "Every man who really loves America will act and speak in the true spirit of neutrality." Even Teddy Roosevelt declared at first, "It is certainly eminently desirable that we should remain entirely neutral."

It was going to be difficult. In the first place, American papers covered European news from London as a rule and the men who did the job were either Englishmen or Americans who had lived in England for years. By and large, they were honest men, but the totally objective reporter is as mythical as the Indian rope trick. What bias there was going to be in reporting this war was going to be in the Allies' favor. Moreover, the circumstances of the initial assault did the Central Powers no good. Austria had attacked "little Serbia," Germany had "raped bleeding Belgium." Historians would be able to see later that it was all a boiling over of great power rivalries going back for years, but at the moment it looked thoroughly as though the big guys were beating up the little guys.

In a note written the night before England declared war, Walter Hines Page made his feelings along these lines clearer than perhaps even he imagined at the time: "The possible consequences stagger the imagination. Germany has staked everything on her ability to win primacy. England and France (to say nothing of Russia) really ought to give her a drubbing. If they do flog Germany, Germany will for a long time be in discredit." Page might feel sympathy for "the poor German ambassador who has lost in his high game," but to Sir Edward Grey, the British foreign secretary, he was bound by all the ties of an American literary man in the great tradition. His biographer observes: "The enthusiasm that both men felt for Wordsworth's poetry in itself formed a strong bond of union." The side Page would take was abundantly clear—and no neutrality nonsense—as early as a month after the war began: "If German bureaucratic brute force could conquer Europe, presently it would try to conquer the United States; and we should all go back to the era of war as man's chief industry and back to the domination of kings by divine right. It seems to me, therefore, that the Hohenzollern idea must perish—be utterly strangled in the making of peace."[5]

A little later and Page would be concocting plans for preventing the American-owned ship *Dacia* from carrying supplies to Germany without getting the British Navy into further trouble for interfering with American trade. It was Page's notion that the French Navy—with which no one was particularly angry at the moment—make the seizure, and Sir Edward Grey thought it was an excellent suggestion.

For a time it appeared that the British trade restrictions might produce some pro-German feeling. The South lost the German cotton market which had taken more than three million bales a year. Then Allied war orders poured into the country and business, somewhat sluggish, began to boom.

And so it began—a feeling against German militarism, an irritation with British trade restrictions, and the general elation of good times at home. It was on May 1, 1915, that the first big crisis began to shape up. Over their morning coffee newspaper readers saw the advertisement inserted by the Imperial German Embassy:

NOTICE! TRAVELERS intending to embark on the Atlantic voyage are reminded that a state of war exists between Germany and her allies and Great Britain and her allies; that the zone of war includes waters adjacent to the British Isles, that in accordance with formal notice given by the Imperial German Government, vessels flying the flags of Great Britain or of any of her allies are liable to destruction in those waters and that travelers sailing in the war zone on ships of Great Britain or her allies do so at their own risk.

On the same day the British liner *Lusitania* left New York with

2,000 passengers and a hold full of rifle ammunition. "Sails Undisturbed by German Warning" was the headline in the *Times*.

And as she sailed, the submarine *U-20* out of Wilhelmshaven, and commanded by Senior Lieutenant Schweiger, was coming west on the prowl for shipping. It was Schweiger's intention to hunt where the main shipping lane to Liverpool runs along the Irish coast.

On May 6 he sank two steamers and Captain Turner of the *Lusitania* was getting wireless messages from the Admiralty advising him that submarines were active in his area. The doughty captain seemed not to have been bothered. In order to ride into Liverpool on the tide, he reduced his speed—an idiotic move in submarine waters—and he was under the incredible misapprehension that the Admiralty orders to steam a zigzag course—a standard anti-torpedo precaution—applied only when a submarine had actually been sighted. It was Schweiger who did the sighting off the Head of Kinsale. He promptly submerged and just after lunch on May 7 slammed one of his two remaining torpedoes into the *Lusitania's* starboard side. Fifteen minutes later the liner went down.

In all 1,195 passengers died. There were 124 dead out of 159 Americans aboard, among them Charles Frohman of theater fame, Alfred Gwynne Vanderbilt, and Elbert Hubbard, the celebrated inspirational writer and opponent of Prussianism.

Wilson was in a Cabinet meeting when a messenger delivered the news. As the details of the casualties came in, the President's eyes filled with tears and he told his secretary, chubby, shrewd New Jersey politico, Joseph Tumulty, "If I pondered over these tragic items . . . I should see red in everything . . . I dare not act unjustly and cannot indulge my own passionate feelings." The New York *World* reminded its readers that those Americans who died had disregarded a German warning not to sail, but no one paid much attention. From Teddy Roosevelt came a cry of "piracy" and in London Colonel Edward House, Wilson's diplomatic leg man, told a doubtless enthusiastic Page, "We shall be at war with Germany within a month."

Certainly House's guess was as good as any other American's and better than most. From being a behind-the-scenes political power in Texas, he had come North to be one of the leaders in the fight to get Wilson nominated in the first place and then stayed on as a behind-the-scenes power in the administration. A colonel by southern courtesy only, he never held an official position, but moved across the international stage much as Harry Hopkins did in the days of Franklin Roosevelt.

In early 1914 he had visited both the Kaiser and Sir Edward Grey in an effort to head off the war, and if the effort failed, this tough-minded, realistic man was certainly the most informed and experienced diplomat we had at the time. This time, though, his guess on war was going to turn out wrong.

A note went to Germany over Bryan's signature protesting that "submarines cannot be used against merchantmen without an inevitable violation of many sacred principles," and added that the United States would not omit "any word or act" necessary to permit its citizens to travel freely. Wilson, who had proclaimed our neutrality and said we wanted nothing from any power, now wanted one of those powers to give up one of its most effective weapons.

The Germans delayed their reply nearly two weeks, doubtless pondering how to blockade Britain if submarines were outlawed—and weighing the advantages of the blockade against the possibility of America coming into the war. Already the split between German diplomats—against bringing America in—and German admirals in favor of the submarine, was developing, and it was going to get worse.

When the reply came it complained that the *Lusitania* had been armed and that she would never have sunk so fast had she not carried ammunition, which exploded. It specifically avoided giving Wilson any assurance that more vessels would not be sunk and more American lives lost. Wilson drafted a second note demanding the assurances and Bryan refused to sign it.

"Germany has a right to prevent contraband going to the Allies," said the Secretary of State, not unreasonably. "I have had to take the course I have chosen. The President has had one view. I have had a different one. I do not censure him for thinking and acting as he thinks best. I cannot go along with him on this note. I think it makes for war. I must act according to my conscience. I go out into the dark."

And he resigned. From London Page growled in a letter to his son: "Again and ever I am reminded of the danger of having to do with cranks. A certain orderliness of mind and conduct seems essential for safety in this short life. Spiritualists, bone-rubbers, anti-vivisectionists, all sorts of antis, in fact, those who have fads about education or fads against it, perfectionists, Daughters of the Dove of Peace, Sons of the Roaring Torrent, itinerant peace mongers—all these may have a real genius among them once in forty years; but to look for an exception to the common run of yellow dogs and damfools among them is like opening oysters in hope of finding pearls. . . .This is the lesson of Bryan."

Teutonic delicacy was not to help matters much. A medal was struck off to celebrate the sinking and the head of the German Red Cross in the United States put it less than tactfully when he suggested that Americans should have stayed off the ship, and ended ". . . anybody can commit suicide if he wants to."

Nevertheless, Wilson, going to Philadelphia to address 4,000 recently naturalized immigrants, said that "there is such a thing as a man being too proud to fight." Partly, it must have been the statement of a man who hated war, a man who as a child had seen the whipped Confederates come home and the devastation left by Sherman's march. Partly, it must have been the statement of a politician who had just talked to Secretary of Agriculture Houston, home from a swing through the West, and been told . . . "the masses of people are not dreaming of our becoming involved in a war."

The martial Northeast howled in frustration, but the rest of the nation was willing to go along. The Des Moines *Register and Leader*, which had written a fire-eating editorial calling the sinking "deliberate murder," produced another urging, "trust the President." In all, three notes went to Germany and the matter was allowed to die. True, we now had a less peaceable secretary of state—New York lawyer Robert Lansing—but the consensus was that Wilson would be his own secretary of state from now on and Mr. Lansing's legal training would simply come in handy when it came to putting the President's feelings into official form.

In November the Italian liner *Ancona* went down in the Mediterranean, and in December the British ship *Persia* in the same sea; American lives were lost in both sinkings, and in some circles in Congress the notion began to germinate that the right of American citizens to travel in foreign ships really wasn't worth it if it was going to drag the nation into a war. In February, 1916, Senator Thomas Gore of Oklahoma introduced a resolution withholding passports from anyone wishing to travel this way, and Representative Jeff McLemore of Texas put a similar proposition before the House. Wilson now swung the other way, fought down both even though it meant a near break with Senator William Stone of Missouri, a fellow Democrat. "I cannot consent to any abridgement of the rights of our citizens in this respect," the President wrote him, seating himself firmly on the horns of a dilemma.

If Wilson's performance was calculated to give the willies to anyone who wanted to see him firmly on one side of the fence or the other, it should not have surprised those who knew him. Like Bryan, he was brought up a Presbyterian, and that creed puts a heavy personal responsibility on a man to be damn good and sure he's right before he moves. Moreover, he was no simple-minded Jonah-and-the-whale Presbyterian; his father was a sophisticated clergyman and professor of theology.

Wilson started as a lawyer, but even the law's discipline didn't satisfy his intellectual probings into the right and the wrong; he moved on to become a professor and later the president of Princeton University. Writing and speaking on political science, he came to national prominence and then the nation had a chance to see that when he did make up his mind, he didn't lack the courage to act. Princeton's academic standards were too low to suit Wilson, its life too dominated by its social clubs. He made changes and the trustees boiled up for a showdown fight. In the end, the trustees won, but Wilson came out of the brawl so bright and shiny that the New Jersey Democratic machine ran him for governor. He won, and the machine was appalled to find that this amateur really meant what he said. In machine-run Jersey conditions were so seamy that it wasn't hard for even a Presbyterian doubter to see the right thing to do. Wilson did right so hard and so often that within a year he had himself one of the most reformed states in the Union and Colonel House was touting him for president.

The Democratic convention of 1912 was held in the steamy heat of a Baltimore, Maryland, June, and it must have been obvious to the delegates from the beginning that they were going to sweat there for some time. The conservative easterners wanted no more of Bryan, but if Bryan couldn't win he had the prestige virtually to name the winner. His choice was Wilson and that did it, although they ran through forty-six ballots before the thing was finally done.

Actually, Wilson was the ideal man to unite the party. He was progressive enough for the West and the South, presentable enough for easterners, fearful of wild-eyed gallus snappers. For the first two years the New Freedom legislation would pour through—lowering tariffs, trust busting, liberalizing the banking system—until the war came to perplex the man who wanted to do right, as he had never been perplexed before. In Mexico he had tried to do right, but in the end had to call out the National Guard, which seemed to him not right, even though it meant training for the troops. Here, though, he could see a way out. Already he had in the works plans for what amounted to a League of Nations for Western Hemisphere nations. Now the experience was about to be repeated on a world scale.

The British blockade—surface warfare—interfered with American commerce. The German blockade—submarine warfare—killed Americans. Neither nation had any real choice; for either side permanently to abandon blockade would mean the loss of the war. To Americans, though, the subs seemed worse—however much German propagandists might cite German babies starved by the British Navy. The number of people the sub killed was infinitesimal compared to the men who died on the Western Front, but, like the German tank early in the Second World War, it had the power to terrify simply by seeming for the moment invincible.

Nevertheless, German diplomacy tried once more. In March, 1916, the French steamer *Sussex* went down in the English Channel. Wilson sent his strongest note: "Unless the Imperial Government should now immediately declare and effect an abandonment of its present methods of submarine warfare against passenger and freight-carrying vessels, the Government of the United States can have no choice but to sever diplomatic relations with the German Empire altogether."

The German diplomats were frightened. Count Johann von Bernstorff, their ambassador in Washington, was in receipt of instructions for sabotaging interned German liners should the worst come. In Berlin our ambassador, James Gerard, saw the situation as "almost hopeless." Then Von Bernstorff hustled around to Colonel House in

Washington and got what he hoped were assurances that if Germany consented to Wilson's demands equal pressure would be put on Britain to let up on the blockade. In Berlin the civilians used Von Bernstorff's maneuver to win one last battle with the army and navy and on May 4 a note came back: "Merchant vessels shall not be sunk without warning and without saving human lives unless those ships attempt to escape or offer resistance." True, it was also stated that if pressure on the British didn't work, "the German Government would be facing a new situation, in which it must reserve to itself complete liberty of decision," but for the moment we were still at peace, with the weapon most likely to pull us into war muzzled. At home there was satisfaction with a diplomatic victory; in London, Page and the English chortled, although perhaps for somewhat different reasons. "The more I think of it," Page wrote, "the better the strategy of the President appears in his latest . . . note to Germany. . . . The Germans had tried to 'put it up' to the President to commit the first unfriendly act. He now 'puts it up' to them. . . . But nobody here believes that they will long abstain from the luxury of crime."

The respite was to last just nine months.

While Wilson tried to hold his people to neutrality—there was even a rumor that Secretary of the Navy Daniels had forbidden American sailors to whistle "Tipperary"—there were a good many Americans who devoutly wished to see us in on the Allied side. Chief Justice White—he who led the cheering when Wilson asked for war— had said: "I wish I were thirty years younger, I would go to Canada and enlist." Vice President Thomas Marshall had obeyed the presidential injunction to keep his pro-Allied sentiments quiet, but once observed: "I am the only American possessed of a voice who followed that request." As early as 1915 General Leonard Wood, a vociferous whooper-upper for preparedness, had organized a volunteer, unofficial, pay-your-own-way "Businessman's Camp" at Plattsburg, New York, at which former Secretary of State Robert Bacon drilled under his son, a "lieutenant," and Bar Harbor and Newport complained of a falling off in social activities, so many eligible young men being away at Plattsburg. Teddy Roosevelt visited this array of militant youth and, pointing to a stray dog that had rolled over on its back to have its stomach rubbed, told reporters, "A very nice dog—his present attitude is strictly one of neutrality."

The British supplemented these efforts with a corps of visiting lecturers and the Germans felt at a loss for a successful counter. There was pacifist sentiment to be encouraged, but if this could conceivably deter aid to Britain, it promised none for Berlin. There were hyphenate-American societies to be formed like the American Truth Society, under a professional Irishman named Jeremiah O'Leary, but about the best these formations seemed capable of were anti-British convulsions.

In time more devious and violent schemes came to the Teutonic mind, and then, suddenly, all came a cropper. In July, 1915, two Secret-Service men followed George Sylvester Viereck, an avowed German propagandist, from his New York office and onto the Sixth Avenue El. With Viereck was an unidentified man who carried a brief case. When Viereck left the El, Secret Service man Frank Burke stayed with the brief-case bearer. He was rewarded by having his quarry nap, then dash off the El leaving the brief case behind. Burke promptly snatched it, left by another door, and ducked behind a crowd of passengers. In seconds its owner reappeared on the platform breathing hard. Burke leaped aboard a streetcar and made off while the gentleman gave chase on foot in a fair imitation of the Keystone Kops.

The brief case went to Secretary of the Treasury William Gibbs McAdoo, a strong interventionist, who promptly leaked the contents to the New York *World*. Shortly Americans knew that the man on the El was Dr. Heinrich E. Albert and that his apparatus had spent more than twenty-seven million dollars on various forms of propaganda and sabotage in the United States. True, none of these schemes had come to any great fruition. Equally true, the British were doing the same sort of propagandizing (and presumably would have indulged in sabotage, too, had it been to their advantage), but the atmosphere being friendlier they could do it more openly.

Wilson toured the country on behalf of preparedness in early 1916, at almost the same time he accepted the resignation of Secretary of War Lindley Garrison, who felt he wasn't going far enough, and replaced him with Newton Baker, who had a reputation for pacifism.

When the Democrats forgathered in convention in St. Louis to re-
nominate Wilson for president, the cry was "Peace!"

Temporary Chairman Martin Glynn of New York led off with "The
policy may not satisfy those who revel in destruction and find
pleasure in despair. It may not satisfy the fire-eater or the swash-
buckler. This policy does satisfy the mothers of the land at whose
hearth and fireside no jingoist war has placed an empty chair. . . . It
does satisfy the fathers of this land and the sons of this land who will
fight for our flag and die for our flag. . . ."

The crowd, a bit more militant, screamed, "Say it again!" and
Glynn deftly added ". . . when Reason primes the rifle, when Honor
draws the sword, when Justice breathes a blessing upon the stands
they uphold."

In praise of the *Sussex* settlement, permanent chairman Ollie
James of Kentucky, a mountain of a man, told his audience: "Without orphaning a single American child, without widowing a single
American mother, without firing a single gun, without shedding a
single drop of blood, Wilson wrung from the most militant spirit that
ever brooded above a battlefield an acknowledgment of American
rights and an agreement to American demands."

All this sounded so agreeable to the peaceable Mr. Bryan that he
agreed, though not a delegate, to make a speech endorsing Wilson. It
turned out to be the battle cry for the whole campaign: "I have dif-
fered with the President in some points of his policy of dealing with
the great war," boomed the matchless orator, "but I agree with the
American people in thanking God we have a president who kept—who
will keep—us out of war."

Charles Evans Hughes, standard bearer for the Republicans,
found himself faced with the Wilson slogan, "He Kept Us Out of
War." Nevertheless, he did have a united Republican party behind
him. After splitting with the conservative Republicans in 1912 and
going off to form his own liberal, trust-busting, clean-politics Progressive party, Teddy Roosevelt was now back in the fold. The split
had brought Wilson to power and that was too much for T. R.

When returns first rolled in from the Northeast on election night
it seemed that Wilson was going down. By nine o'clock New York,
Indiana, Connecticut, and New Jersey had gone Republican and the
newspapers were conceding that Hughes was in. At this juncture

Tumulty received the first of a series of mysterious telephone calls from a man near Republican headquarters urging him to hold on, concede nothing, and wait for the western vote to come in. Tumulty held on, and the next morning the *Times* had an Extra out which saw indications of a Wilson victory as the western vote piled up. The President's daughter Margaret called the news into him while he was shaving and Wilson, who had gone to bed figuring himself whipped, called back, "Tell it to the Marines."

At Hughes' New York home a reporter dropped around and was told by his son, "The President cannot be disturbed."

"Well, when he wakes up," said the reporter, "tell him that he isn't president."

In the end it was a Wilson victory by less than 600,000, and at that the Republicans could draw some solace from the fact that Wilson consistently ran ahead of the rest of the Democratic ticket.

During the summer before the election the air between Washington and London had been blue with American protests over the British black list. If this wasn't quite the anti-blockade pressure Von Bernstorff had hoped for, British stock in America did sink to about its lowest point since the start of the war. Under their Trading with the Enemy Act, the English had made up a black list of about one thousand American firms doing business with Germany. Any ship carrying cargo from these firms was refused coal in British ports. Even Page, according to his affectionate biographer, found this "tactless and unjust." While London would unquestionably have relaxed the black list rather than alienate American opinion, the Germans obligingly took them off the hook with an exceedingly pointless maneuver: on October 7 the submarine *U-53* sailed into the harbor of Newport, Rhode Island, took aboard a few newspapers, left a letter for Von Bernstorff, and then put to sea where she sank no less than nine small ships during the next day.

To have the dread weapon appear thus in their very front yards caused the East Coast citizenry to think a good deal less about the black list, a good deal more about German submarines, and we were back about where we'd been since the beginning—the black list was bad for business, but the submarine was bad for health. Said Colonel House, "if we are to have war, let it be with Germany by all means."

Since the beginning of the war Wilson had had House trotting be-tween Washington, London, and Berlin with one peace plan or an-other, but all of them were doomed. In truth, neither side wanted peace badly enough to be willing to make concessions to get it. After the voting, though, Wilson—more convinced than ever that if the war wasn't ended we would be drawn in—determined on another effort. It took the form of notes, sent on December 18, asking the powers to set forth their war aims in the most general way. It con-tained the phrase "The objects which the statesmen of the belligerents on both sides have in mind in this war are virtually the same. . . ." British and pro-British raged that the lofty aims of London should be confused with those of Berlin. Lord Robert Cecil, Minister for Blockade, summed it up when he told Page, "The President has seemed to pass judgment on the Allied cause by putting it on the same level as the German. I am deeply hurt." The word went out that the British reaction was unfavorable, the last German proponents of moderation went down, and Von Tirpitz and unrestricted submarine warfare took over.

There would be one last effort—a speech to the Senate on January 22, 1917, in which a frustrated Wilson said to his own people what he wanted to say to the belligerents. He spoke, he said, "for the silent masses of mankind everywhere," and called for a "peace with-out victory." He might as well have saved his breath. "This distress-ing peace move," Page called it contemptuously. He could have saved his breath, too; neutrality was a dead duck.

Von Bernstorff had had the telegram instructing him to announce resumption of unrestricted submarine warfare since January 19. The date set for renewal was February 1. On the morning of January 31 he told the crews of German liners which had been interned in American ports when they ran in to escape the British Navy to sabo-tage them so as to make them useless to any American war effort, and then presented himself and his note to Mr. Lansing at the State De-partment. The note set out a war zone and said, "All ships met with-in that zone will be sunk. The Imperial Government is confident that this measure will result in a speedy termination of the war." One American ship a week would be permitted to England under a severe set of conditions, including that she be painted, as one American said, "like a barber pole."

Tumulty recalls that when he carried the bulletin to the President, Wilson read it, read it again, his face reflecting first "blank amazement, then incredulity . . . then gravity and sternness, a sudden grayness of color, a compression of the lips and the familiar locking of the jaw which always characterized him in moments of supreme resolution. Handing the paper back to me, he said in quiet tones, 'This means war. The break that we have tried so hard to prevent now seems inevitable.' " [6]

He began the regular Saturday Cabinet meeting on February 3 by asking immediately, "Shall I break off diplomatic relations with Germany?" The Cabinet was virtually unanimous that he should. The next day the President told Congress, "I think you will agree with me that this government has no alternative consistent with the dignity and the honor of the United States. . . . I have directed the Secretary of State to announce . . . that all diplomatic relations between the United States and the German Empire are severed. . . ."

In London, Page waited anxiously. At nine in the evening the chief of British Naval Intelligence came happily in with a message from the British naval attaché in Washington: "Bernstorff had just been given his passports. I shall probably get drunk tonight."[7]

Still, it was not war, and for the moment, at least, American ships stayed in port rather than risk the submarine. McAdoo and Houston were emphatic that the President should ask Congress for the power to arm the merchantmen, but he reverted to indecision. Houston even felt that he was "somewhat nettled by McAdoo's insistence and emphatic manner and language."

There was little time to ponder the problem; during the evening of Saturday, February 24, Page cabled a tremendous new development. The British had intercepted and decoded a message from German Foreign Secretary Zimmerman to the German minister in Mexico. Sent on January 19, it asked the minister to tell the Mexicans that unrestricted submarine warfare would be resumed, that Germany hoped to keep the United States neutral, but failing that proposed a treaty with Mexico to "make war together, make peace together, generous financial support, and an understanding on our part that Mexico is to reconquer the lost territory in Texas, New Mexico, and Arizona." It also suggested that the Mexicans invite the Japanese into the alliance.

One must wait for the United States Navy's break on the Japanese code before the Battle of Midway in the Second World War to find a more important deciphering job. The British had set up the coup early in the war when they cut the German cable in the North Sea. This forced the Germans onto wireless, which the British could intercept and in due time learned to decode. The more elaborate codes —including the one by which the Zimmerman message was sent— were built around secret books which correlated a group of numerals with a word or phrase. The British had captured the appropriate book for the Zimmerman note from a German consul in the Middle East who had imprudently carried it with him during a raid on a British oil field.

Thus Saturday passed, and events were moving swiftly. Sunday night the Cunarder *Laconia* was running Liverpool bound off the Irish coast, blacked out, lit only by a half moon. A few passengers were dancing to "Poor Butterfly" played on a Victrola, and the American correspondent Floyd Gibbons had just asked an Englishman, "What do you say are our chances of being torpedoed?"

The first fish struck aft with a jolt that answered Gibbons' question. Fortunately, Captain Irvine had drilled his people well on Abandon Ship, and as ship's lights were thrown on, they went quietly into the boats. The single exception was Boat 8. Number 8 was a port-side boat and by the time it was lowered, the *Laconia* had acquired a heavy list to starboard. Consequently, lifeboat Number 8 struck not water, but the side of the sinking vessel. To make matters worse, the forward fall had been let go first so that for moments the boat hung from her after fall, her stern almost straight up in the air.

The crash was enough to hole the boat. Her air tanks kept her afloat, but the passengers found themselves up to their waists in water, unable to handle the boat with oars.

The submarine surfaced near one of the boats and a voice in English "good, but guttural," called out, "What is the name of your ship, her tonnage, and her cargo?"

Some would-be hero suggested, "Don't tell the murderer anything. Let's just sing 'Rule Britannia' at him," but the ship's steward figured discretion better than valor and answered the questions.

Two of the passengers in Number 8 were Mrs. Mary Hoy and

her grown daughter Elizabeth—Americans from Chicago. In recent years they had lived in London with Mrs. Hoy's son Austin, who worked there as an American manufacturer's representative. During the lull following the *Sussex* pledge, they had gone visiting in the States and Austin had repeatedly urged them to stay there until the submarine situation got better. Although the seas were relatively calm, water continually broke over the heads of passengers in the swamped boat. Somewhere around three in the morning Mrs. Hoy died. A little later Elizabeth died, too, still holding her mother's hand.

When Wilson went before Congress at one o'clock Monday afternoon to ask for the arming of merchantmen, it is likely that he did not yet know of the sinking of the *Laconia*. The story was held up by British censorship and it was ten minutes after one before the first flash arrived—a cable from the American consul at Queenstown, Ireland, to the State Department. The President stuck to his prepared text—including the statement that "no overt act" of unrestricted submarine warfare had occurred—but the *Laconia* news was whispered through his audience while he talked.

Came Tuesday and the text of the Zimmerman note was released to the press. "Germany Seeks an Alliance Against Us; Asks Japan and Mexico to Join Her" cried the headlines, and the resulting sensation, as it was undoubtedly supposed to, came crashing around the heads of eleven senators led by La Follette who were against arming the merchantmen. No men to be deterred by storms, though, the eleven—with some side-line cheering from Bryan—filibustered their way through the last three days of the session. Furious, Wilson called them "a little group of wilful men" and went ahead to arm the ships on his own authority.

For the moment there were still a few who doubted the Zimmerman message. Dr. Heinrich Albert's friend Viereck called it "obviously faked," and the Hearst press was skeptical enough to ask their Berlin man to inquire of Zimmerman himself. That incredible diplomat promptly admitted sending the note and bore himself as a man not quite certain what all the fuss was about.

Other headlines were blossoming—"Hoy Sends Appeal to Presi-

dent." Young Mr. Hoy in London was demanding that the United
States take action to avenge a tragedy that he himself had predicted
in the first place. "As an American whose mother and sister were
drowned in the torpedoing of the *Laconia,* I feel I have a right to ask
President Wilson, 'What is America going to do?'" he told a New
York *Times* correspondent. "If this is not the overt act for which the
President was waiting, then I don't know what to call it. . . . I'm going
to telegraph President Wilson asking him, as an American citizen,
that the death of my mother and sister be avenged." He so radioed,
and everyone thought it perfectly splendid of him.

On March 9 Wilson announced that there would be a special session
of Congress on April 16. In the following week three American ships
—our shipping was moving again—were torpedoed, and on March 21
the President moved the special session up to April 2.

By this time the churches were ringing with sermons on the American Christian's duty to go to war with Germany and even Samuel
Gompers, president of the A.F. of L., no fire-eater, was calling together his fellow leaders of labor for conferences on the war period
ahead. In Russia the Czar abdicated and one of the last pacifist arguments—that one of our would-be allies was an autocracy not unlike
Germany—vanished. In a year and a half there was going to be an
American military force in the field against the new regime in Russia,
but when a new great power is being catapulted onto the world stage
for the first time there are just so many things it can think about at one
time. Washington was more concerned with the news that Britain
was on the verge of a financial collapse which could be averted only
by American loans.

From the day of putting the special session ahead, Wilson moved
with a determination that suggests that his mind was made up. During
the Cabinet meeting two days later, Houston reports in his biography,
"The time was consumed in discussing routine matters of preparation,
particularly with legislation which it would be necessary for Congress
to pass." On the next day, March 25, the Council of National Defense
met. This body, whose advisory committee consisted largely of Republican businessmen, had been formed the previous summer to
consider man power and industrial mobilization in case of war, and
now it stated that an army of a million men would be needed and that
a draft was the best way to raise them.

On March 31 Rear Admiral William Sims—in civilian clothes—left secretly for London to discuss ways and means of getting American men and supplies to England. The same night Wilson, unable to sleep, took his own typewriter out and while Mrs. Wilson brought him crackers and milk, he tapped out his war message. It was on the following evening—Sunday, April 1—that he sat with Frank Cobb. "I'd never seen him so worn down," Cobb wrote later. "He looked as if he hadn't slept, and he said he hadn't. He said he was probably going before Congress the next day to ask a declaration of war, and he'd never been so uncertain about anything in his life as about that decision. . . . He said he couldn't see any alternative, that he had tried every way he knew to avoid war."[8]

The President was not quite speaking the truth. He had not tried every way, there was one way he had not tried and, indeed, it is the only way that might—in theory, at least—have worked. April 2 was dawning before the President was through talking to Cobb, and it was too late, but once there had been a way to avoid war if the President and the nation had chosen to take it. It was simplicity itself—no American to sell any goods of any kind or lend money in any amount to any of the belligerents, no Americans to travel in vessels of any of the belligerents. Without American trade and aid there would have been none of the irritations of the British blockade, none of the hazards of submarine warfare, restricted or otherwise, for American ships, no loss of American lives. However, if we are to find fault with Wilson it is not because he never tried the policy—which, in fact, was an impossible one—but that he never put the alternative before the American people. The people did not want war, but they did not want peace at the price they would have had to pay for it. For one thing, our own prosperity was intimately tied to a war boom based on French and British military orders. Later, it would be said that the munitions people got us in out of a concern for profits, but in truth almost every farmer and laborer in America was making money out of the war. Second, the largest—and by and large most powerful and articulate—element in America was tied by blood and language to England, and their sympathies had never been anywhere else since the war started. Perhaps their sympathies should have been elsewhere or neutral, perhaps they should have perceived instantly and brilliantly that this war was the outcome of a century of imperialistic squabbling, but the fact remains that they didn't. Finally, our best minds felt—however much they may have failed to put the fact clearly before the public—that we simply could not afford to let England lose. We could afford a stalemate, but a German victory would mean the upset of a European balance of power on which our own security had rested for more than a hundred years. Conceivably, they were wrong, but the securities of a hundred years are not lightly given up. Certainly what came out of the war in no way advanced American security, but had Wilson made it clear in 1917 that we were not fighting for Bleeding Belgium or Battered Britain or Mrs. Hoy and her daughter, who were foolish enough to sail submarine waters, but because we were trying to make the world safe for America, we might have gone to the peace table with a different set of concepts and left it with a document less calculated to bring on the Second World War in the minimum possible time.

Instead, in London, Page was noting down the beneficent results of the war as he saw them:

1. It will break up and tear away our isolation.
2. It will unhorse our cranks and soft brains.
3. It will make us less promiscuously hospitable to every kind of immigrant.
4. It will re-establish in our minds and conscience and policy our true historic genesis, background, kindred, and destiny—i.e., kill the Irish and German influence.
5. It will revive our real manhood—put the mollycoddles in disgrace as idiots and dandies are.
6. It will make our politics frank and manly by restoring our true nationality.
7. It will make us again a great seafaring people. It is this that has given Great Britain its long lead in the world.
8. Break up feminized education—make a boy a vigorous animal and make our education rest on a wholesome physical basis.
9. Bring men of a higher type into our political life.[9]

Mr. Page was a gentleman of the old school and it was perhaps just as well that his mission to London was almost over; indeed, he had only a few months left to live.

Before the cheering Congress Wilson read on: "The world must be made safe for democracy. . . . We have no quarrel with the German people. . . ." And as he came toward his conclusion the vision of the League of Nations was held before them: ". . . we shall fight for the things which we have always carried nearest our hearts: for democracy, for the right of those who submit to authority to have a voice in their own governments, for the rights and liberties of small nations, for universal dominions of right by such a concert of free people as shall bring peace and safety to all nations and make the world itself at last free.

"To such a task we can dedicate our lives and our fortunes [he didn't add "our sacred honor"], everything that we are and everything that we have, with the pride of those who know that the day has come when America is privileged to spend her blood and her might for the principles that gave her birth and happiness and the peace which she has treasured. God helping her, she can do no other."

He walked quickly through the cheering chamber, stopped briefly by Houston who told him the Supreme Court justices had decided on the spot that they would "give him a favorable verdict on any proposal necessary and designed to beat the Germans," shook hands with his political enemy Senator Lodge, who assured him, "Mr. President, you have expressed in the loftiest manner possible the sentiments of the American people," and went back to his cavalry escort.

Tumulty rode back to the White House with him, the cavalry clattering alongside, and the President said, "Think of what it was they were applauding. My message today was a message of death for our young men. How strange it seems to applaud that."

Back at the White House, he spoke of the criticism of the months past. "It has not been easy to carry these burdens in these trying times. From the beginning I saw the utter futility of neutrality . . . but we had to stand by our traditional policy of steering clear of European embroilments." He then read Tumulty a sympathetic letter from a New England editor, and when he finished, "the President drew his handkerchief from his pocket, wiped away great tears that stood in his eyes, and then laying his head on the Cabinet table, sobbed as if he had been a child."[10]

The nation in general felt no such grief. In New York City the news reached the Metropolitan Opera House just after the third act of *The Canterbury Pilgrims*. Gerard, our ambassador to Germany before the break, stepped to the front of his box and called for the playing of "The Star-Spangled Banner." It was followed by cheers for the President, the Army, the Navy, and the Allies. The enthusiasm was to be dampened a little when, at the beginning of the next act, Margaret Obert, a German singer, appeared, sang a few bars, and fainted away, flat on her back.

At *Out There*—a war drama—Laurette Taylor, playing a cockney, came to the line, "Of course I'm for war—I'm for peace, but once your country is in I don't see what you're going to do 'cepting 'elp," and was greeted with the greatest cheering in the history of the play. At the New Amsterdam Roof Will Rogers searched for something topical and came up with the observation that in two more years he'd have to compete in vaudeville with the Kaiser and the Kaiser's unemployed relatives.

In papers flaunting officers' uniform ads—hand-tailored khakis, $16.00—editorial comment was favorable next morning across the country. Said the Philadelphia *Record*, "We have been dragged into this war by the bad faith of the German Government." In Cincinnati, a city with a large German-American population, the *Commercial-Tribune* was a little more restrained. "The sympathy of the people of the United States, as we understand it, goes out to the German people who are victims of the Prussian militaristic system." On the Coast the San Francisco *Chronicle* felt "the President has resisted war until he could resist no longer," and from the deep South the New Orleans *Times-Picayune* announced, "This nation, forced at last by brutal aggression and outrage to take up the sword, will wage the war in its own and humanity's defense."

Most of the foreign-language press came into line. The New York *Staats-Zeitung* referred to war against the "German Imperial Government" and added, "The President need have no concern as to the loyalty of Americans of German ancestry." In Cincinnati, however, the *Volksblatt* was stiffer: "We agree with the President that war exists between the United States and Germany and that every citizen is bound to comply with the duties arising out of the state of war. All other statements in the President's speech we disapprove and reject."

In Tuesday's New York *Times* there was a ringing ad from Allen's

Foot Ease beginning, "Napoleon once said 'a footsore army is an army half defeated,'" and going on to urge men in service not to be without their product. Out in Thermopolis, Wyoming, a foolhardy soul toasted the Kaiser in a saloon, was promply strung up from a beam, cut down, revived with cold water, made to kiss the American flag, and run out of town. In the *Times* roundup of demonstrations were a number of reports of school kids assembled during the time of the President's address for the purpose of singing patriotic songs, saluting the flag, or both. Three hundred Germans made haste to apply for American citizenship, and a pacifist speaker at Seventh Avenue and 125th Street was roughly handled by a crowd.

In London happy Ambassador Page was in a new world. "The Stars and Stripes," he wrote, "almost instantaneously broke out of private dwellings, shops, hotels, and theaters; street hucksters did a thriving business selling rosettes of the American color, which even the most stodgy Englishmen did not disdain to wear in their buttonholes; wherever there was a band or an orchestra, 'The Star-Spangled Banner' acquired a sudden popularity . . . the editorial outgivings of the British press on America's entrance form a literature all their own. . . . The estimation in which President Wilson was held changed overnight. . . . The President's address before Congress was praised as one of the most eloquent and statesmanlike utterances in history. Special editions of this heartening document had rapid sale."[11]

"The House waits on the Senate; the Senate waits on Senator Robert Marion La Follette of Madison, Wisconsin." Thus the New York *Times* on the first day's effort in the Senate to pass the war resolution. Senator Hitchcock had arisen to ask for unanimous consent for the resolution's immediate consideration. La Follette arose to reply, "I ask that the joint resolution go over for the day under the rules and I object to the request for unanimous consent."

A reporter noted that ". . . the fierce smile which habitually adorns the face of La Follette became, for once, almost a happy one."

A hard-nosed fighter, this La Follette, and used to trouble. A dirt-poor boy who really had been born in a log cabin, he grew up to hate big money, "the interests," and corruption, and became a governor of Wisconsin over the opposition of his own Republican party. He was in the Senate only because his hold on the state's voters was too strong for his party to get him out. Now he was going to make a fight partly because he was anti-British, partly because he was an "agin'" man; if a large group of politicians were trying to rush something through, the La Follette back just naturally went up as stiffly as his spiky hair stood normally.

His colleagues attempted to dissuade him, but La Follette went on with "clearness of enunciation and crispness of voice" to say, "Oh . . . I do not think it quite in conformity with the practice of the Senate to lecture a senator who asks for one day's time on a resolution of this importance. I ask for the regular order."

So Tuesday passed. Several colleges announced that their athletic schedules were being suspended because of the war, but no rush to the recruiting stations was noticeable.

The senators reassembled at ten Wednesday morning before packed galleries. They knew they were going to hear a tiny group of men make a record of their opposition to the war. There were not many of them left—even *The New Republic*, that citadel of American progressivism, had gone over to Wilson. Their arguments were to be compounded of the conviction that war meant an end of social reform at home, that war was an evil per se, and that war was the product of munitions makers hungry for profits. That most of them came from states with large German-American blocs should not be taken as a reflection on their patriotism; no two finer Americans ever sat in the Senate than La Follette and George Norris.

James Vardaman of Mississippi led off. "For the life of me, I cannot believe that war is for the welfare of the world or the people of this nation." Norris made it stronger. He spoke of "the enormous profits of munitions manufacturers, stockbrokers, and bond dealers." He cried, "We are going into war upon the command of gold." Reed of Missouri arose to accuse Norris of treason and Norris calmly replied that Reed would regret the remark in a calmer moment.

Then La Follette began to outline the anti-war position in a speech that was going to last four hours. He talked of "the poor who are called upon to rot in the trenches." He said that we had enforced international law a good deal more strictly against Germany than against Britain. "We have wallowed in the mire at the feet of Great Britain." He claimed that of all our Allies, only France was a true democracy.

They heard him out, but the tide was not to be turned. There were a few more battle cries from the war-minded, and then the vote. An observer found "the senators themselves unusually grave and quiet." Many of them answered to their names in voices that "quivered with emotion."

At eleven-eleven that night the Senate voted 90 to 6 for the declaration of war.

The House started to work the next day and out of a flood of verbiage the speech people were going to remember was the one from Majority Leader Claude Kitchin of North Carolina. Kitchin was brilliant, kindly; there was no more admired man in the Congress. He was one of Wilson's oldest political allies, the man who had steered his New Freedom legislation through the House, but he could not go along with the war. "My friends, I cannot leave my children lands and riches, I cannot leave them fame, but I can leave them the name of an ancestor who, mattering not the consequences to himself, never dared to hesitate to do his duty as God gave him to see it."

On the first ballot Jeannette Rankin of Montana, the first woman to sit in either house of Congress, remained silent. Speaker of the House Uncle Joe Cannon, a politician once characterized as a "foul-mouthed hayseed," went over to her. "Little woman, you cannot afford not to vote. You represent the womanhood of the country in the American Congress. I shall not advise you how to vote, but you should, one way or another."

On the second ballot Miss Rankin stood silent for seconds, then, "I want to stand by my country, but I cannot vote for war. I vote 'no.'"

To their eternal credit, the galleries applauded her.

The papers reported that she voted with "big tears" in her eyes and years later the future mayor of New York, Fiorello La Guardia, who voted "yes," was asked if she really had been crying. "I could not see," the Little Flower recalled, "because of the tears in my own eyes."

It was now three-twelve on Friday morning, and the House had taken sixteen and a half hours before voting for war by a majority of 373 to 50.

Wilson had just finished lunch when they brought the document in to be signed. It said that "the state of war between the United States and the Imperial German Government which has thus been thrust upon the United States is hereby formally declared. . . ." Mrs. Wilson found the President a pen and he wrote, "Approved 6 April, 1917—Woodrow Wilson," at the bottom.

His naval aide ran to a window, wigwagged the news across the street to the Navy Department; immediately a radio message went to all naval ships and stations telling them that we were in it.

We were going to win the war, but we had just lost our best chance of winning the peace. One week earlier England and France would have promised us anything, but we imagined that there was nothing we wanted, simply because we wanted no territory. At the peace table there were going to be a great many things we wanted, the self-determination of small nations, the League of Nations, and all the rest. Then it was going to be tougher to get them.

Chapter Two

"LAFAYETTE, WE ARE HERE"

WE had decided that we wanted to go to war. Now someone was going to have to fight that war. There were some 92,000 Army regulars—a drop in the Western Front bucket—some under-strength National Guard divisions; the bulk of the man power was obviously going to have to come from just plain civilians. And unlike the European nations, we had no fixed mobilization plan whereby millions of men could be brought into the Army in a matter of days.

American tradition called for the volunteer system. The only time we had ever tried a draft—during the Civil War—there had been riots in New York. Nevertheless, everybody at the top knew that it had to be conscription, nothing else would produce enough men soon enough. Wilson knew it, the Army was certain of it, the Council of National Defense was already on record as favoring it.

Secretary of War Newton D. Baker, Judge Advocate General Enoch Crowder, and a hard-driving Major Hugh Johnson—later of NRA fame—drew up a proposal calculated to win the maximum support. The Army would stay out of it. Eligible men would register wherever they normally went to vote, and any problems that came up would be settled by draft boards of home-town folks.

Wilson liked it, pushed it along to the Capitol, and immediately the howls went up. Baker's biographer culled some of the most injured from the *Congressional Record*:

"The conscripts of the Civil War were deserters and cowards, both North and South . . ."

"Worthless fighting material . . ."

"Conscripts are not worth considering . . ."

"It will produce a sulky, unwilling, indifferent army . . ."

"No more abject or involuntary servitude was ever presented to this country, and it is equally un-American . . ."

"Conscription is another name for slavery . . ."

"Supported by munition manufacturers and other selfish interests . . ."

"We shall Prussianize America . . ."

"We will never get a conscript on the firing line in France . . ."

"It will destroy democracy at home while fighting for it abroad . . ."

"No one can estimate the number of officials needed to hunt up the young men whom it is decided to take . . ."[1]

The congressman who told Crowder that his name would become the most odious in America simply didn't understand that frail-bodied, tough-fibered man. The general had already sent the bustling Johnson over to the Government Printing Office to have the ten million forms necessary for registration printed secretly. The printer was glad to oblige, but before long his storage space gave out, the Washington postmaster was taken into the plot, and the overflow stored in his basement.

The draft was bound to pass. Only a Congress gone mad would vote war and then refuse to vote the men to fight it. In the end, most of them went along, there were only eight votes against in the Senate and twenty-three against in the House, where German-born Representative Kahn led the fight for the measure. Long before that Baker had gotten in touch with the governors—and through them with the sheriffs—to tell them what was coming and ship them their registration blanks.

It was May 18 when the draft became law, and June 5 was proclaimed Registration Day. Baker wanted the job done quickly before anti-registration sentiment had a chance to build up. After all, no less a man than Senator Reed of Missouri had promised him, "You will have the streets of our American cities running red with blood on Registration Day."

The senator was wrong. On June 5, 9,660,000 American males between the ages of twenty-one and thirty-one went to their polling places—exhorted by their mayors, prayed for by their clergymen, and wept over by sundry females—and signed up.

Although the police had been prepared for opposition by socialists, pacifists, and members of the IWW, most of the country went out as on a holiday. There were a few exceptions. In Butte, Montana, 600 anti-registration men paraded and the police decided it was the doing of a local Irish social club, although the principal address to the marchers was delivered in Finnish. The Navajo Indians drove off an Indian agent sent to take their names, and the New York *Times* gravely announced that they were considered likely to go on the war-path. The Navajos' neighbors, the Utes, likewise refused, and a number of their young men made off to the hills clad in the traditional bear-dance costumes and considerably liquored up. In Racine, Wisconsin, a man was made to kiss the flag for anti-draft utterances, and one Raymond Moore of Kansas City could be induced to sign only when his sister, weeping copiously, came to the jail in which he'd been put and told him he was causing his mother untold anguish. On the Coast an Indian named White Eagle would have none of the Ute-Navajo attitude and personally carried to the registration place a gentleman unwilling to make the trip.

Thus the men were on the way, and even while preparations were being made for enlarging the bottom of the great army pyramid, a search was on for someone to put at the top of it. Major General Hugh Scott, the chief of staff, was too old to head an expeditionary force. The other likely major generals were Thomas Barry, J. Franklin Bell, Leonard Wood, and John J. Pershing. Barry and Bell were in ill health. Wood had a good Spanish-American War record, a numerous and vocal following in Congress, and had made himself almost a symbol of preparedness with his Plattsburg camp. He had also made himself a symbol of the sort of general who doesn't take orders readily from civilians. During the preparedness row, the War Department had repeatedly tried to tone him down and had had no luck. Secretary of War Newton D. Baker was nothing if not a civilian—a lawyer, a re-form mayor of Cleveland, a man who had come to Washington with some reputation for being a pacifist. He was a quiet man, but he had a mind like an IBM machine and a taste for being obeyed. That let Wood out and left Pershing.

On the Pancho Villa chasing expedition into Mexico Pershing had done a good job with as tough an assignment as a soldier can pull. The supply situation being what it was in any Mexican armed force, Villa's men had to double as bandits—intensely democratic and patriotic bandits—but bandits just the same, and one of their raids took them into American territory in New Mexico. Pershing's instructions had been, roughly: get Villa out of business, but don't cause any serious trouble with the Mexican Government. Pershing had done just that, chasing Villa hard enough to neutralize him, but forswearing the personal glory that might have come from a stand-up fight. And the rest of his record was good; from the beginning he'd been a plugger, a poor boy from Missouri who'd taught school to finance his own further higher education. He was well along— twenty-six—when he finally graduated from West Point and went West to chase Apaches. In Cuba, during the Spanish-American War, his commanding officer called him "the coolest man under fire I ever saw." Sent to the Philippines, he kept rebellious natives in line so thoroughly that Teddy Roosevelt skipped over 862 officers senior to Pershing to promote him to brigadier general.

And he had one further advantage: his father-in-law was Senator Francis Warren of Wyoming, chairman of the Senate Military Affairs Committee. From that gentleman there came on May 3, 1917, to Pershing at Fort Sam Houston near San Antonio, Texas, his headquarters for Mexican operations, a telegram:

WIRE ME TODAY WHETHER AND HOW MUCH YOU SPEAK, READ, AND WRITE FRENCH.

To it the general replied that he was by no means a slouch at French. By his own admission, the answer was "rather optimistic," but he considered it "justified by the possibilities to be implied" from the telegram. Senator Warren amplified the wire shortly after with a letter in which he explained that it had been none other than Baker who had inquired about Pershing's French. Warren had said he didn't really know, but he'd ask his wife, and concluded the letter with "I hope you will wire me promptly so that I may tell the secretary 'what my wife said about it.'"

Actually, Baker had his mind made up before he talked to Warren. A wire to Pershing dated May 2 from the chief of staff told him that troops adding up to a division were to go to France and that he was to command them.

Take it all in all, Pershing was a good man for the job: whipping green civilians into shape so that they could fight beside the veteran armies of Europe. He was tough; the nickname Black Jack had nothing to do with the card game. He had acquired it when he commanded Negro troops in the Philippines, but over the years it had come to refer to his stern, almost dour face. He was all soldier, as stiff as his own stand-up collar. American troops never were quite spit and polish enough to suit him; in his own recollections of the war his most favorable comment on real soldierly bearing refers to some Germans he saw in a prison camp. It must have been galling for him later when a visitor came to his headquarters in France and said that he'd had his doubts about the qualities of the American soldier, but that the headquarters guard impressed and convinced him. Pershing could only tell him the truth: the guards that day were Marines.

Pershing got to Washington on May 10, talked to Scott, then to Baker, of whom he formed a "distinctly favorable impression," and started to get his division organized. It was a few days later that Baker called him back in to say that Wilson had decided to send him not as a division commander, but as commander in chief of the American Expeditionary Force. Pershing grabbed Cavalryman Major James Harbord, long tabbed a comer in the Army, as his chief of staff, and made ready to leave for Europe.

Before he got off for France, a fight started that was going to take more than a year to settle. Both the French and the British military missions were in town and they both wanted American man power. The British wanted them as individuals, shipped over and put straight into existing British formations. The French were willing to take them in small units, to be attached to the French. Pershing said "no," and had to keep saying "no," but it would be the summer of 1918 before he was able to settle the argument for good by rolling a real American army into battle at Saint-Mihiel. Divisions were loaned out in times of crisis, but the "coolest man under fire" had no intention of going to France as the commander of a vast replacement center.

It was May 28 when Pershing and his staff of 63 officers and 146 men assembled at Governors Island, New York, in civilian clothes, slipped through the fog to the British steamship *Baltic*, and headed for Europe. Among those present was a former racing-car driver named Eddie Rickenbacker, taken along because it was considered that he would make an excellent chauffeur for the commander in chief.

Teddy Roosevelt, who at age sixty-eight was having a terrible time understanding that this was modern war and not the old Rough

Rider days, was raising all sorts of hell because Washington wouldn't let him raise a volunteer division and command it himself. Baker and Wilson politely but firmly told him "no" and started about the business of raising an army. Roosevelt wasn't the only man having trouble understanding the new war; among Baker's other duties at the period was the preparation of letters explaining why officers would not be allowed to take their wives to France with them.

The Army said it could handle 687,000 men right away. They were to be chosen from the total of registered men by lottery. The longest list any of the 4,500 draft boards had come up with was 10,500 names. Hence that many numbered slips of paper, each in a black capsule, went into a fish bowl in the Senate Office Building. On the morning of July 20 Baker, blindfolded, reached in and came up with number 258. Thus, 4,500 men around the country bearing draft card 258 knew that they were in the Army now. In areas where the draft list didn't go up to 258, the man holding the number closest to it went instead.

The drawing went on all morning. From time to time a Major General Devol would stir the capsules with a large wooden spoon bedecked with red, white, and blue bunting. There was a pause when one capsule came up empty, but nothing more dramatic occurred either in Washington or around the country. New York City police reported that the city had never been more calm, although large crowds of men gathered outside newspaper offices waiting to hear their numbers come up. A reporter scrounging for a color story had to settle for Andrew Yaros, a Flushing bartender, who had earlier tossed a coin with his brother to see which one would enlist, which one would stay home to support a widowed mother. The brother had gone, only to have Andrew come up one of Flushing's 258's.

We had only some 285,000 rifles and 550 pieces of artillery to issue to these men. The very camps in which they were to train were just being built, but the thing had to start somewhere. The Army ordered draftees to begin to move into cantonments September 1.

Amid much pushing and irritation the National Guard units were already on the move. Since they had tents, the Army decided they could sleep in them and the cantonments with wooden buildings now going up be saved for the draftees. The Guard's heartburn arose chiefly from Pershing's demand for big divisions—29,000 men—rather

than the 17,000-man divisions the Allies were using. Thus, three old
Guard regiments often had to be combined to form a new one, some
famous old outfits lost their identity and didn't like it, and some old
commanding officers lost their commands and liked it even less.
Nevertheless, they moved onto tracts of land the Government pur-
chased throughout the South. The experience of the Twenty-ninth
Division is as typical as any: its first General Order was written by
the adjutant as he sat on a box on the front porch of an abandoned
farmhouse, his typewriter balanced on another box. His camp—Camp
McClellan, in northeastern Alabama—was 19,000 acres of rolling land
and on July 23 not much else. A month later, after as many as 3,000
men a day had been pounding away at the job, the site contained
750 completed structures and 50,000 feet of water pipe in spite of nine
days of what the local Chamber of Commerce referred to as "excessive
rains." When the men began to arrive—in the Twenty-ninth they were
a mélange of National Guardsmen from New Jersey, Delaware, and
Virginia that eventually led to the division being called the "Blue and
Gray"—they were marched over stump-covered fields, turned to dust
or mud according to the occasion, and put to work pitching their own
tents and laying out company areas.

It was actually September 5 before the first draftees began to en-
train, and the scenes across the country were pretty much the same
in small towns and big cities. In civilian clothes, accompanied by the
local band, they marched to the railway station in as military a manner as they could manage. Civil War veterans, often under ragged
old battle flags, marched with them. The great of the community
addressed them, then while the cars drawn up around the station
honked their horns, they boarded the train and pulled out.

It is worth noting that some of them were drunk. Some of them
brought their own liquor, others had had it urged on them by
patriotic barkeepers. One report states that a trainload of cowboys,
Indians, miners, and the like from Arizona, "had one trait in common: they were drunk and not just drunk, but extravagantly and
supremely drunk."[2] In the next twenty-four hours they chucked a
porter off the train (while in motion), looted a bar, lassoed a number
of citizens of Trinidad, Colorado, during a stop, and staged a fight
between a bulldog, a goat, and a tame wildcat which some of them
had brought along as pets.

A draftee's first few days are pretty much the same the world over, and one description of an arrival—at "a desolate wilderness of sand and scrub oak and famous for nothing but our great national bird, the mosquito"[3]—will do as well as another.

"We were marched off over rough, uncompleted roads, thick with dust, around heaps of building material, over spur tracks of the railroad, past half-constructed barracks, all to the tune of carpenters' hammers which clattered with machine-gun-like precision. Reaching a nearly completed barrack, we were halted, and entering were assigned our bunks. To each man was issued his first army equipment, which consisted of two olive-drab blankets, a bed sack to be filled with straw, and a mess kit. We were then introduced to army 'chow' in a manner which became painfully familiar to us. Passing along an ever-tedious mess line to a counter, and armed with our newly acquired eating utensils, which we juggled with a difficulty born of inexperience, we made the acquaintance of army beans and that fluid which some demented people have called coffee. The coffee cup gave us more trouble, perhaps, than anything else, for it seemed to absorb all the heat of its contents. It became so hot that it would have blistered our lips had we attempted to drink from it. When it cooled off a bit we confidently grasped the handle, hoping to wash down a few beans, only to find, too late, that the handle catch was loose, and that the entire contents was being swiftly dumped into the beans. Falling in on another line, we poured what had now become bean soup into a garbage can and completed our first mess by washing our mess kits in soapy hot water and then rinsing them in clear cold water."[4]

They were not an impressive lot, this new army. In the first place, the Government discovered too late that the draftees averaged a good deal bigger than the old regulars. As a result, it was some time before all of them could be gotten completely into uniform. An incipient artilleryman recalled a largish comrade stepping up to the outfitting tables, being unable to find a blouse, overcoat, or pair of pants in his size and coming away with extra shoelaces, dog tags, and a yard of tape.

Equipment for these blowsy draft contingents was rarely present in sufficient quantity. Artillerymen learned their gun drill on logs, a company commander's Ford served for instruction in motor vehicles, many a doughboy learned that a grenade is lobbed, not thrown like a baseball, by practicing with rocks. In all, small wonder that one old-time regular army sergeant put in a few weeks with the draftees, then went AWOL in order to get busted and sent back to his old outfit.

Just to make it worse, the winter of 1917–18 was as dirty a winter as anyone could remember. Most of the camps had been located in the South—over the anguished howls from northern cities who fancied the business they brought—to avoid just that, but it didn't work. An outfit at Camp Greene, North Carolina, noted, "It rained and froze and snowed and rained. The cold, raw wind swept through the trees and over the camp. Morning would find the ground covered with driven snow. Then this would thaw and turn the camp into a vast sea of reddish-yellow mud. It was a thick, viscous clay, of the consistency of library paste and about the color of a new saddle and made progress of any sort almost impossible. An article dropped in it was immediately engulfed. It defied the efforts of the motor-truck company which was supposed to serve the camp. The mud on several roads was up to the floor of the truck bodies."[5]

Sibley stoves were put in the tents—that meant a woodcutting detail out every day and smoke in the tents as the green wood sputtered. In the early days there were even camps where showers were taken al fresco and laundry done in the nearest creek.

They were taught to salute—"the captain made us understand that the fate of the nation, together with the balance of power in Europe, hung on our ability to render a correct salute"—and do close-order drill. Bayonet drill on dummies was in great vogue on the grounds that it instilled a proper fighting spirit. There was gas-mask drill which everyone took extremely seriously after what they'd heard about gas in France, but what most of them remembered out of it was how hot, greasy, and sticky it is inside a mask after perhaps a hundred men have drilled with the same mask earlier in the same day.

The men got thoroughly disgusted with the whole business at times and a Twenty-ninth Division man wrote—he had just been invited to contribute part of his thirty dollars a month to the Liberty Loan campaign—"This intensive training to rush to the aid of bleeding France looks well in the papers, but all our rushing seems to lie in marking time. Imagine! Today is Liberty Loan Day, designated an all-day holiday, with games and mule races to stimulate subscriptions from our pay. The whole business will hardly bring a single extra subscription; all without allotments to dependents have long since taken bonds, but we must go to the mule races by order of the Department of the Southeast! And when, on the five drill days, we do work, they are very severe about making it the full eight-hour day, you bet! But eight hours of what? Well, gun drill on the kind of guns we won't use in France, and detail reconnaissance on the American system which also is not used in France, and time-killing lectures on the Articles of War and Military Courtesy and Hygiene. . . . It's a great life, this rushing to the rescue of France!"

There was more than a little irritation to be training next to civilian construction workers who were making as much in a week as the soldiers were in a month. As though to emphasize the fact, towns near the camps raised their prices until a night out was simply more than the Army could afford. Perhaps the low point was reached at Christmas, 1917. The War Department had announced Christmas leave for 20 per cent of the men in camps before it came to someone in a blinding flash that such a load would swamp the already-overtaxed railroad systems. The number of men was promptly cut to 5 per cent. Out of one division alone more than fifteen hundred men were angry or homesick enough to go home anyway and pull a couple of months' detention for being AWOL.

In spite of it all they began to shape up. Combat-wise French and British officers came over to help and make it all seem a little more real. The day started with reveille at five-thirty and the drill schedule went as follows:

7–7:15–Physical drill
7:15–7:45–Close-order drill
7:45–8–Manual of arms
8–8:30–Bayonet exercises
8:30–9–Extended order
9–9:30–Lectures by officers
9:30–9:40–Rest
9:40–10:15–Grenade drill
10:15–10:45–Aiming and sighting
10:45–11:15–Athletic instruction

11:15–11:30—Close-order drill
11:45—Inspection: men, tents, streets
12:—Mess
1–1:30—Extended order drill
1:30–2—Gas-mask drill
2–2:30—More lectures
2:30–3—Close-order drill
3–3:30—Platoon movements
3:30–4—NCO's drill company and platoons
4–4:30—Rifle instruction
4:30–5—Advance guard and reconnaissance
5–6—Rest
6—Mess

Taps blew at ten o'clock. One soldier described the whole routine as "we have been gassed. We have hurled bombs that flew back at us so rapidly that we received the impression that we had thrown them backward. We have vibrated at the safe end of Chauchat automatic rifles. We have speared dummy Huns on a bayonet run that would discourage the Ringling Brothers. . . . Incidentally, you have no idea what the word discomfort means until you try on a gas mask or respirator. Did you ever try swallowing a hot-water bottle? Did you ever clip a clothespin over your nose and then try earnestly to thrust your head into a rubber boot? Sometime cover your favorite pillow with a slip made of Tanglefoot flypaper and try a nap thereon."

They were marched until a twenty-five-mile hike which had taken three days when they first came in could be made in one; they drilled in dummy trench systems and simulated attacks supported by real artillery fire. In the end there was less talk about the miseries of camp life and a great deal more griping about the delay in getting to France. Outside one camp a touring evangelist had hung his "Where Will You Spend Eternity?" sign, and an infantryman had lettered under it "At Camp McClellan."

Enormous athletic programs were set up, partially in the interests of physical fitness, partly to give the men something to do or watch in their spare time; specialty schools for odd skills such as horse-shoeing were set up, war-risk insurance sold all around. All across the country real infantry divisions began to exist where there had been only crowds of draftees before. In each there were two infantry brigades—with two infantry regiments and a machine-gun battalion each—plus a field artillery brigade of three field artillery regiments and an engineer regiment and a machine-gun battalion. These were heavy divisions—with their supply and repair units they came to 979 officers and 28,050 men, which meant that they were roughly twice as large as a French, British, or German division.

The nation got into the habit of coming down to camp on Sundays to look at them, and a wit at Camp Upton, New York, made out the following table of organization for the "Family Squad": "In charge, One Papa, equipped with package containing pie; One Mamma, equipped with expression 'My Goodness!', One Sweetheart, pretty, never dressed warmly enough for the cold weather (her silk skirt battling with contrary winds); and One Brother, either above or below draft age, looking gawky and out of place in his civilians. The rear rank consisted of assorted Uncles, Aunts, Cousins, and Friends, very poorly drilled."[6]

Ready or not, the Americans were needed in France. So far the war had gone this way: the Germans had started in 1914 with a big sweep across France, the weight of it coming down through virtually defenseless Belgium and then heading for Paris. They almost made it, but two things went wrong. First, a small number of divisions—but perhaps a crucial number—had to be pulled out and sent to the Russian front where the Czar's troops were dying with abandon in defense of the motherland. Second, things moved so fast that various sections of the attack became a little disjointed. The French managed to find a hole in the line during the First Battle of the Marne in September, 1914, hit the advancing Germans on the flank, and send the whole thrust jarring back on its heels.

Both sides then settled down to forming the continuous line across France which became the feature of the Western Front. The Germans turned their attention to chewing up the ill-armed Russians. Winston Churchill tried to take the pressure off the Czar with a landing at the Dardanelles, but the project failed when it ran into surprisingly hard-fighting Turks.

In 1916 the Germans tried to smash through around Verdun, but the French cried, "They shall not pass," and held on. Then in April of 1917 the French commander in chief, Robert Nivelle, decided that all the attack really needed was a little more determination behind it. He bled his army white in an offensive so pigheaded that the men revolted and some regiments threatened to march on Paris. It was May 15 before the government chucked Nivelle out and put in Henri Philippe Pétain, with Ferdinand Foch as his chief of staff. Before the affair was over some 123 French soldiers had been sentenced to death and 23 of them actually executed. In July the British attacked—note that the Allies were so badly organized that the French and the British attacks were not coordinated—and in three months' fighting managed to gain a miserable fifty square miles, and acquire 340,000 casualties.

The Germans understood the need for new tactics. German divisions were sent to bolster the Austrian divisions on the front in northern Italy and in October they slammed through the Italian lines at Caporetto. The technique was new: a short, sharp barrage instead of one that lasted for days, small units going ahead as fast as they could, with strong points left to be cleaned up later. The notion was that it was easier to shock and demoralize an enemy than to kill him outright, and one of the young German officers who studied the lesson hard was Erwin Rommel, who would command the Afrika Korps in the Second World War. It worked beautifully. Before the front could be stabilized, Italy had lost 600,000 men and was almost out of the war.

The Germans were having their own man-power problems, but before 1917 was over the Bolsheviks had taken Russia out of the war. That meant that the full weight of German troops could be transferred to the Western Front and no one doubted that the spring of 1918 would see a major German offensive designed to force a decision before American troops could arrive in quantity. The situation must have looked good to the Germans. They had an advantage of 300,000 men over the French and British; moreover, these were men heartened by the recent victory in Italy. No one knew whether the French had recovered from the revolt which had followed Nivelle's follies, or what the British would be like after the grinding defeats of the summer.

As early as June, 1917, enough transports were scraped together in New York to ship over 14,500 men—elements of the First Division plus a regiment of Marines. The First—"The Big Red One"—so called because of its shoulder patch, contained some of the oldest and best units in the regular army. Its 18th Infantry Regiment had a history going back to the War of 1812 and a distinguished record in the western campaigns of the Civil War; the 6th Field Artillery Regiment had first seen light as Captain Stille's Company of Artillerists and Engineers, organized in 1798. Others, such as the 7th Field Artillery, had been organized just before war broke out by pulling batteries from other regular regiments and filling them out with newly enlisted men. The Marines were companies from the 5th Marine Regiment, veterans of the occupations of Veracruz, Mexico, and Haiti. Eventually they'd become part of the Second Division which was organized in France and took as its motto "Second—To None." In all, the first shipment added up to men for less than half a division, but it gave Pershing something to start with. So far, he'd spent most of his time being hustled to ceremonial appearances for the benefit of Allied morale.

With cruisers as a protection against surface raiders and a screen of destroyers against submarines, the transports made it unscathed in spite of a couple of brushes with the subs and a fan of four torpedoes fired through the convoy. The French jubilantly published the news of their arrival at Saint-Nazaire on June 27 and Pershing promptly raised all kinds of hell in favor of secrecy of troop movements. A few days later he relented enough to let a battalion go up to Paris for a Fourth-of-July celebration.

The general was not entirely pleased with what he saw of his first big parade. "Although these troops were from a regular regiment [the 16th], we were not prepared to make much of an impression from the military point of view as the unit had recently been raised to war strength and about two thirds of the men were recruits. The untrained, awkward appearance of this unit, which was regarded by French officers as representing our regular army, could not have escaped their critical observation."

Whatever the French officers thought, Paris loved it. The New York *Times* reported the next day, "All France celebrated the Fourth of July. Paris turned out a crowd that no American city ever surpassed for size, enthusiasm, and profusion of Stars and Stripes.

"A battalion of the first American expeditionary force about to leave for training behind the battle front had its first official review in France and was the center of the celebration. . . .

"Everywhere the American flag was flying from public buildings, hotels, and residences, and from automobiles, cabs, and carts; horses' bridles and the lapels of pedestrians carried them. . . .

"About the Court of Honor where the Americans were drawn up with a detachment of French Territorials the buildings overflowed with crowded humanity to the roofs. . . .

"The enthusiasm of the vast crowd reached its highest pitch when General Pershing, escorted by President Poincaré, Marshal Joffre . . . passed along the line of the Americans drawn up in square formations. Cheering broke out anew when the American band played the 'Marsellaise' and again when the French band played 'The Star-Spangled Banner' and Pershing received the flags from the President. . . .

" 'Vivent les Américains,' 'Vivent Pershing,' 'Vivent les États Unis,' shouted over and over by the crowd, greeted the American standard bearers as they advanced."

The men then marched out to Lafayette's tomb and "the battalion was joined by a great crowd, many women forcing their way into the ranks and swinging along arm in arm with the men. With wreaths about their necks and bouquets in their hats and rifles, the column looked like a moving flower garden." At the tomb Pershing said a few words, but the honors for the occasion went to his staff officer, Colonel Charles Stanton, who gave the day a phrase to remember by getting up and announcing "Lafayette, we are here!"

A Berlin newspaper trumpeted that it was "firmly convinced that there is little or no truth in the reports of the landing of large American forces in France." Rather, it felt a small contingent was "being taken around there for show purposes to revive French courage . . . there is no American danger within measurable time."

There was some ground for German optimism. The rest of the First Division would come over in July, the regular regiments and Marines which would eventually make up the Second would follow. Then there'd be the first National Guard outfit—the Yankee Division, the Twenty-sixth, from New England—and in October the Rainbow, the

Forty-second. Pershing wanted a million men in France by May of 1918. The Allies watched troop movements and figured he'd be lucky to get half that.

State side, though, things were happening: the Navy was solving the transport problem, and in October Camp Merritt—just up Hudson from Hoboken, New Jersey, port of embarkation—opened as the first of the big embarkation camps. Into Merritt moved an outfit due to be shipped out. It was checked out for equipment down to the last button, had its sick weeded out and its foreigners sworn in as citizens. Then it marched down the steep, winding road to the Hudson River's edge where ferryboats waited to haul the men to the Hoboken piers. More than one farm boy looked at the ferries and wondered how he'd ever make it across the ocean in them. The downriver trip was usually made at night and the men stood around the piers, often for hours, facing a dawn brightened only by Red Cross girls with refreshments. It was estimated that one day's embarkation at New York might involve ten tons of coffee, three tons of rolls, a ton of cigarettes, and several hundredweights of ice cream and cookies. The Red Cross also gave out "safe arrival" cards on which were printed "The ship on which I sailed has arrived safely overseas." The soldier could address as many as he pleased; the lot were kept in New York and dispatched when word came that the ship was safely in France.

They went aboard ships painted in grotesque black, white, and gray stripings—"dazzle painting"—which was supposed to confuse enemy submarines by breaking up the vessel's normal silhouette and thus making sub captains uncertain about which way their targets were heading. In some cases bows were even painted onto sterns, but postwar research indicated that the sub skippers remained remarkably unfooled.

Sailors led the men down to their bunks, four deep pipe bunks so close that a man could hardly get through. A private in the 306th Field Artillery wrote (with apologies to Ring Lardner): "I asked a naval guy on the ship, 'What's the idea?' and he says . . . the idea being that if the boat was captured we could be safe because the Germans couldn't get thru the ailes [sic] to our bunks."[7] The orders were to lie down in the bunks and stay there until the ship was clear of the harbor. After that it was abandon-ship drill, two meals a day cafeteria style, lookout duty until the end of the ride . . . and sea-sickness. The malady was helped along by the pale blue lights used below decks at night which made the well look ill and the ill in an advanced state of decomposition. A Lieutenant Heath of the 168th Iowa got so sick on lookout in the crow's-nest that he had to hang on through several watches before he felt strong enough to climb down. The 168th in general had bad luck going over. On their first sailing, on which the ship had to turn back, they went on the *President Grant.* They were Iowa boys and the ships were new to them anyway; one of them looked around the cramped quarters and announced, "I've eaten like a hog and maybe I've lived like one, but I'm damned if I've ever been crated before." The heads—Navy for toilets—got out of order and water was so short the soldiers were buying it from the sailors at fifty cents a canteenful. One of their medical officers summed it up with, "This was, without doubt, the most unsanitary vessel of ancient or modern times. The conditions were directly due to the colossal ignorance and inefficiency of the naval officers who refused to accept the advice of the competent army medical men on board."[8]

To make it worse, the Iowans felt abandon-ship drill was usually held during meals—so if the ship rolled a bit, a man came back and found his chow on the deck. Fortunately, the *Grant's* boilers gave out a few days out and the 168th came back to the States. Next time they were shipped on a British steamer, and the voyage was un-eventful if one overlooks a riot staged by the men over the food served for Thanksgiving dinner.

The *Grant* was an exception. By and large, the trips produced no more than normal griping and the men tried to keep amused by staging boxing matches, band concerts, and getting out a ship's paper. The Twenty-seventh Division's *Sea Serpent* is typical of the salt-water humorous journalism:

EXTRA
MID OCEAN — 18 U BOATS SENT TO BOTTOM
AFTER NINE HOUR RUNNING FIGHT
The signal for the attack given from the stern where 26 men in the pay of the Imperial German Government secretly gathered and sang "Die Wacht Am Rhine." Immediately, periscopes leaped to the surface.

A doughboy in a New York regiment moaned, "God, I can lick the

Kaiser on land, but I'm a sonofagun, he's got me licked on the water."
One unfortunate lieutenant spent his nights lashed in a deck chair,
too weak to stagger below even when surfeited with lemon drops,
the standard remedy. It was noted that a great many mess kits were
chucked overboard as being of absolutely no use in the immediate
situation.

Over and over again, though, a thrill runs through the narratives
when the edge of the danger zone is reached, the cruiser escort turns
back, and the little destroyers steam out of the mist and into position
around the convoy. A merchant skipper wrote of the little ships making the rendezvous in a dead fog: "The excellent manner in which
they made contact under such conditions has been considered almost
uncanny by the general commanding army forces as well as the
United States senator on board."

If the troop convoys were uncomfortable, the animal convoys
leaving from the Norfolk area were a great deal worse. A sergeant
from the Rainbow Division left a record of a crossing in an "old tub"
with 1,600 horses and mules. "The storm tossed our ship about like a
top. . . . The mountainous waves rolled us around like a ball. The
animals in housings on the top deck were thrown all over the deck. . . .
The screaming and yelling of the animals was pitiful. There wasn't
a thing we could do for them the way the ship was rolling. . . . We
started bailing the water out of number 4 hatch. The animals which
had died in this hatch were torn to pieces. When we stood on the
runway to bail out water, legs, heads, and guts were floating around
in the inky black water. . . . After three days and three nights of bailing we got the water out. We started then to clean up the ship and
get back to our chambermaid duties. There were 250 dead animals
lying around. We tossed them over the side. When we got to the last
ones to go over, they were like butter. The rope which was put around
them just cut right straight through. . . . When we arrived at Saint-
Nazaire [and] started to unload our animals it was just a little more
than some of them could take. They went down the gangplank onto
the dock, let out a heehaw, and dropped dead."[9]

On the long front running from Switzerland to the English Channel
the British held the northern end, the French the center covering
Paris, while the southern end was covered with dribs and drabs, divi-

sions pulled out of the line for a rest and what not. It had been a quiet sector since 1914. Since he'd be dispossessing no one in particular, Pershing decided this was the spot for the Americans. They could learn their business there and when the American army was ready in 1918, drive north to the iron and coal fields and the great rail center at Metz. The general set up shop at Chaumont, an ancient town of about fifteen thousand people in eastern France, and the First Division was ordered to nearby Gondrecourt for training.

NORTHERN FRANCE: The American headquarters was at Chaumont

From Saint-Nazaire to Gondrecourt, a little country town, it was the "side-door pullmans," little French boxcars with *"Chevaux—8, Hommes—40*—8 horses or 40 men—stenciled on the sides and whistles that "emitted thin anaemic shrieks." One soldier noted that the condition of the cars suggested that horses had been the last passengers. They rode for two days and nights, sleeping on straw, eating cold rations, and if the trains were bad, the billets at the end of the ride weren't much better. There were no camps, just barns and lofts, most of them in a state of repair which let more weather in than it kept out. As the autumn advanced, the weather turned just as nasty as it was in the States. Men slept with their shoes on for fear of finding them frozen to the ground in the morning, as damp floors turned icy at night. The food wasn't bad, but not good enough to keep one doughboy from saying, "Captain, I'd just like to get my head in a Camp Hancock garbage can for thirty minutes and get a square meal."

The expression "doughboy" was the soldiers' word for themselves. It was originally an English Navy term for a dumpling, but got transferred to the infantry in the days when troops used pipe clay on their uniforms, that substance producing a doughy mess when it got wet. To our Allies we were Yanks—as the English were Tommies, the French *poilus,* the Australians Aussies, the New Zealanders Kiwis. In the very beginning there was some tendency to use "Sammies," derived from Uncle Sam, but the men never cared for it, and when George M. Cohan wrote in "Over There" that "The Yanks are coming" he clinched the change-over.

The First settled down to work, sometimes harboring the suspicion, endemic among troops overseas, that back home they didn't know there was a war on. Pershing was forced to supplement Baker's efforts by telling the States to issue no passports to the wives or sisters of officers and by October was riled enough to fire off a suggestion that no more good shipping space be wasted on the likes of cuspidors, bookcases, bathtubs, or lawn mowers.

At first training followed state-side lines—French and British officers teaching the rudiments in mock-up trench systems with trench weapons like mortars. Pershing fumed to have the men taken out of the trenches and trained in "open warfare". Moreover, he had a hunch that while the new weapons were all right, nothing could really replace a man with a rifle he could fire accurately. At the moment, though, he was a general without much of an army and no one paid attention. Even some of his own junior officers speculated that the general had "learned nothing since Custer and apparently couldn't learn."

Then it was October, and the decision was made for one battalion from each regiment to go into the line in the Toul sector for ten days with the French. French officers would command, American officers observe.

OCTOBER, 1917: The first Americans went into the line near Nancy. The solid line indicates the front

The spot selected was on the quiet part of the front, just west of Nancy. The infantry moved up in trucks; the artillery had to come farther from the special artillery camp at Valdahon. The brigadier of the 6th Field Artillery got his boys together and abjured them not to let either the 5th or the 7th Field Artillery get in a shot ahead of them. Then he got Battery C—which he'd once commanded himself—off by itself and "with some profanity insisted that it *must* be the winner."[10]

Battery C listened and then started off as if it wasn't going to win anything. The first move was a twenty-mile night march in the rain to the rail center at Besançon. C slipped and slid over the road, horses falling, caissons tipping over. They got lost in the streets of Besançon and staggered into the railroad yard just in time for a staff colonel to chew them out for not having gotten there sooner. Their horses didn't like the *"Chevaux—8, Hommes—40"* any better than the men did, and some of them had to be hog-tied and dragged to get them aboard. The next night they disembarked in the village of Saint-Nicholas du Port, near Toul, found no one to meet them, and bedded down as best they could.

The French, they found, were not at all enthusiastic about anyone firing a first shot. This was a nice, quiet sector, and the French, like sensible veterans, were quite happy to keep it that way. Nevertheless, Captain Idus McLendon commanding C was mindful of his instructions, and on the night of October 22 manhandled a gun across ground too muddy for horses and into firing position. Officers were on the ropes, pulling away with the men. He then repaired to French Major Villers and made an impassioned plea to be allowed to fire. Villers gave in. McLendon discovered that he had forgotten to bring up any ammunition, but by this time Villers was so charged up that he borrowed twenty-four rounds from a French battery. At five minutes past six on the morning of October 23, 1917, Captain McLendon said "Fire!" Sergeant Alex Arch pulled the lanyard, and the first American shot of the war was on its way. The memorable empty case was sent home to President Wilson as a souvenir.

On the night of November 2–3 the first battalions finished their turn and the second battalions moved in. One of them was the Second Battalion, 16th Infantry, the outfit Pershing had sent up to Paris to parade on the Fourth of July. Now they were coming to start payment on the promises they'd made that day and the first one wasn't long coming. It was three that morning, with the Sixteenth dug in along the top of a bare hill, when the Germans put a box barrage down on them, cutting off one platoon from help from the flanks or the rear. Then the German raiding party came on, blowing gaps in the barbed wire and diving into the trenches for a vicious little close-in fight that was over almost before it started. The raiders pulled out with 11 prisoners and left three dead men, one shot, one with his throat cut, one with his head bashed in by a rifle butt in the trench.

They were Corporal James B. Gresham, four-year veteran of Evansville, Indiana, Private Thomas Enright, eight-year veteran of Pittsburgh, Pennsylvania, and Private Merle Hay, wartime volunteer of Glidden, Iowa. These were the first Americans to die in combat, and when the news got back home a few days later, the newspapers hurried around to their next of kin. Gresham's mother was hanging out her wash when they told her. "God help me to endure," she sobbed. "Yes, he's a hero and for his sake I ought to be brave. But I'm not a hero. I'm just a mother." Enright's closest relative was a sister, and she hadn't even known that he was in France. Hay's father said, "I'm proud of my boy." His mother collapsed and could say nothing.

Christopher Morley produced a verse for the old *Life* magazine:

> Gresham, Enright and Hay!
> There are no words to say
> Our love, our noble pride
> For these, our first who died.

In all, there would be 116,516 American dead before it was finished. Now, we had barely that many troops in France, but the training period was over.

Chapter Three

"DO YOUR BIT"

BACK HOME: APRIL, 1917–JANUARY, 1918

Two days after Wilson had signed the Declaration of War came Easter Sunday. This time, though, the traditional Easter parade along New York's Fifth Avenue had a new look—drab. There weren't many people out walking, and the clothes were a great deal more sober than usual. The moralists concluded that people were getting the war spirit; the cynics noted that it had been a cold, gray day and decided there would have been very little parading, war or no.

In truth, no one knew quite how to react to the war because so far not even the men at the very top knew what it was going to be like. The more sophisticated could guess that all the young and youngish single men would go into uniform, that many of them would fight overseas. Indeed this was so evident that New York's City clerk Patrick Scully noted the boom in marriages and remarked, "I have reluctantly come to the conclusion that this unprecedented increase in the number of applications for marriage licenses is due in a very great degree to the recent announcement that all single men between nineteen and twenty-five may be drafted for military service. Any man who thus seeks to hide behind a woman's skirts is a moral and physical coward."

We knew a little about putting masses of men under arms from the Civil War experience, but there was nothing in the past to prepare us for the way the home front was going to be involved, the whole production capacity of the country harnessed to the armed forces. There was going to be almost a whole year of feeling our way before we really got the thing rolling.

On April 11 the baseball season started as though nothing unusual were going on . . . or almost nothing. The Boston Red Sox, with a good left-hander named Babe Ruth pitching, whipped the Yankees 10 to 3. The only martial note was a drill put on by the Yanks, using bats for rifles, and a sports writer noted that they drilled better than they hit. In the National League the champion Brooklyn club—variously called the Robins or the Superbas—lost to the Phillies without any drill at all and the Giants got rained out.

On the same day, though, the American flag went into battle for the first time. One William Clancy, who had enlisted with the Canadians, tied it to his bayonet during an attack at Vimy. Rumor had it that Clancy was a Texan, which seemed to please everybody; in due time, however, he turned out to be from Boston. It was hard to say just how far our patriotism was carrying us. On April 13 it was noted that volunteering had slumped off in spite of vigorous efforts to promote it. On the other hand, demand had driven the price of American flags sky high and Assistant Secretary of Treasury Norton felt the situation serious enough to denounce the flagmakers as profiteers.

At New York's Hippodrome Mrs. Harry Payne Whitney's Junior Patriots put on an evening of "living pictures—they were posed by men and women prominent in society." Ernest Thompson Seton, the wild-life author and chief of the Woodcraft League, urged his young followers to plant potatoes and take as their motto "The hoe behind the flag." Up at Callicoon, New York, we took what may have been in a sense our first war casualty: banker John Dering was shot while seated in his living room by a National Guard sentry who let fly wildly, without realizing how far his bullet would carry, at what he thought was a skulker in the underbrush. During a performance of Barnum and Bailey's Circus a Russian bear attacked an animal trainer of German extraction; newspaper reporters found some in the audience who thought they saw a portent of things to come, others were simply delighted to have a German bitten.

Even so early in the game it didn't pay to have a German name. Mrs. Hugo Heisinger—daughter of the St. Louis beer baron Adolphus Busch—found herself under suspicion of spying simply because she had a wireless telegraph set in her house. The set turned out, undramatically, to belong to one of her servants who was studying wireless at that hotbed of sedition, the local YMCA. A munitions plant in Chester, Pennsylvania, blew up, killing 125, and the public leaped to the conclusion that it was German sabotage. Down in Alabama federal agents seized two men "believed German" who were thought to be inciting Negro miners to go to Mexico. On Broadway George Arliss opened in a revival of his great hit *Disraeli*; for his curtain speech he reminded the audience that Dizzy had always warned against the Prussians. Across the country people were alerted by patriotic organizations to watch out for "gloaters"—characters who seemed to smile or otherwise exhibit satisfaction at news of German victories.

The country resounded with urgings to "do your bit," and as the draft legislation went before Congress, it was clear what the men's bit was going to be. Just what a woman could do was less certain. Stern's department store took note of her traditional role with an ad, "Women's Correct Attire for Mourning Wear," but the traditional role wasn't going to be enough. Women were moving out of the kitchen. The more militant had been stomping around the country demanding the vote and something called "equal rights" which in plain English seemed to include the right to lead premarital sex lives. Already they were seeping into war industry—half the dead in the Chester munitions explosion had been girls and ads urged women to come to school to prepare themselves as electrical workers and in other defense specialties. B. Altman offered a "Military Suit for Women—The Fusilier," then Franklin-Simon went them one better with "Military Khaki Dresses for Girls Fourteen to Twenty." Even the well-bred young ladies of the very social Lenox, Massachusetts, summer colony were announced as having completed a course in type-writing to fit themselves for "patriotic work" in addition to their previous studies in canning and preserving fruits. Some girls, of course, went along as though they didn't know there was a war on. In New York City a maid in the home of a professor was arrested for slipping roach powder into the family's food. This, the papers said, came as a great disappointment to the maid since it was alleged she had been hoping that the milkman was going to get blamed, he having been an intimate of hers and (in the journalese of the day) "treated her unkindly." In the same city a Mr. Cahane was asking for a divorce because his wife insisted on living next to a graveyard even though she knew full well that Mr. Cahane was scared to death of ghosts.

Down in Washington the cold spring turned hot and steamy and the Government tried to organize the country for war. The draft was off and running; for the home front, they had the old Council of National Defense, a purely advisory body, to build on. It had been around since 1916—some Cabinet officers backed up by the Advisory Commission of the Council which consisted of Bernard Baruch, the Wall Street operator; Julius Rosenwald of Sears, Roebuck; Daniel Willard, a railroad man; Dr. Hollis Godfrey, the head of Drexel Engineering Institute; Samuel Gompers, president of the American Federation of Labor; Howard Coffin, an automotive engineer; and finally Dr. Franklin Martin from the American College of Surgeons.

To this was added, shortly after the Declaration of War, the General Munitions Board. Obviously, the Government was about to become the chief purchaser of everything and the General Munitions Board was supposed to keep the various departments of the Government from beating their brains out—and incidentally raising prices clean out of sight—by competing with each other. In the long run the Board was going to get its own brains beaten out, but we were new at the industrial mobilization business. There was a root problem: the best way to run a war is from the top with sundry czars saying who can do what. Against this: the sense of the nation was against industrial combination; we'd just come through our "trust-busting" period. Combination in business was good for efficiency in wartime, but it was going to take Washington a year to figure that out. The Board was told it would be a perfectly splendid thing if various government bureaus didn't fall all over each other trying to get supplies in the open market, but it was given no authority to slap them down when they did so. Accordingly, the agencies went their own way and the Board was not long for this world. Later, the control of business would become, according to an industrial historian, ". . . . absolute. There was no freedom of individual enterprise. The control was autocratic, as powerful as any which ever reigned in the Russia of the Romanoffs."[1] First, though, there was going to have to be a near collapse of the entire production program.

Here was the problem: there were army camps, guns, planes, ships to be built; to get the raw materials with which to build them, the manufacturers—decently patriotic men, anxious to "do their bit"—were chasing raw materials for the job around the market. The requisite steel for a given job might go, for example, to the most diligent chaser rather than the manufacturer of the commodity most needed at the moment. Clearly someone had to say who would get what raw materials when and—lest the Government be bankrupt in the process—what price would be paid for them. Moreover, the demand for cannon—to take one instance—being what it is in the normal peacetime market, some people were obviously going to have to go into the cannon business who hadn't been there before. Again, someone was going to have to say who was to do it. Finally, with all these raw materials, finished products, and army man power moving around the country, the nation's railroad system—a collection of Toonerville Trolley lines—was going to jam up unless there was someone to say what moved where and when.

By July, 1917, the all-bark, no-bite General Munitions Board had had it, and the Council of National Defense produced the brand-new War Industries Board to replace it. At first it amounted to a resounding increase in title, but real control was coming. Baruch, who was going to wind up running the whole show, slid over into the new setup as the man in charge of raw materials.

That wasn't the only change in July. Over at the Shipping Board—created by Congress in 1916 as a peaceable sort of defense measure since it involved only merchant ships—the chairman and the general manager came into headlong collision over steel vs. wooden ships (not to mention the question of divided authority), and both resigned. Everybody knew the American merchant marine didn't amount to much—only about 10 per cent of our trade traveled in American bottoms—and since ships, lots of ships, were clearly necessary if American men, guns, and food were to make themselves felt in Europe, there was loud public outcry and Edward Hurley, a Chicago businessman and early Wilson backer, was summoned to take charge. His previous government service consisted of some time on the Red Cross War Council, but shipbuilding experience or no, he did have a sense of urgency. He promptly issued an order taking over the shipyards. The yards howled bloody murder, but henceforth they were working for the Government. Involved in the take over were 431 hulls which the yards had down for private firms and various foreign governments; they now belonged to the Fleet Corporation, the operating arm of the Shipping Board. In addition, existing American vessels over 2,500 tons were requisitioned and contracts let for the construction of new shipyards. The largest of them—it would be the largest shipyard in the world—was signed in September. It was to be built on Hog Island, a dismal marsh in the Delaware River. When completed it would have building ways for 50 ships and fitting-out piers for another 28. To supplement the fleet until all this new construction should become real, Hurley even brought steamers through from the Great Lakes, 12 of them being cut in two, then reassembled to get them through the locks in the Welland Canal.

Out on the Pacific Coast two visionaries set about building concrete ships as a means of getting the necessary tonnage quickly, but Fleet Corporation eyed them coldly and proceeded along different if similarly novel lines. Its notion was the "fabricated ship," a vessel made from standardized parts in the same way that Henry Ford rolled his cars off an assembly line. Since every ship in the world at that point had been handmade there was no precedent to go on; to Theodore Ferris, naval architect, went the task of designing one suitable for fabrication. What he came up with was no beauty, but her components could be mass produced anywhere, even far inland, and shipped to the assembly site.

Thus the shipbuilding program, and it was typical: ambitious, vigorously pushed, and seemingly well adapted to the American mass-production genius. It was also going to be an almost total failure in the sense that very little that it produced ever went to war. The first ship delivered by fabled Hog Island, that self-proclaimed Eighth Wonder of the World with its 846 acres, 250 buildings and $65,000,000 construction cost, was not to arrive until after the war was over. In the summer of 1917, though, no one could see that far ahead, least of all the general public. It had been proclaimed that "A Bridge of Ships" to France was in the making and the public expected just that, overnight or possibly just a little bit sooner.

Not the least cause of great expectations for this and other programs which never flew so high as expected was the work of that remarkable man George Creel. The marvelous Creel, a one-time crusading magazine journalist from New York, may be said to have been the first man to bring Madison Avenue to Washington; it would not be amiss if the host of public-relations men, public information officers, communications counselors, and the like now infesting that community were to erect a statue to him as their founding father and patron saint. None exists; by the time Creel left Washington there

were very few local citizens who would have contributed a dime to
such an enterprise.

Creel got into the act through a letter to Wilson while the President
was considering the censorship problem directly after the Declaration
of War. It was his suggestion that the Government go beyond something so negative as censorship to something positive, the war being
"a plain publicity proposition, a vast enterprise in salesmanship, the
world's greatest adventure in advertising." It was, in fact, his notion
to "weld the people of the United States into one white-hot mass in-
stinct with fraternity, devotion, courage, and deathless determination." Wilson took him on as executive secretary of the Committee
on Public Information, the committee itself consisting of the secre-
taries of state, war, and navy. If he imagined that a mere three
Cabinet members would hold Creel in check, he misread his man.

According to those who knew him, Creel in private was a jolly soul,
given to funny stories and good at mimicry, a form of humor much
admired by the President himself. In public life, however, he has been
called "a man of primitive violence," a man "compounded of the
berserker qualities of Danton, Marat, and Charlotte Corday," a man
who became "blind drunk . . . the minute he opened his public
mouth."[2]

These qualities would become apparent enough later on—particularly in his relations with Congress—but for the moment he appeared
a jet-propelled Godsend. The newspapers feared a genuine censorship.
The various government departments felt it safer for the moment to
exercise a rigorous self-censorship rather than release any news which
could conceivably be of value to the enemy. Creel promptly sent his
staff swarming through the Government, routing out any bit of news
they could lay their hands on, preparing releases and restraining the
papers only to the extent of a simple document entitled "What the
Government Asks of the Press." It contained a list of eighteen items
on which the papers were asked not to publish information—troop
movements, experiments in new weapons and the like—and concluded
with the note that ". . . enforcement is a matter for the press itself."

Telling people what not to print was the smallest part of Creel's
plans; he now set about selling the war to the American people and,
finally, selling America to the rest of the world. Seventy-five million
copies of pamphlets written by scholars to explain America's history

and war aims were distributed in this country and more overseas. A bevy of French and English lecturers were imported to whoop it up; Creel's favorites were Captain Paul Périgord and Countess De Bryas. The captain, a priest when the war broke out, had won his commission leading a charge at Verdun. He was possessed of "a voice like an organ note"; Creel kept him on tour for seven months, at the end of which time he collapsed from exhaustion. The countess, a beauty, was found particularly apt at mingling with defense workers. She kept her white gloves, thus dirtied by contact with the proletariat, as souvenirs until she, too, had a breakdown. A man of feverish energy himself, Creel added a domestic model called The Four-Minute Man who lectured his community for four minutes on various subjects Creel considered important. These gentlemen—75,000 in all—were dropped into the middle of movie programs, armed by Creel with two or three suggested versions of addresses on "Why We Are Fighting," "What Our Enemy Really Is," "Food Conservation," and the like Creel estimated that in all they made 755,190 speeches, "every one having the carry of shrapnel." A grateful nation nicknamed them The Stentorian Guard.

For those unable or unwilling to read or listen Creel organized a Division of Pictorial Publicity headed by the country's most distinguished popular artist, Charles Dana Gibson. Urging his forces on with the cry "Draw till it hurts," Gibson lined up the graphic talent of the nation and a flood of posters followed. The most famous of them all—James Montgomery Flagg's pointing Uncle Sam with the caption "I want you"—is probably still the best known of all the representations of our national figure.

The infant art of the motion picture was also brought into play with epics like *Pershing's Crusaders* and *America's Answer*, put together out of Signal Corps clips. Popular at home, there was some difficulty in getting them shown in neutral countries abroad. Creel promptly arranged to have American theatrical films withheld from non-cooperators; faced with a no-propaganda-films, no-Mary Pickford threat, the foreign distributors got into line.

Thus the propaganda machinery was going full blast even if the assembly lines weren't, and Creel's great work—making Woodrow Wilson and his Fourteen Points the hope of the people of the world—was still ahead of him. For the energetic one, though, troubles were beginning. When Rear Admiral Albert Gleaves' first troop convoy of June, 1917, got through safely, the admiral sent back a report which, along with less exciting details, told of submarine attacks on his ships. Creel worked it up into a statement for the secretary of the navy, and if his version of the sub attacks lost nothing in the retelling, it did not go beyond the statements Gleaves had made. The nation rejoiced mightily, then thought twice when an Associated Press story from London said that there had been no attacks at all, that green seamen had fired their heads off at floating sticks and fish. The press denounced Creel for a "Fourth-of-July hoax," Senator Boise Penrose, Republican boss of Pennsylvania, demanded an investigation. Eventually the original of Gleaves' report took Creel off the hook; he was free to proceed to troubles of his own making.

Despite the Creel exhortations, there were a few people who had not been in favor of the war, were not in favor of it, and intended to remain so. It had scarcely been declared when the editor of the anarchist *New Era* called for a strike against it and got himself arrested. Come September and an assortment of convinced pacifists, socialists, anarchists, members of that leftist labor union, the International Workers of the World—the Wobblies—and some just plain crackpots were assembling in the Midwest under the title People's Council of America for Democracy and Peace and looking for a place to meet and protest. Delegates converging from the East and West had been trying to assemble in Minneapolis, Chicago, or Milwaukee and in the face of official displeasure in all those cities were about to move on to Washington, D.C. Meanwhile, a Labor Loyalty Conference—pro-war—set up in Minneapolis, its delegates having sped thither in a train Creel entitled "The Red, White, and Blue Special."

On September 3, however, Mayor Big Bill Thompson of Chicago— he who was later to offer to punch the King of England in the snoot— decided that the protesters could come to his town. "Sure, go ahead," he told them, "just as long as you behave yourselves," and even provided police protection since it was just time for the draftees to move to camp and the chances of violence correspondingly good. Governor Frank Lowden, who had already told the pacifists they couldn't meet in Illinois, sent troops to break the whole thing up, but they got there too late—the pacifists met for a short session and adjourned in what may have been record-breaking time while they still had their health.

Just what turned Thompson into a flaming civil libertarian is hard to estimate; perhaps his large collection of Irish voters who were anti-English, hence anti-war, is as good a guess as any. Chicago didn't even bother to ask why, the papers blasted Thompson and urged impeachment. The mayor listened attentively, then sued the Chicago *Herald* for $250,000, the *Tribune* for $500,000, the *Daily News* for $250,000, and various private citizens who'd had harsh things to say for a total of $600,000. In all, the suits came to $1,600,000, and Thompson went right on being mayor of Chicago.

Just as Wilson had predicted to Frank Cobb, though, there was going to be very little spirit of tolerance around the country in wartime. In June Congress had passed espionage and sedition laws which took in an awful lot of territory—a man could get into trouble for saying something likely to hurt the sale of war bonds, making pro-German statements, and, of course, for speaking against the Government, the flag, or the armed forces. In all, 1,600 people were arrested, and the cost to the German war effort was zero, the gain to the American effort just about the same. The first big raid came right after the Chicago peace rally. Across the country IWW offices were raided and after a a trial that lasted four months, 95 Wobblies went to jail. In New York, *The Masses*—a Greenwich Village magazine whose circulation scarcely exceeded the total of the immediate families of its contributors—had its mailing privilege taken away. In the New York *Times* there was a story predicting that as many as 100 "radical" papers might be suppressed. Just what harm any of these people were doing to the war effort would be hard to say. That the Wobblies advocated and practiced violence as a means of bringing pie in the sky for the working stiffs in the mining and lumber camps of the West is true enough. That they were seditious or even gave much of a damn about the war one way or another is dubious. *The Masses* had printed a number of reports from Europe by the Greenwich Village Golden Boy John Reed which said, "This is not our war," but it would be hard to show that they represented any clear and present danger.

The truth is that the old safe-and-sane nineteenth century was passing and the change frightened a lot of people. The labor unions were coming on—conservative ones such as Sam Gompers' A.F. of L. and rowdy ones like the I.W.W.—and the conservative grip that had been on the country since the Civil War was slipping. Teddy Roosevelt had ridden to power on the first wave of protest against business rule, Wilson had followed, and now people were worried about how far it was going to go. If the radicals at home weren't bad enough, there were the Bolsheviks in Russia. That Russia would be out of the war by the end of the year wasn't completely obvious to the home-front American in the summer of 1917, but it was clear that the middle-of-the-road Kerensky government had thrown its army in for one last offensive and been beaten. Now the soldiers wouldn't fight any more—or at least they wouldn't fight Germans—and even then it seemed at least likely that they'd shortly be fighting their own government with a man named Lenin egging them on. Hopefully a report came out of Russia that the terrible Lenin was really dead and had been since 1916; the man running around Petrograd using his name was really someone named Zaderblum.

In all, these Bolsheviks were clearly people who would take Russia out of the war if they could seize the power, and clearly the radicals in America were in sympathy with them: Q.E.D., they were dangerous and better off in jail. Eugene Debs, long-time socialist candidate for president, followed the Wobblies off to prison.

Back in 1914, when the war was brand new, Ambassador Page in London had commandeered an American mining engineer living there to help Americans stranded by the outbreak to get back home. The tourists packed off, Page was looking around for a man to administer American food sent to Belgium. As Page recalled it, he simply had the engineer in during a conference at which the Belgians explained their plight and at the end of it turned to him and said, "Hoover, you're It!"

"Mr. Hoover made no reply; he neither accepted nor rejected the proposal. He merely glanced at the clock, then got up and silently left the room. In a few minutes he returned and entered again into the discussion.

" 'Hoover, why did you get up and leave so abruptly?' " asked Page, a little puzzled over his behavior.

" 'I saw by the clock,' came the answer, 'that there was an hour left before the Exchange closed in New York. So I went out and cabled, buying several millions of bushels of wheat—for the Belgians, of course.' "[3]

When in May, 1917, Wilson needed a food commissioner Herbert

Hoover had made a record for humanity and efficiency in Belgium which left him the only possible man for the job. For once in the war, an administrator got the powers to do the job promptly—or almost promptly. England had to have wheat, the American wheat crop promised to be none too good; controls had to go on if there was to be enough to go around. The Lever Act to give the President authority on food and everything that went into producing it went before Congress in June, was wrangled over with pitiful crying about czars in Washington lording it over little farmers on the prairies, and finally became law in midsummer. The pattern for running the war was beginning to emerge—one-man control: Hurley for shipping, Creel for publicity, Hoover for food. The War Industries Board was still Hydra-headed, but changes were coming.

September and the first draftees went off to camp, but through the pleasant autumn the country still seemed half at war, half at peace. The Friends of Irish Freedom still demonstrated on the streets of New York; the cops had recently discovered that the easiest way to break them up was to run an automobile back and forth through the gathering. John McGraw's Giants and the Chicago White Sox were moving toward the pennants with comfortable leads that saved the populace the stress of a tight race in such trying times. Just to let people know we really were at war, though, the making of whisky stopped on September 8. This was not exactly prohibition, but a war measure to conserve grain; the thirsty still had legal access to such booze as had been produced prior to the deadline.

Harvard University went along with militant feminism by announcing that it was going to admit women—that is, girls from Radcliffe could go to Harvard Medical School—and in movie houses around the country there was a film called *Polly of the Circus*, starring Mae Marsh. It was the first production of a new outfit called the Samuel Goldwyn Company.

Unready yet for fighting in Europe, the troops managed a few skirmishes for home consumption. In Kentucky southern draftees and Negro civilians got into a brawl at a town fair; then out on Long Island the Rainbow Division staged a beauty. The boys in its Alabama regiment thought it was just a crying shame to be so close to the big city they'd heard so much about and yet see so little of it. Accordingly, a bunch of them got together one night, rushed past their own sentries who didn't put up much resistance, and then ran smack into the sentries of the Rainbow's New York regiment. Whether any of the boys in the head-cracking that followed knew it or not, the direct ancestors of these two regiments had met once before—at First Manassas during the Civil War. The children proved worthy of their fathers; it was a wonderful brawl that ended with the New Yorkers holding the line as if they were the French at Verdun. Surprisingly, it all made for mutual respect rather than bad blood; when the Rainbow got to France, the Alabams and the New Yorkers went into battle next to each other and the liaison couldn't have been better. The public noted the fight approvingly and anticipated what these tigers would do when turned loose on the Hun who now—according to some Allied propaganda genius—was showering France with poisoned candy dropped from airplanes for French kids to pick up.

The harsh winter which so plagued the training camps came on, and the mood of the people began to turn cold with it. Partially it was the result of the public just not understanding how long it took to organize a modern army. The old picture of Paul Revere riding through the night yelling, "The Redcoats are coming" and Great-great-great Grandfather grabbing his musket down off the wall to take his place on the firing line next morning, was a hard one to down. Instead, here was the New Year coming on, the war almost nine months old, and all we'd managed was to get the First Division into the line in a quiet sector. To make it worse, people were beginning to find out that Creel's happy handouts and the facts were two different things. Families with sons in camp heard about the wooden guns and the rocks making do as hand grenades. Parents were perhaps even more disturbed by shortages of warm winter uniforms and inadequate heating in barracks. The Christmas-leave fiasco made it plain that the railroads were in a terrible muddle. Coal was short. There were mutterings that Fuel Administrator Harry Garfield was after all a college president, and who could expect a professor to get a practical job of work done right? When Garfield tried to get priorities for coal shipments, Hoover protested that he was interfering with food deliveries and the public was treated to the spectacle of the mighty quarreling among themselves.

Congress went back into session December 3 with a good many things, some big, some small, to worry about. From overseas came

the news that the Bolsheviks were in control and definitely making
an armistice with Germany. On the Western Front the Germans were
pushing the British back around Cambrai. Behind the lines an American private made bad publicity and was hanged for raping a seven-
year-old French girl.

At home, too, besides the railroad snarl and the fuel shortage, some
of the unglamorous details of war were cropping up. A fraud indict-
ment was being handed down against a uniform manufacturer, the
coming declaration of war against Austria-Hungary meant disloca-
tions in the brick-producing field, where a vast number of workers
were Austrian, the number of American millionaires had increased
by the astonishing number of 7,925 to bring the total to 22,696. Clearly
someone was making money out of the war. Around the country vice
was booming near the camps in spite of the law against selling drinks
to men in uniform. A United States marshal raided one joint in New
Rochelle, New York, to discover a couple of hundred drunken soldiers
and sailors being attended to by young ladies in tights whose profanity, according to the marshal, was "the most sickening I have
ever heard."

Down in Dyersburg, Tennessee, a mob took a Negro accused of
raping a white woman away from the sheriff and burned him at the
stake in the town square while thousands watched as "the mob carried
out the execution quietly." Of course, a great nation at war had no
time for such matters; it was a few lines buried inside the papers
even though the acquittal of the beautiful Mrs. Blanca De Saulles in
New York for shooting her divorced husband was page one. The
jury estimated that Mrs. De Saulles was not quite of sound mind at
the time she gave her ex the business, and juror William Jones drew
a mild rebuke from the judge for smiling and winking at the lady
while the verdict was being announced.

However, Congress was coming back into session and the New
York *Times* reported that it would "convene tomorrow . . . at a time
when the situation of America . . . is more difficult, more filled with
the material of pessimism than at any time since this country entered
the war."

The session started quietly enough with war declared on Austria-
Hungary; then two disasters occurred further to upset the jittery
legislators.

At nine on the clear morning of December 7 the French freighter
Mont Blanc was working her way into Halifax, Nova Scotia, with
1,000 tons of ammunition aboard plus an on-deck cargo of benzine.
It was not a promising combination. She came to the narrows at the
entrance to the harbor just as the Belgian relief ship *Imo* was coming
out. The two vessels exchanged whistle signals and should have
passed easily clear, since even the narrows were half a mile wide.
They did not. The whistle signals were misunderstood; *Imo* rammed
Mont Blanc in the port side and the deck-loaded benzine caught fire.
Her crew tried to fight the flames, but fell back before them and
abandoned ship. Seventeen minutes after the accident, *Mont Blanc*
blew up.

The hills rising on either side of the narrows made it a trough, acting to contain the explosion and re-enforce it. Two square miles of
Halifax were flattened, and what was left of the wooden buildings
was in flames. Windows were broken 61 miles away, a telegraph
operator four miles away was killed by the blast. In all, 1,800 people—
many of them children caught in schoolhouses—were killed and 3,000
were injured. A tidal wave driven by the explosion roared into the
dock area, tearing ships from their moorings and drowning dock
workers.

Halifax's first thought was that it was a German air raid or fleet
bombardment, then they realized that it was a civilian disaster, the
greatest of the war, and set about burying their dead and housing
the 20,000 homeless. Next day a blizzard shrieked through the bleeding city to bring rescue work almost to a standstill.

It was a disaster, not an American disaster, not enough to change
the course of the war, but one more piece of rotten news. To pile it
on came the next word—the American destroyer *Jacob Jones* had been
torpedoed by a German submarine. Our first warship had gone down.

There was some partisan politics in what followed—Republican
congressmen chivvying a Democratic administration—but most of it
was sheer frustration at the way things were going. An investigation
went into the camp and arms situation. Secretary of War Baker said
we were doing very well considering how short a time we'd been at
it. The army chief of ordnance, General Crozier, endeared himself
by blaming the whole mess on Congress, then changed his mind and
decided to blame it all on Secretary Baker.

In the northeast, temperatures were sinking; half the coalyards in New York City were closed because they had nothing to sell.

General Crozier now changed his mind again and announced that the War Department was responsible for the lack of rifles and machine guns. The machine-gun manufacturers decided to say a word and declared the whole thing to be General Crozier's fault. In truth, the blame was about fifty-fifty between Baker and Crozier. On May 11 both had been told on excellent authority that the new Browning heavy machine gun was a wonderful weapon; they stalled around until September before doing anything meaningful about it.

Northeast temperatures dropped lower still, and the day after Christmas Wilson announced that the Government was taking over the railroads, so one authority could coordinate troop and supply movements. Secretary of the Treasury William Gibbs McAdoo, who'd made himself a good reputation running the first Liberty Loan drive, got the call to administer them. By New Year it was sub-zero in New York and New England; McAdoo grabbed all the rolling stock he could find and rushed coal thataway. It was a grand gesture, it thawed out the frozen citizenry, but by the time McAdoo and Fuel Administrator Harry Garfield had time to look around they found themselves faced with something much, much worse. Between the bad railway situation and their gallant efforts to keep the northeast at body temperature they had completely frozen up all of American industry east of the Mississippi River. There was no coal left to keep the wheels going around.

On January 16 the country read with amazement, horror, and a general sense that it was enough to make a man cuss that Garfield was closing down every plant east of the Mississippi—except food plants—until the railroads and coal could get straightened out. People read it and thought, "He can't mean munitions plants," then read it again, and realized that he did. The *entire* war-production machine was to come to a dead stop for five days and thereafter close down nine consecutive Mondays.

The Senate—which had felt all along that it was not being told enough about the conduct of the war—realized that things were even worse than it had imagined. On January 18 Senator George Chamberlain, of Oregon, Democrat and chairman of the Senate Committee on Military Affairs, had a date to speak in New York City before

the National Security League. It was a predominantly Republican audience, but Chamberlain put his party affiliations behind him and
told them, "The military establishment of the United States has fallen
down. . . . There is no use to be an optimist about a thing that does
not exist. It has almost stopped functioning. . . . The reason it fell is
inefficiency in every bureau and department of the Government of the
United States. . . . I speak not as a Democrat, but as an American
citizen." He then went on to demand a bipartisan war cabinet and
they cheered him with Teddy Roosevelt cheering louder than anyone
else. Teddy had been suggested by various parties for a post that
never existed, munitions administrator, and the job appealed to him.

In his shock and in his bitterness at being misled by George Creel's
"great adventure in advertising," Senator Chamberlain had over-
stated his case. In spite of the woes of poor Garfield, the establishment had not broken down. It was, in fact, just beginning to get
going. It was never going to be a tremendous success in terms of
getting American ships, artillery, or planes overseas in significant
quantities—they didn't get there, the war ended too soon. If it had
gone on until 1919—and in 1917 everyone expected at least that—they
would have been there and in bulk. Benedict Crowell, who was assistant secretary of war from 1917 to 1920, summed it all up with an
old story about a man who missed a train in spite of running hard to
make it and said afterward, "I ran fast enough. The trouble is, I didn't
start soon enough."

So American war production. Almost nothing had been done up
until the day we entered the war. How much preparedness the nation
would have stood for no one can tell, but certainly Wilson hadn't
pushed for it, Baker hadn't pushed, and the Army hadn't even
bothered to revise its antiquated purchasing system whereby various
service bureaus competed with one another.

Testifying before Congress, Baker kept his temper, tactfully admitted past errors, and kept repeating that we really had done pretty
well considering the time we'd been on the job. On March 4 Wilson
further soothed an already somewhat mollified Congress by moving
Bernard Baruch up to chief of the War Industries Board. Baruch had
the power to set priorities throughout industry, the old scrambling
days were over. Wilson set it out in the letter asking Baruch to take
the job. He could create new sources of materials, convert existing

facilities, advise the various government agencies on prices to be paid, and finally make "the determination, wherever necessary, of production and of delivery and of the proportions of any given article to be made immediately accessible to the several purchasing agencies when the supply of that article is insufficient, either temporarily or permanently."

Just to make certain there were no remaining loopholes in the power structure, Wilson then rolled one more bill through Congress, the Overman Act, which gave him the power, for the duration, to alter, create, destroy, or just plain tinker with any government agency or bureau he saw fit. It took in so much ground that an amendment was jokingly suggested, to read, "If any power, constitutional or not, has been inadvertently omitted from this bill, it is hereby granted in full."

The bill passed in May; it had taken us just a little more than a year to move from a peacetime, free-enterprise system to one run on order from the very top.

If the industrial plant had been stuttering, its woes compounded by George Creel's happy utterances, the propaganda mill was simultaneously achieving its great triumph, and to Creel must go part of the credit.

On January 5 Lloyd George had delivered an address outlining British war aims. Wilson had been working on a similar speech, then suddenly decided to deliver it in a hurry on January 8. To Congress he gave "scant notice of his coming, notice barely sufficient to enable the Senate and the House to make the necessary arrangements for a joint session."

Next day the newspapers played hardest the fact that in the speech Wilson for the first time came out flatly for the return of Alsace-Lorraine to France after the war. There was very little comment on what eventually came to be known as the Fourteen Points, which were to be the basis for the peace. They were, in brief:

    I   Open covenants of peace, openly arrived at . . .

   II   Absolute freedom . . . upon the seas . . .

  III   The removal, so far as possible, of all economic barriers . . . among all the nations . . .

IV Adequate guarantees . . . that national armaments will be reduced to the lowest point consistent with domestic safety.

V A free, open-minded, and absolutely impartial adjustment of all colonial claims . . . the interests of the populations concerned must have equal weight with the equitable claims of the government whose title is to be determined.

VI The evacuation of all Russian territory . . . and unembarrassed opportunity for the independent determination of her own political development and national policy. . . .

VII Belgium . . . must be evacuated and restored . . .

VIII All French territory should be freed . . . and the wrong done . . . in the matter of Alsace-Lorraine . . . should be righted . . .

IX A readjustment of the frontiers of Italy should be effected along clearly recognizable lines of nationality.

X The peoples of Austria-Hungary, whose place among the nations we wish to see safeguarded and assured, should be accorded the freest opportunity for autonomous development.

XI Rumania, Serbia, and Montenegro should be evacuated . . . international guarantees of the political and economic independence and territorial integrity of the several Balkan states should be entered into.

XII The Turkish portions of the present Ottoman Empire should be assured a secure sovereignty, but the other nationalities which are now under Turkish rule should be assured an undoubted security of life . . .

XIII An independent Polish state should be erected . . .

XIV A general association of nations must be formed under specific covenants for the purpose of affording mutual guarantees of political independence and territorial integrity to great and small states alike.

The reaction was very favorable, but certainly no indication of what was to come. Even Senator Chamberlain, embroiled with the President on other issues, said, "It is one of the greatest state papers the President has ever delivered." A few Republicans muttered that the third item sounded suspiciously like free trade, but the best reaction gage was a long editorial in the New York *Times* which spoke well of the speech, but ended by saying that there had been enough talk about war aims and "may we now hope that some further and satisfactory progress will be made in fighting Germany." Perhaps Creel really did sense what a weapon had been forged; at any rate he had his boys turned to pumping the Points all over the world by wireless telegraph.

There had been war for three and a half years. We were new to it, our casualty lists were still small, it would be Fall again before the real human price of the thing began pressing down on us. In the rest of the world, though, they'd had about all the killing they could stand. In England a peer of the realm, the Marquis of Lansdowne, was suggesting a negotiated peace. Russia really was making a separate peace and the *poilus* and the Tommies going into their fourth year of fighting couldn't help but think that Russians wouldn't be pushed up in Nivelle offensives until the outfits making the push simply didn't exist any more. Even in Germany, men were asking whether it was still possible to win.

Wilson would later be accused of a document too idealistic for this imperfect world. In fact, half his points were cagy offers to Germany's allies showing them how they could get out of the war without getting out of existence: Austria-Hungary could go on living, the Turks could keep most of what they had, Bulgaria would have herself guaranteed.

For the rest, they were an answer to men asking, "Why die for a few yards of French mud?" From now on this was not just a war to defeat Germany, but a war to prevent any such war from happening again. Wilson was overoptimistic, but he had given a new meaning to the slaughter. Perhaps the war would have ended on exactly the same date without the Fourteen Points, but Creel spread them around the world, and it is worth noting that when the end came it was to the Fourteen Points that Germany appealed as a basis for peace.

For the moment the German press unloaded on the speech, calling it a "clumsy trap," and denouncing Wilson's "demagogic devices." The *Norddeutsche Allgemeine Zeitung* even christened the Points when it used the phrase "fourteen points" for the first time, then went on to call them "a real symphony of will to no peace." Note, though, that a lot of German papers thought the speech a little hot to handle; they denounced it without bothering to tell their readerships what Wilson said. There were cracks in the wall, too. The *Frankfurter Zeitung* found the speech conciliatory and said that if Wilson could get his allies to accept the same terms "there will not yet be a basis for peace negotiations, [but] we will have come much nearer to a possibility thereof."

For now the *Frankfurter Zeitung* was still a lonely voice. The peace party in Berlin was overwhelmed by the military; there would have to be more fighting.

Chapter Four

"HOMER, WHICH IS YOU?"

THEY called it "The Valley Forge of the AEF." The winter blasted on and Pershing now had four divisions either in the line for brief periods on the southern end of the front, for training; or drilling outdoors at simulated open warfare. They were the First and the Second; the Twenty-sixth—Yankee—Division, the New England crowd which had won the race to be the first National Guard outfit overseas; and the Rainbow—Forty-second—Division, with its Guardsmen from all over the United States. Shoes were particularly short; the Rainbow did a hike from one training site to another and in spite of makeshift cardboard inner soles, the marchers left a lot of bloody splotches in the snow.

The Rainbow and the Yankee divisions got into the line during February. The Second—a jury-rigged outfit consisting of a brigade of Marines and a brigade of regular infantry—made it in March.

"The Line"—the vast trench system from Switzerland to the North Sea—was that winter undergoing a change based on estimates of the German attack in the spring. Instead of a line, it was becoming a defense in depth, a zone. Out front would be 25 or 50 men in a strong point, with orders to hold on no matter what. They were there to give the alarm and not much else. Behind them was the first real line of trenches with pillboxed machine guns for added strength. Behind that another trench line—sometimes two—with barbed wire strung between. In each were dugouts going down thirty, forty feet or more into which the men could dive in a bombardment or gas attack. From each line connecting trenches—*boyaux*—ran back to the next. Often these were trapped with obstacles to hinder raiders, some had wire mesh over the top of the *boyaux* so that grenades tossed at attackers couldn't be heaved out of the top of the trench.

Depending on the ground, some of the trenches were dry, some stayed knee-deep wet no matter how much housekeeping they got.

In all of them lived the cooties—the lice that got into the men and into their clothes and could be gotten out only by a thorough steaming at a delousing station in the rear. In all of them lived rats, also grown gross, the gruesome diet in No-Man's Land being what it was.

The basic weapon was the rifle, and by general consensus the French shot badly, the Germans well, and the British very well. American regulars and Marines, brought up on the tradition of the frontier squirrel shooter, would outdo them all when they got into action. At the end of the rifle was a bayonet and with this much blood was supposed to be let. In fact, the opposing units rarely got that close to each other, but the bayonet was much admired by troops on the march because they could carry an extra loaf of bread speared on it. In addition, the infantry carried hand grenades which were effective once a man got within throwing distance. To increase the range, experiments were made with rifle grenades—grenades fired from a special fitting put on a rifle—but the effect was no howling success.

The French also developed—with some success—an automatic rifle which was the forerunner of all the sub-machine guns, machine pistols, and burp guns of wars to come. It was officially the Chauchat, and Americans who used it called it variously the Sho-Sho, the Sure Shot, or, when it jammed as it did regularly, the Sure something else. As a further experiment in a weapon that didn't have to be aimed too carefully when a man was in a hurry, the Marines even tried out sawed-off shotguns and the Germans denounced them as barbarous.

In close support of the infantry were trench mortars, flame throwers, and machine guns. The trench mortar—a little stovepipe cannon which pointed up—was useful for lobbing shells into unfriendly trenches. The Germans called them *Minenwerfer*. The flame thrower was terrifying to behold and would assuredly frizzle a man if it caught up with him, but it was an unwieldy device of extremely limited range.

The king was the machine gun and it was the machine gun that made this war different from all those before it. There had been experiments with machine guns as early as the American Civil War, but now it was an effective, mass-produced weapon. The German Maxim, which the Americans faced, could fire 500 rounds a minute although it was usually fired in shorter bursts. It could be aimed accurately up to 800 yards and for simply spraying an area it was good up to fifteen hundred yards. Clearly, advancing infantry didn't have a chance against such a weapon, that could be dug in and deliver such a rate of fire. Authorities have estimated that as many as 80 per cent of all the casualties in the war were inflicted by machine guns. Even if the figure is high, it was the machine gun—a defensive weapon—that had reduced the Western Front to a stalemate.

The first offensive reply was to beef up artillery support in an effort to destroy the machine guns before the infantry went over the top. At the beginning of the war the standard light fieldpieces on all sides were guns of approximately three-inch caliber, of which the French 75 mm. was the most famous. The standard heavy was a six-incher, although as the war went on bigger and bigger pieces were brought up until naval guns were being trundled around France on railway cars and the Germans had a Big Bertha which could drop shells into Paris from 76 miles away. The greatest change, however, was not in the type of artillery, but in the quantity. At the beginning a gun for every 20 yards of front was considered sufficient to support an attack. By the end, there were enough guns for every ten or even five yards. As a prelude to the British attack at Arras in the spring of 1917, some 2,700,000 rounds of ammunition were fired and even then the gains were slight. Not only did so much bombardment remove any chance of surprise, but it churned up the battlefield so badly that it was impossible to move guns, tanks, and supplies forward rapidly if an advance did get started, particularly since most artillery was still horse drawn.

The high commands racked their brains for another offensive weapon. The Germans found one first in poison gas. In April, 1915, they took advantage of a favoring wind to send clouds of chlorine drifting toward the British and French lines at Ypres. The men in the front died or fled, but the Germans weren't really ready to follow up a break-through. Moreover, the favoring wind dropped and they soon found themselves among their own gas clouds. Gas masks—crude at first, later well made—came to the front and gas was no longer a decisive weapon.

The British reply came in the fall of 1916 when the first tanks appeared along the Somme. There were only 11 of them, they lumbered along at less than four miles an hour, and they broke down just about the way you'd expect a new, untested vehicle to break down, but a decisive weapon had been found. There were never really enough of them, but they could get to the machine guns. Artillery could knock them out, eventually, but the only true counter, a light, mobile anti-tank gun, was still years ahead. Strangely, the Allies let the weapon slide after the war, but the Germans didn't: the triumph of armored warfare came with the Nazi *Blitzkrieg* years later.

As 1917 came to an end, though, the front was static; the men froze in the miles and miles of dreary trenches and waited for the German push which everyone knew was coming in the spring.

The first trip into the line was an occasion for much inspirational talk. A colonel of the Yankee's 102d Infantry sent his boys in with, "Men of Connecticut—you blue-bellied, shad-eating Nutmeg Yanks, damn your Yankee hides to hell! Heads up. Stick your chests out! You're from the best fightin' stock in the world. Do you know it? Now let me see you smile. That's it. Grin! Hold it! Now I want just one thing, spirit! I'm the old man, the boss, see? But I'm going to give you all the grub and shoes and clothes I can beg, buy, or steal, and as long as I'm colonel of this regiment you're going to get everything that's coming to you and there's no damn staff officers are going to say me no. But I want spirit! And here's a secret. Gather in close—right around me. That's it! We're going to fight! Now! Right away!"[1]

Thus fired up, an outfit might go in and find nothing more to fight against than a gas attack with nine or ten thousand gas shells dropped on them in a few hours. The gas-filled artillery shell had replaced the earlier crude technique of getting the stuff over the lines by wind power. In general, two sorts of gases were in use. One sort made a man choke; phosgene with its scent of new-mown hay was typical. The other was a burning gas, like mustard or lewisite, which attacked the skin and eyes.

The Rainbow got hit with such a gas attack shortly after they moved in and a man who was there remembered later a doctor tearing off his mask to operate on a casualty, and later "... men were going blind one after another and being ordered to the hospital. Often, by the time they got to the ambulance, the man leading was himself blind and both got into the ambulance together. ... By ten o'clock in the morning fully two thirds of the company had been blinded."[2]

For variety, high explosives could come over instead of gas. A doughboy was in a dugout when a shell "hit very nearly in the center of the roof. Forty feet of earth poured in as if from a tunnel. The men in the center of the room were covered by it almost immediately. After the first roar of falling timber and earth subsided, I heard someone ask Norman how he was. Norman answered, 'I have a plank through my stomach.' . . . he did not die immediately, I could hear him in a constantly weaker voice giving comfort to those who were dying near and with him."

The narrator himself was buried in dirt up to his chin with more filtering down all the time. "I was terribly frightened. I prayed. I prayed for my mother and father individually and collectively. I prayed for all I knew. I recited the Lord's Prayer. I made my peace with God and was unafraid. . . . It was only by shoving . . . earth over my left shoulder . . . that I kept from being completely buried."

He was trapped twelve hours before two buddies found him and scooped him out with their helmets.[3]

The ultimate in Germanic attentions was a raid. First came a bombardment. "Suddenly, with the instantaneity of a lightning flash, the whole north seems to rise up in flames and hurl itself forward . . . there is no need to waken anyone; air and earth tremble with the concussion of bursting shells . . . terrified bodies come rushing, flipping, stumbling, splashing to the dugouts, dodging bits of flying debris, ducking showers of dirt, their faces lighted by flashing explosions."

When the barrage lifts, the men are ordered back up into the trenches to face the Germans following close behind their shelling and firing as they come. "Six of them reached our dugout just as its four occupants had started up the steps. Without the slightest warning, a grenade burst in the midst of the Iowans and hurled them all to the bottom. Private Byron Van Raden fell dead . . . [the rest] . . . were badly wounded."[4]

Less seriously, it fell to two of the Yankee Division to be convoying a large can of doughnuts to the forward positions one night when they were set upon by seven raiders. The Yankees returned the fire, killed one doughnut snatcher, and arrived in the line with the report, "Never lost a doughnut."

There being no way to learn the gentle art of raiding but by raiding, the Yanks began to make their own sorties, faces blackened, helmets wrapped in burlap to keep them from rattling on the barbed wire. On one of the Rainbow's first raids, no less a personage than its chief of staff, Colonel Douglas MacArthur, strolled into the raiding party togged out in a turtle-neck sweater and an overseas cap (the colonel scorned helmets) and went all the way to the German trenches with them. The Germans had figured the raid and pulled their men back, but the Rainbow was not to play permanently in such bad luck. A patrol from its 167th Alabama went out and suddenly found itself with all the Boche it could handle. A "big Hun shot by Sergeant Hall, as if crazed by the pain from the wound, leaped into the trench and dived at him. Hall, as he fired at the other Germans, threw the man down and Corporal Homer Whited grappled with the Boche, striking him over the head with his pistol butt."

The German wouldn't stay down, though, and Corporal Whited's buddy, Corporal Freeman, raised his rifle to do the man in, tried to aim, and then plaintively asked of the men grappling in the dark, "Homer, which is you?"[5]

In one way and another they learned their business and took their losses. There was a raid on the Second Division one night and word drifted back that "I" Company was wiped out. Roaring into the line came old Mess Sergeant Wiggins, a forty-year veteran, with a long carving knife flashing in the air and the cry " 'I' Company's never wiped out as long as I'm here." The 106th Infantry even achieved the insouciance of using a dead and buried German's leg projecting into its trench as a place on which to hang helmets.

On March 21 the storm, that everyone had known was coming, broke. Using a short, heavy barrage instead of a long one which would give the defense time to adjust, the Germans poured their infantry at the junction of the British and French lines between Saint-Quentin and Arras. The French gave toward Paris, the British toward the Channel, and for days it looked as though the line might part. Montdidier, only 40 miles from Paris fell, and Amiens was threatened. In all, the Germans had gained 14 miles by March 25.

One small American unit managed to get in the fight. A construction detail from the 6th Engineers was building a railroad in the British sector when the blow fell. They weren't supposed to fight, they weren't equipped to fight, but somehow they managed to find a mess of machine guns in a machine-gun school. They didn't know how to use machine guns, but being engineers they figured the weapon out, betook themselves to the line, and stayed there.

SPRING OFFENSIVE: The German push of early 1918, showing the front line as it was on May 27, just before the First Division attacked at Cantigny

On March 25 Pershing hurried to General Pétain near Compiègne and told him that for the moment the American army could wait; while the crisis lasted our troops were his to use where and as he needed them. The First, Second, and Rainbow Divisions were in the line on the quiet southern end of the front, the Yankee in the central sector but still south of the German push. The push ran out of steam just short of taking Amiens and scared the Allies into something they should have done years before—appointing one commander in chief for all Allied armies. Marshal Foch got the job just in time to see the next push begin, the Germans driving the British back on the sea at the extreme northern end of the line near Ypres.

Ferdinand Foch had had his ups and downs in this war. Promoted and decorated for his work as an army commander, in stopping the German rush toward Paris at the beginning of the war, he had been relieved of command following the unsuccessful Somme offensive of 1916 when the casualty lists sickened even men used to the blood-soaked Western Front. Brought back after the Nivelle fiasco, he was now in charge of it all, and if the French and the British and the American troops could be sure of anything, it was that this stocky, cocky little man would keep whipping them forward to the offensive. If French enthusiasm for attack, attack, attack had been dampened a little by the discovery that sheer audacity was no match for machine guns, Foch was still a driver who believed that the best way to deal with an enemy attack was to punch back at it.

It was April 17 before orders came down sending Americans into the fight. The First Division was told to move up to Cantigny, a flaming hell of a sector right at the point of the big German salient bearing down on Paris. German artillery rained down on it so steadily that no trenches had been dug, no wire strung. It was nothing but wheat fields lying in a shallow valley with the shell holes providing what protection was to be had. The French apologized as they pulled out. "We are not turning over to you a sector, but a good place to make a sector." The men lay in the shell holes all day with the artillery drubbing them, an average of 3,450 shells a day on a 5,000-yard front. In one night they took three and a half hours of gas shelling and 800 casualties.

Chiefly, though, the night was for digging, deepening the shell holes, connecting them into a trench line. Ration parties—every doughboy's nomination for the unsung heroes of the war—scrambled back through the dark to bring the one square meal of the day forward and enough water for half a canteen a day per man. All too often they were hit and died and the men in the line went hungry.

On the far side of the valley there was a line of hills and on them sat the little village of Cantigny. The First knew that hidden in its ruined buildings were the German artillery observers calling down the fire on them, but at first no one had any plans for doing anything about it. That had to wait on a fight down at the southern end of the line.

The Yankee Division was still in the line at the south, and on the night of April 19–20—two days after the First moved into the inferno at Cantigny—the Yankees found their front "as clear and quiet . . . as one could ask for." Companies C and D of the 102d Infantry moved out in front of Seicheprey village to relieve companies M and L. At 3:16 A.M. German artillery blasted the line. Seicheprey was cut off. It was dawn before improvised patrols of runners, cooks, and telephone men pushed through into the town. It was strewn with American dead and not a few Germans. C and D had been ordered to hold at all costs if attacked, and hold they had, even when 1,500 German shock troops descended on the 500 Americans. They were almost all killed or captured, but from the few survivors the 102d heard how they'd gone down, fighting with shovels, meat cleavers, and rocks after they ran out of ammunition.

The Germans made big propaganda use of this episode. They displayed the prisoners, broadcast it as a major American defeat, and generally let it be known that American infantry wasn't worth a hoot. Both for their own morale and that of their Allies the Americans were going to have to hit back somewhere. Cantigny was the spot selected.

Cantigny was about a mile from the American lines, on the hills, and the center of a salient—that is, a position that stuck out like a pie wedge ahead of the main German lines. The First's 28th Infantry was going to do the job, so they pulled them out of the line and drilled them on a mock up of the German positions. To make doubly sure the attack went through, French tanks were brought in on the job and drilled with them. There would be a French flame-thrower detachment, too, and artillery capable of getting rid of an ammunition dump totaling 200,000 rounds, 5,000,000 pounds' weight of metal. The Americans had a trick of their own to add: machine-gun battalions would be placed all the way forward to support the infantry during the advance.

Secrecy was everything—only four officers to a regiment knew that an attack was coming. The Germans sensed something just the same; there was too much activity along the front to suit them.

During the night of May 26–27 they dumped 15,000 gas shells into the lines and put over a raid to find out what was going on. Fortunately, the prisoners they took knew nothing.

During the night of May 27–28 the French tanks came into the line, the infantry stood to in the trenches talking the night away, too worked up to sleep. At five forty-five on the twenty-eighth, the first American assault of the war began: 386 guns pounded the German salient, a mile and a half of front. One hour later—six forty-five—the officers said, "Come on, boys," and the First moved out in three lines into a misty morning, the sun just beginning to break through the ground haze. They walked their mile quietly, right into Cantigny, with nothing but a few bad jokes about "Boches for breakfast" for conversation. The barrage moved nicely, 25 yards to the minute, and the infantry kept up with it, tanks moving with the first wave. Once inside the village, the French flame-thrower crews came up to burn the Germans out of their dugouts.

It had been a surprise, after all; they caught the Germans in the middle of a relief, one battalion coming into Cantigny, another leaving, and before the sun was all up, 250 Boche left in the other direction as prisoners.

They'd known all along that it was going to be easier to take the town than to hold it, and only five minutes after they arrived the first small counterattack came in. Artillery smashed it, and the infantry had time to dig in before the Germans came on again late in the afternoon. There would be five counterattacks in all before the town was secured, but this one was the only one that ever showed any signs of getting through. They found one weak spot in the line, but before they could take advantage of it Colonel Theodore Roosevelt, Jr., brought a battalion of the 26th Infantry up and plugged the gap.

In all, the Americans suffered 1,067 casualties in doing the job, but the first American offensive was a fact—no more big propaganda could be made out of Seicheprey. It wasn't much, a one-regiment job on a town the Germans could live without—and were holding with second-line troops, kids, and men in their forties—but it was a fact just the same, a first, a small sign of the turn the war was taking. If there was to be an American army, there had to be men capable of handling it, and the First had proven that there were men around who could get things organized. It is worth noting that one of the men who did the organizing on the First's staff was Colonel George Catlett Marshall, a man destined to go on quite a long way.

It was a good time for a success. On May 27 the third thrust of the big German victory offensive had broken out on the Central Front, rolling toward the Marne and Paris. By the first of the month they had grabbed Soissons, were on the Marne at Château-Thierry, and had 60,000 French prisoners in the bag.

Foch had some French reserve divisions he could have put in, but he hesitated to commit his veterans while the German offensive was still rolling under full steam. Better let the Americans take the shock if they could, and save his reserve for a counter. Orders went out to the Second Division, training around the village of Chaumont-en-Vexin, and the Third at Château-Villaine, to get going.

The Third had never been in the line on even a quiet sector and just to make things worse, its general, Joseph Dickman, was off inspecting the front. The men waited for the French *camions*—trucks— to arrive and the 7th Machine Gun Battalion, which had its own trucks, went bowling off ahead, destination Château-Thierry on the Marne River. All night they rode, and at dawn the trucks dumped them off amid a French Colonial outfit which wasn't really expecting them. The Germans were descending on the north bank of the Marne, the French had the south, and all hands agreed that the situation called for holding the two bridges across the river. Just in the nick of time the 7th hustled its 48 machine guns up to the riverbank and dug in.

Once the Germans tried to force the narrow bridges and the Africans and the gunners cut them down. Twice they tried and failed. Then the French finally got around to blowing the bridges and for the moment the south bank of the Marne was secure. Late in the day, the rest of the Third came puffing up to Château-Thierry, sore at having missed the fight.

At Chaumont-en-Vexin, northwest of Paris, the Second was told to be ready to move on the evening of May 30. The transport was *camions*—French trucks with canvas tops, hard wooden benches down each side, and enough room for 30 men, their rifles, and their 60-pound packs. The men mustered at 6 P.M. but the *camions* didn't show so the men, having hurried, lay down in the open fields to

sleep and wait. Someone had changed his mind. Originally the call
had been for a movement to Beauvais. Now the word came down
to go to Meaux, about twenty miles northeast of Paris. Then the word
was passed that the division would move by train. At 2 A.M. on the
thirty-first another word came and they were back to *camions* again.
To make it more complex, someone up the line figured that there
already were too many trucks in Meaux and decided to route them
north of there through May-en-Multien.

At 4 A.M. the *camions* actually showed up driven by little brown
men from Indo-China. They moved out in units of 50 trucks, enough
for one battalion, and by ten-thirty in the morning the whole show
was on the road: a peculiar division consisting of the 9th and 23d Infantry regiments of the regular army, and the 5th and 6th regiments
of Marines. At the end of the column came Lizzie. Lizzie was a
Ford truck fitted out as an ambulance and presented to the 6th
Marines by the kind Miss Elizabeth Pearce of New York City. Since
the French had provided ambulances, Lizzie had been converted to
a general delivery truck, and of Lizzie much more anon.

The day was blazing hot, and as they drove through the little
French villages, the people turned out to throw flowers and wave
little American flags. The Tonkinese drivers had been hauling re-
enforcements for seventy-two hours in some cases and from time
to time one of them would go to sleep at the wheel and drive into a
ditch. At May-en-Multien French liaison officers gave them the rest
of their directions. They were to go into the line northwest of
Château-Thierry near a town called Belleau. It had all been a quiet
sector before the German drive started, with Frenchmen working
their farms right up the line. Now they were streaming back, calling "*La guerre est fini,*" and jamming the roads. The whole trip was
only about 80 miles, but it was midnight of the thirty-first before the
first units left the trucks seven kilometers behind the lines and
started to march toward the front.

The men were cocky; a rookie asked where the line was, and an
old sergeant told him, "Line, hell! We're going to make a line."
Higher up, French General Degoutte inquired of the division's chief
of staff, Colonel Preston Brown, whether his men could hold.
"General," Brown snapped back, "these are American regulars. In a
hundred and fifty years they have never been beaten. They will hold."

It sounded good. Actually, the units were regular, but the men were green. The 6th Marines figured they had, out of 3,000 men, only officers from captain up and some fifty noncoms who had really seen service. The rest were kids, 60 per cent of them college boys.

All through June 1 they rolled in, their supply trains far behind and the men living on emergency rations of hardtack and bacon. Colonel Artemus Catlin of the 6th Marines set up his first command post at the tiny village of Lucy-le-Bocage. The men set up in rifle pits, six feet long, two and a half feet wide, and three feet deep, called "graves." On June 2 the French got a chance to see what they could do. Three times the Germans came on at the 5th Marines and gave way under rifle and machine-gun fire. On the next two days they decided shell fire was cheaper than man power and contented themselves with artillery fire which cost the division 200 casualties.

Encouraged, the French and Major Benjamin Berry's battalion of the 5th Marines moved up a little on June 5 to take Hill 165 and loop the Marine line so that it now lay west as well as south of a mass of dark trees called Belleau Wood.

It was a wood, no forest, only about two kilometers from north to south and a kilometer wide. But it stood on ground higher than the surrounding country and if the trees weren't much—only five or six inches in diameter—they were set so thickly that a man could see scarcely more than fifteen feet. Inside the wood, according to Second's history, were concealed "a variety of contours . . . knolls rise abruptly; great jagged boulders suddenly thrust themselves from the ground; particularly is such an outcropping seen crowning the heights on the southern face of the woods—grey, enormous stones, festooned with moss, a veritable citadel for the defense."

It was two o'clock on the afternoon of June 6—the same date as the Normandy landings twenty-six years later—that the 4th Marine Brigade was ordered to take Belleau Wood. Degoutte expected a German sortie soon and hoped to beat them to the punch; besides, the Wood was far too good a base for future German operations. It was three forty-five in the afternoon when the orders got down to the Marines. Colonel Catlin went around to Major Benjamin Berry's battalion, which was to make the assault from the west, and looked out unhappily over the 400 yards of wheat field the men would have to cross before they got to the Wood. He doubted that they'd be able to do it. Most of the men—500 of them, the attack was to be made at half battalion strength—were lying down in a gully, waiting, smoking, talking. Catlin fished around for something appropriate to say to them and finally settled for, "Give 'em hell, boys."

They had half an hour's artillery preparation, but the guns hadn't been registered in and they didn't hit much. Promptly at five the barrage lifted, the officers' whistles blew, and Berry's kids moved out. Floyd Gibbons, covering for the Chicago *Tribune*, reported that immediately "the air was full of red-hot nails." A few minutes later Gibbons was going to lose an eye and acquire the eye patch which became his trademark.

Berry got it in the arm, but kept going. Two hundred yards through the wheat—winter wheat it was, thigh high, still green and full of scarlet poppies—the whole line wavered. Legend says a sergeant shouted, "Come on, you sons of bitches! Do you want to live forever?" The veterans and the college boys made it to within a hundred yards of the Wood before the German machine gunners cut them to pieces and they had to hit the dirt for good. At dark Berry's boys were withdrawn to their own lines.

From the southwest Major Berton Sibley's battalion of the 6th Marines—Sibley was a quiet, studious man, usually called "Ma" Sibley—also jumped off promptly at five. They had a slightly better situation—only two hundred yards to go. The men walked five yards apart in four ranks, twenty yards between the ranks. They walked in silence. Later reporters claimed they shouted, "Remember the *Lusitania!*" and sang "Yankee Doodle," but nobody there at the time recalls it. The Germans kept their fire low, men went down from leg and belly wounds, but the lines kept moving. Catlin crowded forward to see how they were doing and a sniper knocked him out of the fight.

Sibley's men hit the edge of the Wood and went in, crowding forward to get to the rear of the tormenting machine guns and put them out of action. They discovered that a shrewd old German major, named Bischoff, had arranged his guns so that they supported one another and a man attacking one was likely to find himself under fire from two others. The Marines kept plugging away at it, though, until they hit the German main line of resistance at eight-thirty.

By that time they had a toehold all along the southern edge of the Wood.

On their right Holcomb's battalion of the 6th had orders to move up, keep even, and take the village of Bouresches. Captain Donald Duncan and Lieutenant James Robertson got into the village with 400 men. Duncan died with a bullet through the mouth, and before Robertson had taken Bouresches his 400 men were reduced to 20 and most of those out of ammunition. In the rear Lieutenant William Moore and Sergeant Major John Quick heard about it, loaded a truck with the necessary, and got through in a wild night ride with shell fire splitting the sky like lightning. Then Lizzie and her driver, Private Morris Fletz, heard about a shortage of rations and came through, too, at the cost of 12 bullet holes in Lizzie. She kept on for the next five days and at the end of them, the former ambulance had one tire off, her radiator smashed, a wheel hit, and 40 bullet holes. The Marines painted a Croix de Guerre on her hood.

Through the seventh and the eighth they kept picking away at the machine guns in the Wood. As a private from North Carolina saw it, "German machine guns were everywhere. In the trees and in small ground holes. And camouflaged at other places so they couldn't be spotted.

" . . . Believe me, there were some bullets whizzing around. They came so close at times I could almost feel their touch. My pack was shot up pretty much but they didn't get me.

"After that I thought I was bullet proof and didn't care a damn for all the Germans and their machine guns.

"Soon we all charged forward again. I saw one Dutchman stick his head out of a hole and then duck. I ran to the hole. The next time his head came up it was good night, Fritz.

"We were running along when a German pops right up from the weeds on the roadside and shot at a sergeant with me. The bullet got the sergeant in the right wrist. I got the German before he dropped back into the weeds.

"Every blamed tree must have had a machine gunner. As soon as we spied them we'd drop down and pick them off with our rifles. Potting the Germans became great sport. Even the officers would seize rifles from wounded Marines and go to it.

"On the second day of our advance my captain and two others besides myself were lying prone and cracking away at 'em. I was second in line. Before I knew what had happened a machine gun got me in the right arm just at the elbow. Five shots hit right in succession. The elbow was torn to shreds, but the hits didn't hurt. It seemed just like getting five little stings of electricity.

"The captain ordered two men to help me back. I said I could make it alone."[6]

It was a two-mile hike to the dressing station and he almost made it before he fainted from loss of blood.

The hospital corpsman at the front—Navy pharmacist's mates—did a good job of getting the men back; a corporal said of them, "Those fellows deserve a gold medal or the highest award they can receive," but once the men were back there simply weren't enough doctors to take care of them. More were rushed up, but many of them were not surgeons and they lacked equipment. One remembered working in a barn, the floors slippery with blood, with no more equipment than he could carry with him and no nurses allowed so far forward. When it was all over, the doctor in charge was threatened with a court-martial, but a medal would have been more appropriate considering the job he did under such circumstances.

The machine guns were too much. One company went in with 200 men and came out with 11. On June 9 everybody was pulled back to the edge of the Wood and 200 guns went to work on it. After that things improved a little. The reporting back home was purple. "The Americans remain in the highest spirits despite the terrific fighting," one correspondent wrote. "Their only regret is that they have to stop while they sleep." Marine enlistments jumped 100 per cent. One of the boys on the spot wrote less enthusiastically. "They gave us a bombardment which lasted about five or six hours, which none of us will forget as long as we live. It tore the woods all to thunder; the trees looked like someone had cut them down with a scythe."

On June 12 the artillery treatment was repeated, and this time it was Wise's battalion that went forward, "groups of men, under any officer or sergeant who happened to pick them up, working forward independently, attacking gallantly each machine-gun group as they found it, firing from the hip as they moved." At one point they made it all the way to the northern edge of the Wood, but the Germans still held the northwest corner. An Army regiment from the Third Division was thrown in to help out on the fifteenth and by that time the Marines were too exhausted to object to what would have been taken as a mortal insult at any other time.

Finally, on June 25, a fourteen-hour artillery preparation was laid on. From 3:00 A.M. to 5:00 P.M., they fired and then sent it forward in a rolling barrage. The Marines followed, and the last of the Wood was cleared nineteen days after the fight started.

The casualties had been terrible. Sibley's battalion lost 42 per cent of its officers and 40 per cent of its men, and the record for other units was as bad or worse. In all, the Marines took 5,711 casualties. The casualty lists went home and what lay ahead came into focus. Cantigny had been a nice, quick win and the losses hadn't been bad. Now we were going to realize that for the first time since the Civil War we were engaged in a bloody, heavy casualty affair. Until then the only people back home who really knew that war was hell were Yanks and Rebs in their seventies and time had softened most of their memories.

Even Catlin, a great Marine, felt the need to reassess the situation. He lay in the hospital, shot through the chest, and told visitors, "Don't feel so bad about me. It's my own fault. I shouldn't have been so close to the front in a first-class war."

They were fighting and dying in the near-perfect days of late spring and early summer. "Almost to the front-line trenches the country was buried in lush grass and simply wild with flowers. The beautiful beech woods passed through their wonderful first-leaved stage, when their ineffable green was the most thrilling color imaginable, to the deeper hue of the full leaf. Acacias were ablaze along the roads, and everywhere in and out of the *camion* trains ran the little children who still lived among the vineyards close to the lines, their arms full of bouquets of lilies of the valley."

Whether it was the season or the dying or both, the men in the lines changed. Their language was a good deal less gamey than it had been in the rear areas, there was a good deal more consideration of one man for another. A doughboy claimed, "You never know when a man speaks to you that those words aren't going to be the last he ever will speak. That makes you listen, and when you answer him, it makes you more careful what you say."

On the Marines' right the Second's two regular army regiments had waited through the Belleau Wood fight, anxious for a fight of their own, but with no orders for one. Plans were being made, however. There was a dent in the middle of their position; it could be eliminated and the line straightened out by taking the town of Vaux.

Vaux was something of a problem, a small town, but built almost entirely of good stout stone buildings. An easy town to get into—artillery could drive the enemy into the cellars—but the very devil to get the Germans out of. Each stone house was potentially a small stone fort. Accordingly, Division Intelligence set out to know Vaux so thoroughly that the infantry would be familiar with every crook and turn of it when it came to fighting inside the town and cleaning out the houses.

They got the general layout from aerial photographs, then stumbled on a bonanza of picture post cards which gave a ground-level view of the streets. Best of all, they turned up the old village stonemason who'd worked in most of the houses in town at one time or another. Fortunately, he was a man with a good memory; when the time came the doughboys knew how most of the houses were laid out inside. When the attack was made, each infantryman went over with a small personal map of Vaux in his pack and a definitely assigned house out of which to flush Germans.

The artillery went to work at six in the morning of July 1. All day they fired, the gunners stripped to the waist in the July heat; at three minutes to six in the evening they stopped pounding the little town and set up a barrage, rolling it forward one hundred yards every two minutes. The infantry got up and walked behind it. . . . "In one long-drawn, well-aligned wave," the New York *Times* reported, "they crawled from their trenches or shelters and closely hugging an almost perfect barrage without getting their noses into it, set out all along a two-mile front at an evenly smart pace. Their slight dip down into the long, gentle scoop of a ravine, a not difficult scramble up the opposite slope, and their bobbing tin hats were gone into the roaring evening. In twenty-four minutes they were in Vaux."

The barrage moved to the far side of the town and stood, dropping a wall between Vaux and any help that might try to come to it. It had done its work well, there were scarcely enough Germans left to be worth cleaning out. The regulars rejoiced in a straight line and one captured town, and were relieved that only 46 men had been killed.

During the big Spring crisis the British had suddenly discovered that they could provide a lot more shipping than they'd offered before. Accordingly, American troops had been pouring into France during May, June, and July. Among them was the Thirty-third Division, an Illinois National Guard outfit. There were too many new boys to train them all in the old Toul sector, so the American 2d Corps was formed as a training command behind the British. To it went the Thirty-third. It wasn't considered ready to fight yet, but General Sir Henry Rawlinson, commanding the British Fourth Army, went around to the American 2d Corps commander, and wangled four of its companies for a party he had planned. The word leaked out to Pershing and they were almost withdrawn, but Australian Lieutenant General Sir John Monash, commanding the attack, said it was too late, if they took back the Americans the whole show would have to be called off.

The object in view for the 33d and the Australians was not unlike Cantigny: some high ground which provided the Germans with altogether too much observation on the Allied positions. The objectives were the town of Hamel and two clumps of woods nearby.

Considering the job was going to be done by three Australian brigades with only 1,000 Americans attached it couldn't really be called a big American effort, but it was a first. Up until now all the American attacks had been made by the regulars and Marines of the First and Second divisions. Now a National Guard Division, albeit just a little chunk of one, was going to try its luck. Just to make it more dramatic, the attack was scheduled for the Fourth of July.

Just after midnight, July 3, they crawled 400 yards out into No-Man's Land, then waited for three hours until the barrage went in. There is some dispute over whether the barrage was short or the infantry went too fast in the dark. At any rate, some of it fell among the advancing troops and it didn't do the job it was supposed to do on the German barbed wire. Undeterred, they cut their way through the wire and went after the machine guns with bayonets and grenades. Corporal Thomas Pope rushed one single-handed, bayoneted some of its crew, and held the rest off with rifle fire until help could come up. When they heard about it back in Washington they figured it was pretty good going for a man in combat for the first time and gave him the Congressional Medal of Honor.

In all, it took about an hour to get Hamel. The men dug in, held on through a counterattack the next day, and secured the position. The National Guard could fight. Even the Australians, who had a great reputation as assault troops, admitted it; one of their colonels who came around to say a few words to the Americans finished by departing from his prepared text to say, "Yanks, you're fighting fools, but I'm for you!"

Pershing wasn't in the least pleased. He considered it a British effort to get their hands on his troops and raised the devil. Now they listened: there were 26 American divisions in France. Seven were in or near the line, 15 in training or quiet sectors, two in depots, and two just arriving. Everyone knew there'd be one more big German push, but it looked now as if it could be held. After that there would be an offensive and Pershing figured to have the American army he'd waited so long for.

Except for little actions like Hamel and Vaux and winding up Belleau Wood, the front had been quiet since June 15. They had been defensive-offensives: that is designed to keep the enemy off balance, to gain better ground on which to meet the coming German drive. No one knew where the drive would come, but the smart money was on the Château-Thierry area. It was the deepest German penetration, only fifty miles from Paris. There was only one more river to cross—the Marne—and the Germans would have open country through which to race for the French capital.

On Bastille Day Paris was happy. Big Bertha might shell the city and German planes bomb it at night and the rumble of guns from the Marne front be heard on a still night, but there was a sense that the tide was turning. To the Bastille Day parade came a battalion from each of the Allied nations and they marched that day as part of a special French bond-selling drive. The French swung by first, then the Americans, then the Belgians followed by the British, and so down the line: New Zealanders and Australians, Italians, Poles, Czechs, Greeks, Portuguese, and even a Russian contingent.

The last man had scarcely filed past when messengers were all over Paris ordering American officers and men back to their units. The word was out that this was the night and, for once, the word had it right. At midnight, July 14, the artillery crashed and the last German push of the war started. As predicted, it was a drive to get across the Marne at Château-Thierry. There were four American divisions in the area. At Belleau Wood the Yankee Division's National Guardsmen had replaced the worn-out Second. They were a little too far west to get hit hard. On their right was a French division, then the Third American at Château-Thierry where they'd been ever since their machine gunners had come charging up to the river-bank six weeks before. Then came another French outfit and next the pea-green Pennsylvania National Guard—the Twenty-eighth—which had no line time in even a quiet sector. They were fed in by companies to fight with the French. Farther east there was the veteran Forty-second Division, the Rainbow.

There have been some good defensive fights in American history: the Alamo, General George Thomas and his Union men at Chickamauga, Bataan, the paratroopers at Bastogne. Sometimes the defense won, sometimes it was overrun in the end. That night and the next day the 38th Infantry Regiment of the Third Division made a stand that deserves to rank with the famous ones, and it won.

The 38th was in line just west of where the Surmelin River flows north into the Marne. The Surmelin runs northwest and down either side of its gentle valley there ran two good roads which went south into the main Paris highway. This was to be the main German track, the route by which guns were to move south and help exploit a breakthrough.

The 38th's colonel rejoiced in the resoundingly martial name of Ulysses Grant McAlexander, and if any memories of Grant rallying his men on the first awful day at Shiloh helped him out, his parents are to be congratulated. He was a Minnesota man, a West Pointer, and for a while he'd been with the First Division. He was something of a sloganeer; he was fond of telling his regiment that it might get killed but that it could not be conquered. In the event, though, he was more inclined to rely on good works than slogans, and when the event came, it found him remarkably well prepared. Down by the river he put Major Guy Rowe's 2d Battalion. The 1st Battalion, only half strength, was farther back in the support, and the 3d Battalion even deeper in reserve.

Along the river Rowe's men had three companies in line—G, H, and E, from left to right—each with two platoons dug in down on the riverbank, two more about three hundred and fifty yards back behind the embankment of the east-west Paris-Metz railroad. The railroad was raised up on a constructed embankment about nine feet high and so wide that it was very difficult to fight from behind it. On his right flank stood F Company and McAlexander had arranged them in an unusual way. Instead of facing the river, they faced northeast in a specially dug line of trenches running back from the main line. The colonel knew the French favored a yielding defense and with the French One Hundred and Thirty-first Division on his right he wanted to be sure his flank was covered.

Having made these preparations, McAlexander crawled as far down toward the river as he could, turned around, viewed his position as it would appear to the enemy and announced, "Let 'em come!" He then borrowed a rifle, took a few pot shots at the Germans across the fifty-yard-wide river, and crawled back to wait.

The night of the fourteenth was altogether too quiet to suit McAlexander. Fairly early in the evening he put out the word, "Stand by to repel the enemy." At midnight the Boche obliged by opening up with 84 batteries. Phosgene and mustard-gas shells were mixed in with the explosives, so the 38th yanked on their gas masks. At first the bombardment was deep; the men along the river weren't being hit too badly. It was 2:10 A.M. when Rowe sent a message back by runner, "I was at the riverbank when it started . . . much gas . . . I believe that everybody is standing it well. *We will hold them.*"

At two-thirty the first Germans came across in boats, just a patrol sneaking into Mezy, a little river-front town just west of the 38th's position. Lieutenant David Calkins, commanding the first platoon of G Company, had been down inspecting his men along the river when they spotted him and let go with a shot that broke his right wrist. Calkins promptly dived into a shoulder-high wheat field, switched his pistol to his left hand, and popped up among the raiders shooting. He got two of them before he was flattened by a rifle butt over the head. The raiders hauled him back across the river for quizzing.

Calkins blandly told them there were nine divisions waiting for them and got thoroughly kicked around for lying.

At 3:00 A.M. the shelling shifted down to the riverbank and a smoke screen began to build up on the water. The German Tenth Division was getting ready to come over. It was a good outfit, including the 6th Grenadier Guards. The 38th lay in its rifle pits at the river, dying in the shelling, listening to pontoons and boats being dragged down to the opposite bank.

At 4:00 A.M. they came. In front of E and H companies, it was boats and the doughboys beat them off with rifles, machine guns, and hand grenades. In front of G they got a pontoon bridge over and Calkins' platoon took a terrible beating. The Germans got almost all of them, but they paid a price for it. Later, they found one man dead with an empty rifle and pistol beside him, 12 dead Germans around him. Another bayoneted five before a machine-gun bullet cut him down.

On came the Germans, charging across the three hundred and fifty yards from the river to the railroad track. G drove them back, got grenaded for its pains, and then drove them back when they charged again. Most of another platoon went under in the process. G, in no mood to be sporting, put a captured German captain up on the railroad embankment to get a little breathing space.

At about 5:00 A.M. the French on the right started to fall back in accordance with their doctrine of a yielding defense, and McAlexander's flank was right where he'd figured it was going to be—up in the air. At first light the crack 5th Grenadier Guards came charging down on what should have been a wide-open hole and instead ran smack into F Company in the Thank-God trenches they'd been digging right up until the time the bombardment started. They bounced back, whereupon Lieutenant Ralph Eberlin went into the open with two platoons and chased them back to the riverbank. Eberlin got himself wounded, but his men made it back to the lifesaving trenches. Lieutenant Cramer took them over and they spent the rest of a wild morning in forays which convinced the Germans that they couldn't get into F's rear and kept them flowing straight south with their own flank open. Eventually the line got too long for F to handle and McAlexander put in his half-strength 1st Battalion to help out.

It was 10:30 A.M. when poor G Company, which had been getting the worst of it all along, suddenly looked up to find 250 Germans advancing eight hundred yards in its rear. The Third's 30th Regiment had been forced back; the 38th was now left with both flanks open to take the consequences. G already had all the fighting it could handle, there wasn't anything like 250 men left in the entire outfit, but Captain Wooldridge got a handful of his tigers turned around, put them down in some rock piles at the rear of Mézy, and drove off the new threat.

At this point McAlexander was surrounded on three sides and his total front was eight and a half miles long, most of it on the right flank. No cut-up battalion and a half should ever have been able to hold anything like that much real estate, but there they stayed until four-thirty in the afternoon, when they were ordered to pull back even with the rest of the line. They had taken 1,087 casualties out of 1,500 men engaged, but they figured they'd cost the Germans 3,000 dead and wounded. Whatever the exact figure, the Boche was quite content to sit along the railroad embankment and let them go in peace. On this front the big German push had gone as far as it was going. Ulysses Grant McAlexander's namesake could scarcely have done the job better.

The Twenty-eighth Division—the Pennsylvania National Guard Division—had never been in the line before, but the emergency being what it was, it had to be some help anyway. Accordingly, it was moved up into a second line of defense behind the Third Division and behind the French on Third's right. Unfortunately, the French had a few weak spots in their line and to fill these four companies from the Twenty-eighth were moved right up to the river line, each of them to be sandwiched in between two French units.

They were green, so green that one company had just taken off their gear and sat down to eat when the bombardment started even though it had been pretty general knowledge that the attack was coming at midnight. For youngsters they did well. The men along the river did a good job on the Germans trying to cross in front of them, those a little farther back held up through the cannonading. No one had told them about the French yielding defense, though, and suddenly it was the 38th Infantry's situation all over again: the French began to filter to the rear, the Americans understood they were to hold at all costs, and before they knew it, they were simply isolated groups surrounded on what once had been the river line.

One platoon wheeled around and fought with its back to the river until a five-to-one rush wiped it out. Another managed to sneak through the tall wheat, find a weak point in the enemy line, and fight its way through. It was the exception; one platoon that didn't get out told its story later: "A runner came down with an order from Lieutenant Hayman for the men to retire. A patrol was sent forward to ascertain the conditions. The patrol returned with the information that the Germans were advancing in the rear of our forward lines in great numbers. In the meantime Sergeant Walter Roth had gone back to the P.C. [Post of Command] for verification of the order to retire and was not seen afterward. Our position was covered by a severe harassing fire. We then proceeded toward the Marne, it being impossible to retire as ordered. We took an easterly direction and ran into a large force of the enemy which assumed an attitude of surrender. Lieutenant Guy, carrying a rifle, advanced toward them, and one of the Germans, who had a pistol concealed in his hand, shot the lieutenant in the forehead. The bullet penetrated his helmet, took a downward course, crashed into his forehead and eye, and lodged in his gas mask.

"We immediately dropped to the prone position and opened fire. With command of the position we were able to swing around the Germans, forming a half circle . . . the fighting continued at this place until about 2:00 P.M. when the enemy retired. . . .Those who were able to walk preceded up the banks of the river until we came to a battery of German light artillery. Here we changed our direction, moving closer to the stream and hoping to be able to move in a circle and rejoin the company. About three-thirty we decided to rest the wounded until darkness fell, but got a surprise from the enemy, as we discovered we were completely surrounded and prisoners of the Germans."[7]

In all, one company got 36 men home out of 210 engaged and the losses, shot and captured, in the other three ran about the same. Before the day was out two more companies got into the fight on the second line, helping out McAlexander's flank, and when Pershing heard what they'd all done their first time out, he was well pleased. "Why, they are iron men," he said, and the Twenty-eighth promptly took unto itself the title Iron Division.

The aptly named Rainbow Division had units from no less than 26 of the states on its roster and some of its outfits and personalities were as colorful as its title. One of the infantry regiments was the old New York National Guard Fighting 69th, federalized as the 165th United States Infantry, and it carried on its rolls Colonel Wild Bill Donovan, who would go on to OSS fame in the Second World War, and Father Francis P. Duffy. The 167th Infantry was an Alabama National Guard unit and it had a reputation for being composed of wild men. There is a legend that some of them dressed up as Indians one night and staged a raid on the German lines. The other two infantry regiments were the 168th—the Iowans who'd been shipped out on the *President Grant*—and the 166th from Ohio.

Its chief of staff was, of course, none other than Douglas MacArthur —son of a famous general, the most brilliant West Pointer of his day, the man responsible for getting a National Guard division organized and hustled to France. He was also already something of a character. His cap was worn without its wire stiffener, much in the manner of the Second World War air-force cap, and his most usual weapon was a riding crop. Like his father, he had a reputation for a self-confidence that was sometimes hard for his superiors to take, but he was going to come out of the war with a record that would take him up to the Army chief of staff's job before many years were out. He was off to a tremendous head start over the man who was to be his chief rival down the years and who spent the war impatiently at a tank training camp in Gettysburg, Pennsylvania—Major Dwight Eisenhower. By the time poor Ike got his orders overseas the war ended. His only decoration for the war came ten years later—a distinguished service medal awarded for state-side achievements.

The Rainbow Division had been in quiet sectors off and on for five months, but had no experience with anything big when on the night of July 3 it was taken out of the reserve and marched through a cold, rainy night to the Champagne sector. This brought it under the French Fourth Army and General Henri Gouraud, a one-armed, gimp-legged first-class fighter who went about with his kepi rakishly on one side of his head.

Gouraud had his boys hard at work digging defenses against the coming offensive, and the Rainbow pitched in beside them, hacking away at the miserably hard chalk soil of the Champagne which yielded life to some scrubby pine trees and endless expanses of blood-red poppies. The defense was in depth. The old front lines were actually abandoned. The only men there were observers, left to do one job: fire red warning rockets when they saw the Germans come over the top. After that they were free to get back to their own lines if they could do it. The rest of the old line was booby-trapped. Behind it lay a belt of strong points manned by sacrifice squads. They weren't free to do anything but stay there and die. Nobody expected them to stop the Germans; they were there simply to get the attack off balance so that it would hit the real line of defense—the so-called intermediate position—in bits and pieces rather than in one big hammer blow. Behind Intermediate Position lay Second Position and beyond this the Germans must not be allowed to go. Gouraud had given up as much as two to four kilometers in depth along his old front, but he counted on bleeding the German attack to death as it crossed that ground.

On July 7 he issued the men an order which began, "To the French and American soldiers of the Fourth Army. We may be attacked at any moment," and ended, "Each shall have but one thought: to kill a plenty, until they have had their fill. Therefore your general says to you: You will break this assault and it will be a happy day."

The Americans were scattered through the two French divisions in companies. The Alabamans were on the right, the Ohio boys in the center with one section of Company I detailed out front as a sacrifice squad, and the Irishmen from New York on the left. The Iowans were back on the Second Position.

They knew they were in for a terrible pounding when the artillery started. General Michael Lenihan, commanding the 83d Brigade, had even taken his machine gunners out of all the old pillboxes, preferring to have them take their chances in shell holes rather than stay in positions the Germans certainly had plotted. In the event he turned out to be right—every one of the old pillboxes was torn to bits.

At first they expected it on the night of July 13–14, but it passed, and the Iowans even got up a football game the next afternoon to celebrate Bastille Day. Then at nine that night a French patrol went out and came back with a prize: German assault troops who knew that the bombardment was due ten minutes after midnight and the infantry assault at four-fifteen in the morning.

Gouraud opened up his own artillery ten minutes before midnight, caught the German infantry moving into their jump-off positions, and punished them badly. Nevertheless, the German bombardment came on schedule; the Rainbow's men thought it was the heaviest of the war. They put on their gas masks, huddled in the dugouts, and quickly turned ghost-white as the explosions showered them with chalk dust. In the dugouts "the air became so foul that the candles went out and a match would flicker only for a moment. Men were placed on the steps to fan the air down, but that did not relieve the situation. In order to avoid suffocation in one of them where a number had already fainted, the occupants were ordered to move in a circle going out one entrance and in another. This was kept up for hours, and every now and then someone was struck, but it was better than letting a whole company die from lack of oxygen." [8]

A private in a Maryland trench mortar battery had no dugout and had to hug the forward face of a trench. "After laying in this hell-fire for what seemed to me like a century I heard a shell coming which I was sure had my name written all over it. My feelings were indescribable. The only thing I remember flashing across my mind was I wonder what my mother will say when she hears that I am dead. . . . With a shriek like the fiends out of hell the shell hit in the back of the trench, burying all of us . . . to be truthful I thought I was dead as I felt those big lumps of chalk hit me in the back. I was afraid to move. Then the thought struck me that maybe I was not dead but just buried. . . .I was starting to suffocate so after kicking and squirming I got myself out." [9]

The beautifully plotted fire searched for every gun position, every strong point. The French artillerymen gave it back while they had a gun left to serve. An Iowan remembered later a French battery firing and singing *Madelon* " '*Pour le repos*'—crash!—'*la plaisir*'—slam! —'*du militaire*'—bang!" until a shell wiped them out. An American crew on a French 75 lost men until there was only one doughboy left, but he went on alone, loading and firing, keeping his piece in the fight.

It was four-fifteen when the red signal rockets fluttered up along the old front line and they knew the Germans were coming. The

Ohio men out with the sacrifice squads saw figures moving past their post in the morning half light and opened up. The Germans returned the fire and the first casualty was a man who'd sneaked out of a hospital to be with his outfit. Then the senior noncom was killed, the lieutenant went down wounded; the enemy closed in and killed or captured the rest.

The assault lost time on the sacrifice posts, though, and the artillery Gouraud had kept out of the first part of the fight began to cut big holes in it. German planes controlled the air, but strafing the trenches couldn't keep the riflemen and machine gunners down. An Alabama sharpshooter—who admitted to having done a lot of practicing on revenue men back home—even got one of them by killing the pilot with a rifle shot.

On the right they made one small hole in the Intermediate Position. Two Alabama companies joined two French companies to drive them out again. On the left they came at the New Yorkers so fast that the gunners couldn't stop them. Lieutenant Kenneth Ogle rushed his platoon out with fixed bayonets and drove them off with bare steel. By 11:00 A.M. it was clear that six German divisions were getting nowhere against two French divisions and one American division. The gray lines began to fall back, the artillery lashing them as they went. There would be another attack at six in the evening and two small ones the next day, but the storm was over. The Rainbow Division took 1,567 casualties for its part in what was going to be called the decisive day of the war. For the gray lines were falling back not for the day, but for good; the *Friedensturm*, the peace offensive, was over. There would be no successors because the German man-power edge was gone. With troops brought from the old Russian front, the Germans had enjoyed a superiority of 200,000 men over the Allies when they attacked in March. They had inflicted great casualties and taken many prisoners, but the Americans came too quickly. Now there were 26 American divisions in France, seven of them in or near the line in the Château-Thierry area, the rest scattered in rear training locations. The man-power situation was even up and from now on the Allies would pull ahead. They could attack now: the next news was going to be that the Americans were across the Marne and into Château-Thierry and, with the French, were chewing their way into the base of the German salient at Soissons.

Chapter Five

"THE COMMAND IS 'FORWARD'"

JULY, 1918–SEPTEMBER, 1918

SINCE mid-June, 1918, Marshal Ferdinand Foch had contemplated the three big German salients pushing into his lines—at Amiens, Château-Thierry, and Saint-Mihiel—and wondered how to deal with them. His decision was that the Château-Thierry salient must be the first to be wiped out. It was the most threatening, the closest to Paris. It would be the scene of the coming German attack, hence the troops massed for defense could also be used for the counter. Finally, the German assault would fill the pocket with men and equipment; if one attack could zip across the top of the pocket while another kept the Germans too busy to withdraw, the take in men and guns captured might be tremendous.

Accordingly, a double attack was laid out. One prong would drive due east just south of Soissons where the line made a right angle and the salient began. Just a short advance here would cut the salient's main highway—the Soissons-Château-Thierry road—and deprive the Germans of their chief means of supplying the front, their best means of withdrawing from it. The second prong would come from the south, across the Marne, back through Château-Thierry, and then on north. The aim was not to gain ground, but to make the enemy stand and fight, too closely engaged to be able to pull out before the exit door was slammed shut.

Obviously the push at Soissons was the big show. If that didn't go through, the southern attack simply didn't matter. To make sure that it did go, Foch turned the job over to his best attacking general, "Butcher" Mangin. The tender-minded might object that Mangin was nothing if not lavish at expending man power, but he knew how to get a smash going and keep it moving. To do the job for him there were to be three divisions—the American First and Second and the French Moroccan. The Americans might well be flattered by the company. The Moroccans had started off as a combination of

COUNTER ATTACK: The front line when Marshal Ferdinand Foch launched his attack in July, 1918

Moroccans and the Foreign Legion. Driving for Mangin had cost them so many casualties that the outfit was now mostly Senegalese, but regardless of race, creed, or color it had a reputation as a ferocious fighting division with a marked distaste for taking prisoners.

The final fillip to the scheme was surprise—complete, total surprise. The Germans would not detect the attacking force because it simply would not exist until the moment when it did attack. The men would not be moved to the front until the very night of the assault. There would be no bombardment, just a rolling barrage with the men moving out behind it.

The First Division had come out of the line at Cantigny on July 5. It was July 9 before the Second Division got the last of its elements back from Belleau Wood and Vaux—the Yankee Division taking over—and set to work filling its shot-up formations. The men got deloused, swam in the Marne, and figured they were good for at least two weeks. One outfit—the First's 7th Field Artillery—was actually on the road to a rest area when the word caught up with them on July 14. They had come to a fork in the road when a hurrying staff officer stopped the column. The right fork led toward Paris, a chance to rest, to wash, for passes into the city for the fortunate. The left fork led back toward the front. The regiment waited in the night while a few officers huddled over the new orders; then they moved again, swinging to the left and back to the fight.

Actually, the movement of artillery forward had started on July 12. They marched at night and hid in the woods by day to avoid German reconnaissance planes. By the fifteenth it was obvious that the horses just wouldn't be able to get the guns up to attack at dawn on July 18. Up rushed trucks, onto them went the guns and cannoneers to jolt the rest of their way forward. Onward, unencumbered, went the horses and drivers and they had to get there on time because even a truck couldn't drag a gun into firing position, much less roll it forward once the shooting started. They still didn't know where they were going: it was one check point to the next and at each a French officer to give them the next destination.

First Division infantry went onto the *camions* on July 12. They were old hands now. When they were told their rolling kitchens would follow right along behind them, they believed not a word of it and took the kitchens aboard the *camions* with them. Little good it did them. They were hidden out in the Compiègne forest with no cooking fires allowed. Just to make it worse, it rained. The Second's infantry were similarly hidden in the Forêt de Retz and thus things stood in the afternoon of July 17. One of the Second Division's Marine outfits was sitting by the side of the forest road when "the call came that 'Father Murphy is receiving confessions.'" Then "we knew we were going into another battle": that night they were to march over ground they had never seen, take over a line they'd never seen, put their guns into positions they'd never seen, and at 4:35 A.M. on July 18 attack Germans they'd never seen.

There were three roads and a host of unmarked forest trails leading to the front. Night fell, and 67,000 men, 3,000 vehicles, and 5,000 animals emerged from the woods, the cellars, the barns, and the gullies where they'd been hiding and tried to use them all at once.

At first, as the men swung along the back roads leading to the main ones, the forests—manicured by a fastidious French forestry service— were magnificent in the dusk. The great oaks, eighty and ninety feet high, were in full leaf, throwing a canopy over the trails, cutting out the sky and the German aerial observation. In the cleared spaces between the trees lay endless rows of ammunition boxes and with them artillery, French infantry, and the natty French cavalry all waiting to join. They did, and the roads began to clot up. On the side came the infantry in single file, hungry, tired, and panting for water. In the center of the road moved the heavy stuff. A Marine left an account of what it was like:

"The tanks are new to us. There are big tanks and little tanks, all with their weird camouflage in colors of green, red, and brown. They rattle and crunch and groan and snort along, and no one argues with them in the matter of right of way. Through the slit at the base of the conning tower of each small tank protrudes a machine gun. The larger tanks carry three-inch guns. . . .

"On the right side of the road moving forward in a never-ending stream plods a single line of drab-colored infantry. . . .

"The center of the road is a jumble of the machinery of war, heavy howitzers propelled by squatty, low-built, powerful caterpillars; roan, black, and sorrel horses, hitched in teams; the graceful French 75's and their caissons drawn by six horses, with eight larger horses tugging, struggling along, pulling the heavier 155's.

"Occasionally a heavy gun or caisson slips into the ditch somewhere ahead and the diversified column jams up, remaining in a solid, almost motionless pack, and amid a jamboree of sounds, squawks, horns, whistles, and shouts, sways back and forth a few times and moves on, the crippled gun having been heaved over to the side of the road out of the line of traffic.

"A horse's leg is broken. He is dispassionately pistoled. Nothing is permitted to interfere with the forward movement of the troops, the transport, the machinery of war, the balance of power of the big drive just in the offing.

"Interspersed with the heavier traffic are the rolling kitchens, water wagons and combat wagons, each drawn by a span of mules. Ever attempting to forge ahead are the despatch riders on motor-cycles with officers in their sidecars—with now and then some general officer's staff car in the van. There are the never-ending trains of heavy ammunition trucks, loaded, rumbling, groaning, and grinding, ever holding to the center of the road.

"On the left, winding through the trees, are the famous French horse, the Dragoons, picturesque indeed with plumes and lances, men and horses alike, big and well conditioned. Just inside the trees in the ditch on the left of the road patiently plugs the French *poilu* in faded blue, now gray with dust, with the inevitable drooping mus-tache—his much-too-long rifle, and enough paraphernalia, pots and pans, etc., on his back to start up light housekeeping.

"Between the guns, caisson, tanks, supply and ammunition trucks, in other words, between the heavy transport that ever holds com-mand of the center of the road, and the single drab column of Ameri-cans on the right, is a Moroccan machine-gun outfit, each individual a tall, dark, rangy cuss. . . ."[1]

The storm began at about ten o'clock, no patter of rain breaking through the forest curtain, but a torrent, a tropical downpour, a blast of water that made the dark of the forest night impenetrable. It soaked the men's packs, making them twice as heavy. It had been two days' going without food now, since rations couldn't get forward, and a day's forced march, but they staggered on, each man grabbing the pack strap of the man ahead of him to keep touch in the dark-ness. Now and then one of them would stumble and splash into the watery ditch at the side of the road and his cursing would mingle with the thunder and the clanking of the tanks. An occasional flash of lightning showed the tanks the road, for the rest they groped along behind a walking guide whose hands had been daubed with phosphorescent paint.

If the downpour made it doubly certain that the men on the roads would be hidden from German planes, it was making it doubly un-certain that the infantry and guns would be in the line for the four thirty-five jump-off. Officers, gray with fatigue, pushed their men forward, searching for the French guides who would lead them into position.

Somehow most of them made it. The last leg was a steep hill that led up to the line. They panted up it and flopped down gasping, dazed with exhaustion. The storm went as suddenly as it had come, and perhaps in the new silence the Germans heard something. At any rate, a single red rocket went up in front of the First Division and some light artillery fire came down on the Americans. The men just lay there, husbanding their strength through the last few moments before their own guns would open.

It was still too dark to see, but ahead of them lay a broad plateau. At its north edge it sloped down to the valley of the Aisne River; to the east it fell into the valley of the Crise down which ran the Soissons-Château-Thierry road and the cutting of that road was the main task that lay ahead of them. Over most of its area the plateau was one wheat field, the wheat waist high. Here and there were little villages and running in from the river valleys, ravines. It would be the ravines that gave the worst trouble before the work was done.

Twenty minutes before jump-off a Marine colonel was still calling back for his machine guns and still being told that the road was so blocked that they couldn't come up. "Very well," he said, "we'll take the Boche machine guns." Minutes later artillery opened and the men went over. Some units still hadn't reached the line when it started. As they heard the guns go, they broke into a run, hit the line running, and kept right on going.

The attack had the First Division on the north with all four regiments in line—the 28th, the 26th, the 16th, and the 18th reading from north to south. The Moroccans had the center and the Second Division the south, with 5th Marines, 9th and 23d Infantry in line, 6th Marines in reserve.

For the first hour it was a joy. The surprise was complete and the German outpost lines thinly held and lightly wired. Desperate signal rockets went up, but the German artillery had been well pounded by the French and American and the reply was weak. The First Division infantry and French tanks routed out the German machine gunners until they came to their first objective, a road running northeast from Dommiers about two kilometers from the jump-off position. Here the barrage stood for twenty minutes, the men re-formed, and

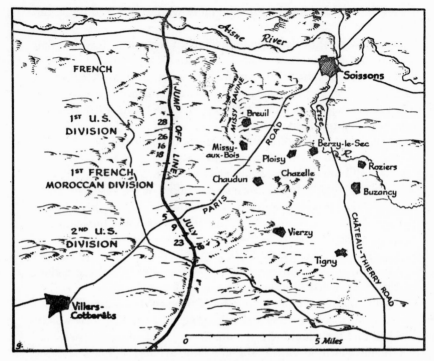

SOISSONS: The line of battle and the ground over which the attack moved

then jumped off for the second objective, which included Missy ravine.

The Second Division got off a little raggedly when the 9th Infantry in the center found the Marine company on its left was late on the starting line, leaving an open flank which some embattled Germans in a farmhouse began to pepper with machine-gun fire. The 9th turned north to deal with it, then the Marines caught up, and together they cleaned out the farmhouse. From then on it went smoothly, the men dropping down when they found machine guns ahead of them while the men to the left and the right moved up to flank the guns out.

As they moved out past the first objective line, they were already outrunning the range—6,000 yards—of the 75's, so the word went back to the artillery to move up. The word "Cease firing, march order!" went out, and while half the batteries kept up the fire, the other half limbered up and sent their horses forward at a trot. It was light by now; German planes had taken control of the air and strafed the gunners as they came.

Missy ravine is a long finger thrust into the plateau from the north. It is about a kilometer wide with steep sides and a marsh and a deep stream at the bottom. The Germans had filled it with artillery and the sides were high enough to keep the Allied guns from having gotten to it.

Two companies of the 28th with five French tanks helping out dived into the ravine to clean it out and were blown to pieces. Two more companies went in, going for the village of Breuil, around which a lot of the heavy stuff being thrown at them was concentrated. It was north of their sector, but the French couldn't move and the strong point couldn't be left hammering at the flank of the advance. The companies made a little ground along the muddy bottom of the ravine and got themselves thoroughly cut up in the process. The assault battalion was down to half strength, the support battalion came up, the French to the north got themselves organized for one more rush. All together they went forward, hip deep through the marsh, and this time they made it. On the right the 26th kept pace, fought its way across the southern tip of the ravine in spite of machine-gun fire that chewed big pieces out of it, and as the two regiments made a line for the night, they were halfway to the Château-Thierry road. No one doubted that a start on the rest of the trip would come at first light in the morning.

On the right prong of First's attack the 16th and the 18th made better time. No Missy ravine lying across their track, they got across the Paris-Soissons road in spite of a hail of artillery fire and went right on into the village of Chaudun down in the Moroccan territory. The speed opened up a bad gap between the 16th's left and the regiments hung up on the ravine. Accordingly, the 16th dropped units off facing north to keep the hole covered.

The Second Division slugged ahead against the machine guns, losing officers until most of its companies were commanded by sergeants, but making their day's ground, except for the shot-up hamlet of Vierzy, by noon. Prisoners poured back and the Marines were forced to defend one group of them against the Senegalese, who

had a feeling that a dead prisoner was even more desirable than a
live one. A luckier group captured something which had by that time
become infinitely more fascinating—food, a barrel of sauerkraut.
They smashed it in and went on eating the sauerkraut in handfuls. In
spite of the casualties, the dead-tired men and the units hopelessly
muddled, they got one more attack organized by seven in the evening and went smashing into Vierzy before they quit for the night.
Then they lay down, and as one lieutenant admitted, ". . . we took
turns watching, but we were so dead tired I believe the entire German army could have advanced unseen."

During the darkness those who were still awake could see the
signs of their victory—fires lighting the sky as the Germans burned
stores they knew they couldn't get out of the shrinking salient.

Toward the end of that first day they saw something which no
man would ever see in war again. From the rear of the Second's
position, out of the Forêt de Retz came columns of French cavalry,
lined out as on parade. The Germans let them come as the columns
were flung out into line, the sabers drawn, and a cavalry charge in
the grand tradition spurred forward. The Light Brigade at Balaclava
faced no surer ruin. The machine guns opened and in what came out
again there were more riderless horses than men.

During the second day, the First flung itself against the machine
gunners and made inches. The surprise was over; the German right,
covering Soissons, had been beefed up during the night and was
holding. The 16th and 18th did manage a small advance, but it only
made the bad gap between the 26th and 28th worse. The northern
arm had to move up, the hole had to be closed. The artillery pushed
forward to plaster the ground; at five-thirty the 1st Battalion of the
28th and 1st Battalion of the 26th went out through the wheat with
the dying sun at their backs and made the two kilometers needed to
bring the line up even with the 16th and the 18th on the south.

The Second found itself up against game Germans who kept firing
until they were killed on their machine guns. Nevertheless, the 6th
Marines, which had been held out of the first day's fighting, made
it all the way through to the Château-Thierry road, got tossed off it
by a German counterattack, got back on it again, again got pushed
back, and finally had to settle for a line at Tigny. That did the job,
though—the road now lay between the two lines and nothing coming

out of the Château-Thierry pocket was going to travel that way. It had taken 4,000 casualties to do the job; that night the Second pulled out, and was replaced by a British division, taking their memories with them. One of the men wrote in his diary, "I came across a most interesting sight this afternoon. There laid a German, a man I should judge about thirty years old; he looked about six feet tall, laying on his stomach, his head toward our lines. Facing him in practically the same position was a little Moroccan about five feet, three inches tall. Both were dead, both were cut something terrible; both had their trench knives in their hands. It must have been a terrible struggle, a fight to the death. Both paid the penalty. They had made the supreme sacrifice. They surely were enemies when they met."

There was no rest for the weary First. Through a long third day of battle they went forward with the Moroccans, going for Berzy le Sec and the Ploisy and Chazelle ravines. They got some of the high ground around the village, but it wouldn't fall. On the morning of the fourth day what was left of the division pulled itself together for one last try. Every rear-area man was moved up to fill out the blasted ranks of the infantry and at four forty-five in the morning the 16th and the 18th went out, across the Crise, across the Château-Thierry road, and there was no stopping them until they had pushed right up the heights to the Buzancy plateau beyond and secured the job. At eight-thirty, the 26th and the 28th went for Berzy le Sec after a three-hour artillery preparation and this time Beaumont Buck, their brigadier general, led the charge in person. A division historian noted ". . through the clouds of dust and smoke our infantry advanced and finally every soldier in the attack, able to move, disappeared from sight over the crest. The artillery fire of the enemy became visible only as drifting clouds of smoke. With the diminution of the enemy's artillery fire came a great increase in his machine-gun fire. . . .

"Near the old wooden shed on the crest over which the infantry had passed appeared long files of men returning. They wore the unmistakable German helmet . . . shortly after our wounded hobbled past, pale, worn, and bloody . . . they stated proudly that they . . . had taken the town of Berzy le Sec, the last objective of the division."[2]

The First had taken a lacerating 7,000 casualties and even the French were beginning to wonder whether we weren't overdashing in our approach to the machine-gun problem. The French, at the bottom of their man-power barrel, necessarily went forward more slowly, hoping to save men by maneuver. Pershing felt that it simply meant larger losses in the long run and that the all-out smash was preferable however badly a single day's statistics might look as a result. In a sense, both were wrong. Men with rifles going against machine guns were going to suffer badly whether they went slowly or quickly. The answer was tanks; the armor available at Soissons had done a job until the artillery knocked it out. At the same time, the French and the Americans down at the bottom of the salient were being asked to go forward alone in bad tank country. They were going to gain some ground, but they weren't going to gain it until the Germans were ready to let go of it and they were going to take vicious losses in the process.

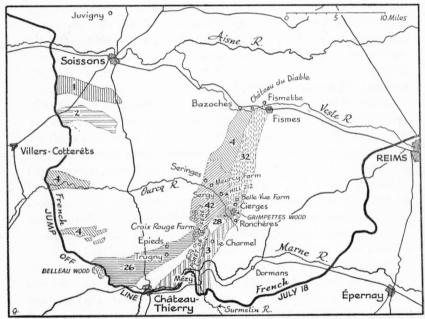

THE OURCQ-VESLE OFFENSIVE: The ground covered by American divisions as they fought up to the Vesle River. At the top left, Juvigny, to which the Thirty-Second Division drove under the command of French General Mangin

Around the tip of the salient there were three American divisions. Up the west face was the Fourth, new to combat, and put in by regiments with the French. On the blood-soaked ground at Belleau Wood stood the veteran Yankee and farther south, just east of Château-Thierry, was the Third, now know as the Marne Division, doing business at its same old stand.

On the night of the 17–18, the Fourth and the Yankee got drenched in the same downpour that soaked the men moving up on Soissons and thought nervously of the morning. It was the Fourth's first anything and the Yankee's first attack. The Fourth went ahead steadily alongside the French, taking out the machine guns in the way and showing their greenness only by having too many men bunched together at the front of the attack by the time the day was over. The Yankee went roaring ahead, even its divisional photographer taking prisoners, the Germans apparently mistaking his camera for a secret weapon. Their divisional historian was bound to note, though, "This was our boys' first fighting against machine guns, and at the beginning they had many losses because they would insist on charging the guns frontally. The French never did this; if they were held up, they telephoned back for artillery and sat down until the big guns had reduced the 'nests.' "

Next day the Fourth got a taste of it. Surprised by the attack, the Germans brought up more machine guns and on the nineteenth and twentieth, the Fourth took 2,000 casualties. They, too, felt that raw courage was a bad answer to the machine-gun problem: ". . . for the results achieved, their losses had been too great."

The Yankee spent the nineteenth marking time while the French on their flanks came up and then that night got the glorious word that the Germans were pulling out, that they could go hell for leather in the morning and leave their flanks as open as they liked. They jumped off at 4:00 A.M. and didn't stop until they'd gone nine kilometers and run smack into the next German line at Epieds and Trugny. Obviously the Germans really were pulling back, so that night—the twentieth to twenty-first—the Third started across the Marne near Château-Thierry. They had no trouble crossing the river, but through the twenty-first it became apparent that this was no rout. Throughout the day forward elements of both the Third and the Yankee found themselves up against solid opposition. The cross-country dash being over, a general attack was scheduled for the twenty-second.

In front of Epieds the Yankee walked out against the machine guns and though its 102d Infantry did get into the town, not enough men were left by the time they got there to fend off a German counterattack. They tried it again the next day, but with scarcely any better luck, and to the south the Third spent the same two days trying to get to Le Charmel with equally bad luck and high casualties. McAlexander's old 38th Infantry—which now firmly believed it could do anything—actually did get into the village, but its flanks were barer than Mother Hubbard's cupboard and not even the 38th could get away with that twice.

Sergeant Alexander Woollcott, who'd later be a very great drama critic, but at the moment was a writer for the soldier newspaper *Stars and Stripes,* followed the Yankees forward that day and when it was over, he filed a story. It concerned a Yankee Division captain who'd sat down beneath a tree when his men stopped for a rest and was mortally wounded by an enemy shell. The rest—in Woollcottian prose:

" 'Good-by, boys,' he said, and his head sagged forward.

"Then it was as if, somewhere in the universe, a Commander Invisible had called 'Attention!' Captain Leahy raised his head. With clearing voice, he spoke the name of the officer to whom it would be his duty to turn over the battalion in the event of his being called away.

" 'Lieutenant Hansen,' he said, 'the command is "Forward." See the boys through.'

"Then he died."

A brigade of the Twenty-eighth— the Pennsylvanians—was turned over to the Yankee to beef up the assault on the twenty-fourth. They moved out, not greatly heartened by what the Yankees had been telling them, to try their luck. "Just at the break of day, July 24, Captain Cain was reconnoitering the terrain over which the attack was to be made at six-fifteen. The Yankee pointed out a wheat field, saying, 'You are not going to hear a shot until you get to the edge of that wheat field, but from then on you are going to catch hell. That is just where they gave it to us day before yesterday, when they let us come right up to the edge of the wheat and then opened up on

WAR COMES: President Woodrow Wilson (*above*) went before the Congress on April 2, 1917 and asked for a declaration of war against Germany. (*Below*) Wilson on rostrum. (*World Photo Inc.*)

VOLUNTEER: Before the declaration of war, the Army had been increased by voluntary enlistments. (*Above*) James Montgomery Flagg's famous Uncle Sam poster.

DRAFT: When the war came, though, a modern mass army had to be raised by conscription. Here, Secretary of War Newton D. Baker, blind-folded, draws the first draft number. (*U.S. Army Signal Corps*)

GOODBYE: The men marched away and a sweetheart (*left*) and a mother (*right*) in New York City watched their particular man go with the 7th Regiment to Camp Wadsworth, South Carolina. (*Underwood and Underwood*)

SHOTS: Rookies are pretty much the same the whole world over. Here, they are lined up for shots in a camp near Atlanta, Georgia. (*Tracy Mathewson*)

SOLDIERS: A few days later, the rookies were in uniform and drilling. This line-up is against a typical barracks. (*Tracy Mathewson*)

THE RETURN OF THE *MAYFLOWER:* To get the Army overseas, the Navy had to lick the German submarines. Here, the first American destroyers arrive in Queenstown, Ireland, in May, 1917. (*From a painting by Bernard F. Gribble*)

KAMERAD! And lick the submarines the destroyers did. This is the *U-58* surrendering to the U.S.S. *Fanning.* It turned out to be our only confirmed submarine kill of the war.

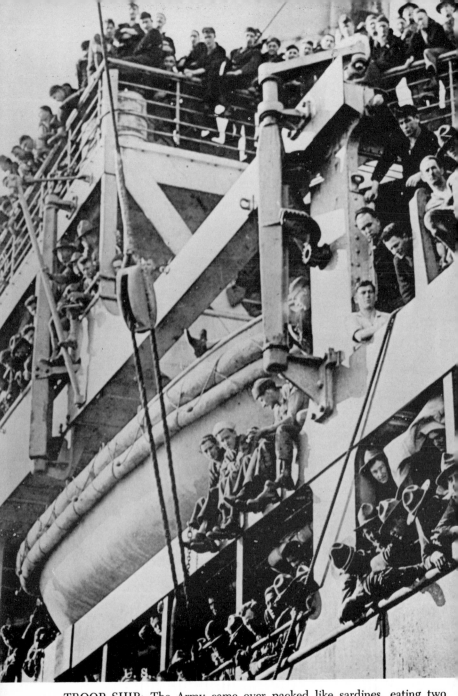

TROOP SHIP: The Army came over packed like sardines, eating two meals a day cafeteria style when it wasn't too seasick to eat. (*The National Archives*)

"LAFAYETTE, WE ARE HERE." The doughboys marched off the transports to spend their first night in France in ancient French barracks which went back to Napoleon's day. (*Underwood and Underwood*)

"40 AND 8's": Then it was across France in midget box cars which were said to carry 40 men—but nothing in regulations said that they had to carry them comfortably.

NO MAN'S LAND: This was the front in 1917—a waste of shell holes and strong points lit by distant flares. (*From the drawing by Georges Scott*)

THE TRENCHES: They made a long, crooked line across France as the doughboys went into the line for the first time. (*The National Archives*)

STAND BY! Then the training period was over and we were really in it. Here, Second Division artillery goes into action at Soissons. (*The National Archives*)

MOVE UP! At St. Mihiel an American Army went into action for the first time. This is First Division following up the break-through, with threatening Mont Sec in background. (*The National Archives*)

ON GUARD: We sent some excellent artists overseas. One of them, Harvey Dunn, painted this doughboy on lookout with a few liberated German potato-masher grenades. (*The National Archives*)

REAR AREA: Another artist, Wallace Morgan, caught these men getting washed up in a French town in spite of the *"eau mauvaise"* of which the sign warns. (*The National Archives*)

TAKE TEN: Finally, troops who have just gone through at St. Mihiel are caught in the smashed-up village of Hattonchâtel by combat artist Captain W. F. Aylward. (*The National Archives*)

BIRDMEN IN TRAINING: British and French planes on the most important American training field—Issoudun, near the village of the same name (*background*) in southeast France. (*The National Archives*)

DAWN PATROL: Americans out over the lines in a French two seater, the Breguet. They are from the 96th Aero Squadron. (*The National Archives*)

LUF AND RICK: (*Left*) This is the Lafayette Escadrille hero Raoul Lufbery after he had switched to the American Air Service. (*Below*) Eddie Rickenbacker, the greatest American ace, with his "Hat in the Ring" insignia. (*Wyndham Press Service*)

BRIDGE OF SHIPS: The great Hog Island shipyard, which would have made even more history if the war had not ended so soon.

DO YOUR BIT: Girls of the Wadleigh High School, New York City, cultivating over here to feed the boys over there. (*Underwood and Underwood*)

LIBERTY LOAN: Douglas Fairbanks—Senior—with Charlie Chaplin on his shoulders during a Liberty Bond drive in New York. (*Underwood and Underwood*)

COMMAND: Allied Commander in Chief, Marshal Ferdinand Foch, with the American commander, General John J. ("Black Jack") Pershing. (*U.S. Army Signal Corps*)

THE LOST'S LEADER: Major Charles Whittlesey, who led the Lost Battalion and, in the great tradition, got his people through. (*The National Archives*)

SQUIRREL SHOOTER: Sergeant Alvin C. York of the Eighty-second Division. He captured 132 prisoners and Foch called him "the greatest . . . private soldier of the war." (*The National Archives*)

ARMOR: French tanks with American crews moving up to the attack during the offensive in the Meuse-Argonne Forest area. (*The National Archives*)

ATTACK: Infantry of the Twenty-seventh Division going out through barbed wire. The Twenty-seventh Division was an American outfit serving with the British. (*The National Archives*)

COMBAT: This is perhaps the greatest action picture of the war. It shows men of the Second Division's 23d Infantry on the attack. (*The National Archives*)

PINNED DOWN: Again, the Second Division. Here, riflemen hit the dirt during the attack on Blanc Mont while serving with the French in October, 1918. (*The National Archives*)

SUPPLY LINE: Food and ammunition move up while the wounded come back through a ruined village on the Meuse-Argonne front. (*The National Archives*)

PRISONERS: A doughboy herds Germans to the rear during the last days of the Meuse-Argonne drive, when the enemy infantry was beginning to crack. (*The National Archives*)

LIBERATED: French men and women, many of them in German-held territory since 1914, turned out to greet the Americans as the last push went forward. (*The National Archives*)

THE WAR COMES TO AN END :
Men of "M" Company, 6th Infantry
Regiment, Fifth Division, celebrate
the Armistice. (*The National Ar-chives*)

"PRAISE GOD FROM WHOM ALL BLESSINGS FLOW": Part of the New York crowd with an effigy of the Kaiser on Armistice Day. (*Times Photo Service*)

us with machine guns and the men fell like flies without a chance to fire a shot. Be very careful to keep your men with good interval and distance when you get to that wheat field.' Captain Cain . . . thought the Yankee was certainly giving him a dismal picture of what they were to encounter and said nothing about it to any of his men. At six-fifteen the attack started, the men traveling light, having left their packs in the woods because bayonet action was anticipated. Gradually they approached the wheat field; they were twenty-five yards from it and not a shot had been heard. The first wave entered the standing grain and the captain held his breath. 'Here is where it starts and God help us.' The second wave entered the wheat, the third, the fourth. 'What are they going to do—get us all up close and kill us all at one time or take us off piecemeal?' And still not a shot, but the advance continued, the tension grew tighter, and the sound of a machine gun would have been welcome and no surprise. Suddenly came a message from the left, saying the Boche had gone. . . ."[3]

The German right had fallen back as far as the Forêt de Fere: the Pennsylvanians and the Twenty-sixth Division were whipped forward with command still hoping to turn it into a rout. Next day, though, command decided both outfits had had all they could take for the moment and put the Rainbow in to relieve them. The same day the Third clawed its way back into Le Charmel, this time for keeps, but the Germans, making a good thing of the ridges rising back from the Marne, gave up just the town and no more. Indeed, from a château on the heights above the town they kept up a machine-gun fire which made it impossible to use the streets by daylight.

The Rainbow got out of their *camions* at Epieds, took no stock in any stories about a German retreat, and pushed up through the Forêt de Fere in battle order. "Great shells were snapping full-grown trees like matchwood and plowing up the damp, fragrant earth." Presently, on the twenty-sixth, the 84th Brigade—the Alabama and Iowa regiments—found themselves near the center of the forest, facing a natural mantrap. The trees gave way to a wheat field that ran up a slope crowned by a nest of stone buildings connected by walls and trenches. This was La Croix Rouge Farm, a natural strong point, infested with machine guns looking out over clear fields of fire. Behind the clearing the trees took up again, offering cover for more guns.

On the afternoon of the twenty-sixth word came down for the Alabamans to take the farm, the Iowans the line of the road running from the farm southeast to Le Charmel. Bill Screws, the Alabama's colonel, almost bit his cigar in two when they told him. He figured it was madness to make the attack in daylight without artillery preparation. Up top, though, they wanted to keep the front moving and the word remained "Go." Just before the 4:50 P.M. jump-off an artilleryman asked Screws where he was going. The colonel chomped his cigar and replied, "Damn if I know, but I'm on my way."

They moved out on schedule and ". . . . the instant the low-lying Boche caught sight of their helmets, a murderous fire from half-a-hundred concealed guns swept upon them, tearing great gaps in their ranks. No order was necessary. In a second they were flat on the ground, formed into a skirmish line, and replying to the fire, although they couldn't see the enemy. The air was a tumult of shell crashes, shouted commands, snapping bullets, crackle of machine guns, and calls for stretcher-bearers. The ever-thinning line, more by crawling than by rushing, slowly gained ground toward . . . the road."[4]

By dark they had the road and the farm, and the Alabamans had the heaviest casualty list they were to have in any engagement of the war, the Iowans almost as bad. There were barely enough men to carry the wounded back, but they kept at the task until the stretchers blistered their hands and for part of the way to the rear, particularly in front of the farm, they had to walk on dead men to get there. It rained through the night and at dawn they found the Germans gone again, but none of the men in the line doubted that they had simply gone back to another line which was not to be seized by hastily mounted, badly backed rushes. Up at command, though, they were not so certain.

The Germans had indeed found themselves a new snug hole. This time they were behind the Ourcq River. The Ourcq isn't much of a river, only five yards wide and waist deep most of the way—one doughboy opined that they'd call it a creek back home. The ground on its north bank, though, is a good deal higher than the ground to the south; the attacker would have to come on with the enemy looking down his throat.

For some reason command thought they were going to go bowling through. Perhaps hoped would be a better word. This was the biggest

American attack so far. The Rainbow was on the north, the Pennsylvania had been put back in to replace the French division in the center, and the Third was still plugging north from Le Charmel down south. Command wanted a good show; on Sunday, July 28, the three divisions were to get across the river, push the Germans off the high ground, and keep going. What they were going to get was one of the dirtiest days of infantry slaughter since Grant lost his head at Cold Harbor.

The Third got itself solidly across the river into Ronchères, a cluster of stone houses. The Pennsylvanians sent in their 110th Infantry and showed they were learning their business by scuttling the men forward in small combat groups instead of nice even lines to be shot at. The Germans let them come on up and around Hill 188 until they were within three hundred yards and then opened up. The men tried to make the rest of the way crawling, but there wasn't enough cover. At dark they were back on the riverbank.

The Rainbow went in with its favorite assault formation: Iowa on the right, Alabama next, then New York and Ohio on the left. On the right, the plan called for pinching out Sergy—the Iowans were to take the heights to the east of it, the Alabamans those on the west. It was four-fifty in the morning when the Iowans started filing down to the river, rifles at high port to keep them out of the wet wheat. For the moment they were screened by the mist along the river bottom and they picked their way across the water, a few men scurrying at a time, without casualties. Ahead of them lay Hill 212, bare except for the inevitable wheat. The assault battalion spread out around the base of the hill, started forward, and as they came ghost-like out of the mist the slaughter started. It was rifles and bayonets against dug-in machine guns and artillery.

In spite of the losses, they began to get the machine gunners, not in a bravura charge, but by little groups of riflemen keeping a gun crew down while one or two men slipped forward to kill them in the gun pits. Battle cries are a good deal more common in the press than on the battlefield, but men who were there say the Iowans really did go forward shouting, "Give the squareheads hell, give 'em hell!" Halfway up the hill they went, then slipped a company around to the left where it took the Germans on the flank and then they went all the way to the top.

The Iowans could go no farther. Men kept dropping and the regi-

mental historian was an honest enough man to note that ". . . it became so hot that minor wounds which automatically reversed one's
direction were welcomed."[5] Most of the men were pulled back under
the crest to give them a little protection and a patrol pushed into
Sergy. Five men went out, got bushwhacked inside the village, and
one got back.

Late in the afternoon came the counterattack, a barrage followed
by two waves of gray infantrymen walking quietly. There were three
lieutenants and a sergeant left to command the men on the hill and
their best hope was their two machine guns. A shell wiped one out
and the crew of the other took flight. Rifle fire wasn't stopping the
attack. Privates David Binkley and Ferdinand Prien—neither had
ever fired a machine gun in his life—made a dash for the abandoned
gun, somehow got it going, and the Germans fell back.

The sun went down blood red that night and in the little daylight
that was left all the Iowans had to do was hold on through a gas
attack, an air raid with Fokkers coming in low to strafe the hill, and
one more counterattack which the artillery smashed up before it fell
on the exhausted men.

Pushing up to the high ground west of Sergy, the Alabamans had,
if anything, even worse going. A machine gunner who was with the
advance found that "as we reached the crest of the hill, instead of the
five or six Germans I had been firing upon, a solid line of Germans
arose stretching all across the hill. Machine guns opened up upon us
from the woods on the right and from the church steeple and buildings from the little village of La Ferte on our left, pouring a terrific fire into our ranks. Hearing a groan at my side, I turned and saw
little F. H. Dent of Macon, his shirt on fire; a bullet had struck a
clip of cartridges in his belt, exploding them, setting his shirt on fire
as well as badly wounding him."[6]

There they lay, the Germans in Sergy pouring it in on the flank to
add to the fire from ahead. Late in the day two companies of the
Ohio were pulled out of division reserve for a go at the town. They
got in, but there weren't enough of them left to hold against a counterattack and as the day ended, the Germans still had Sergy.

On the left the New Yorkers were supposed to get across the
Ourcq, then fight their way up a valley which ran down to the river

from Meurcy Farm. Their artillery was unable to support them, the officers had no faith in the move. They jumped off with "angry blessings from the colonel," and Captain Merle-Smith, who had one of the assault companies, left a vivid record of what followed: ". . . we came down across the fields to the River Ourcq under scattering enemy fire. We came down just where the little stream has broadened out into a still water about thirty feet across. It looks deep. The line hesitates; a couple of men drop. Awful thought—the captain must lead and I never liked a cold bath in the morning; however, I jumped from the bank expecting to swim but my feet touched a muddy bottom and the water wasn't too cold. All the line in the water now. Up the other bank through the bordering woods. A small German detachment overrun, two more Germans shot out of a tree, and now on the side of the hill in front appear open wheat fields. One hundred yards ahead five machine guns in fox holes on the hillside; bravery must be granted to the German defenders, firing until our men were sometimes within twenty feet, then 'Kamerad,' expecting no quarter and getting very little. . . . On up the hill now quite heavy enfilade machine-gun fire from right and left, both front and rear. No target to be seen, men now dropping fast but the line too excited to notice. An artillery barrage comes down. It seems wise to hurry the men up through and inside the German barrage. I get shot in the arm giving the double-time signal, which causes some amusement among the men near, as they had suffered from that signal in the training area.

" . . . The damaging fire was coming from our left and right, a source completely invisible, but yet a sheaf of bullets through the young wheat. A man crouches to run forward. He is shot through the legs, drops to hands and knees, is hit in the legs and arm; down flat and is again hit in the head. A bullet cuts my coat on the back of my shoulder but barely scratches. The men of my headquarters company are all hit but one—a terrible feeling of helplessness because there seems no one to fight against and it is the officers' responsibility to pick the targets and reduce the enemy fire by your own . . . 180 degrees of emptiness. . . .

"The men are very steady but there are only a pitifully few of them left."[7]

On the far left the Ohioans came up just in time for the attack—Benson Hough, their colonel, remembered asking directions in the blackness as they marched: "I was directed to proceed on the road I was traveling until I arrived at a crossroads, where the identifying marks were said to be nine dead horses. . . ." He got his boys there in time to receive just one order, "Put your regiment in over there." It was the same story as the rest of the line: infantry, without tanks or artillery, dying in front of dug-in machine guns.

As dawn came on the twenty-ninth, corps command was still talking cheerily about an advance clear to the Vesle. The Third Division and the Pennsylvanians spent the day hacking away at Grimpettes Wood. Three times they attacked, and night found them no closer to the Vesle than they'd been in the morning. On the Rainbow's front the Ohio got into Seringes to stay, the New Yorkers got into Meurcy Farm but found it too hot to stay there, and on the right two battalions from the Fourth Division were borrowed for another try at Sergy. One of them was commanded by Major Troy Middleton who in another war later on was going to have the whole of the Anzio Beachhead to worry about as a major general.

Sergy wasn't much—a farm village of 256 people in ordinary times, and as one of the men who fought for it said, "It was not noteworthy for its beauty nor was it overly clean. . . ." This day, though, its 78 houses were small stone forts from which the gunners could cut up the advance to either flank. One of the Fourth's battalions was to hit it from head on, a pick-up force from the Iowa Regiment to take it on the eastern edge. Later, both units would claim to have been first into the town; whatever the case, it was ours by nightfall, and one of the strong points on the Ourcq line was done for.

That night what was left of the Third Division was pulled out of the line—they'd been in since June 1. The Thirty-second, Michigan and Wisconsin men, all fresh and unshot at, went in in its place. One of its colonels left a remarkably honest record of what it felt like to go in for the first time. He was reconnoitering forward in the area his men were to occupy. "After perhaps twenty minutes we reached the timber. . . . I struck something with my foot that yielded like, maybe a sandbag. When I touched it I felt that it was a coat—yes, a coat upon a dead man. I did not like this woods. . . . Just a little way ahead, perhaps 200 yards, shells were constantly breaking and sometimes fragments purred down towards us . . . I was not comfortable a bit.

"I call to the runner, 'Boy, that last shell was gas; put on your mask.' With that last word I dived into mine. I couldn't see a thing inside the mask, but I could hear every shell that broke plainer than ever. I couldn't see my guide and I stumbled around like a blind man. I decided I could pull down my mask and leave the tube in my mouth and the clip on my nose until I reached the guide.

"I decided I had to take a chance on gas. I might die a slow and lingering death, but if we stopped much longer there the laws of chance indicated a quick death from high explosives. I pulled off my mask."[8]

On the thirtieth the Rainbow plugged ahead and even when they gained ground there were never enough men left to hold it. "The Tragic Thirtieth," the Iowans called it because of the fearful beating they took in an attack on hills north of Sergy; they knew they couldn't succeed. "We had to crawl from the start," wrote a captain who led what was left of his company into the machine guns that day. "The bullets were just skipping over the top of the ground, in a seemingly solid wave. Shells were falling thick and fast around us and they had the range to a foot. . . . There was not a breath of wind stirring and the heat rose in shimmering waves. Here a man went hurtling into the air to fall to earth a shapeless, quivering mass; there another was swirled completely around by the impact of a bullet full in the body. The distant horizon seemed to weave before the clouded eyes of the survivors. It seemed to be but a question of time until they were annihilated. Their frayed nerves could stand not much more. One man went stark, staring mad and ended his misery with a bullet from his own gun."[9]

On their right, though, the Pennsylvanians finally made it up Hill 188 on what amounted to the sixth try in three days. The men were in a fury at the hill; when the wounded in the rear heard that one more try was going in, they threw away their diagnosis tags and went back into the line to be part of it. Their artillery had gotten organized behind them this time and they went over the top of the hill so hard that they drove right into Grimpettes Wood and, along with the Thirty-second, took that, too, in furious hand-to-hand combat that went on into faceless fighting in the dark. One of them wrote back, "You can tell the folks that more fellows are converted over here by shell fire than ever hit Billy Sunday's sawdust trail." Stretcher-bearers carrying back the wounded worked until their hands gave out and

then wired the stretcher handles to their wrists in order to keep on
working.

Since the American right and left were attacking in converging directions, the line was slowly growing shorter, and that night it was
practical to pull the Pennsylvanians out and leave the 32d with the
whole right. Ahead of them lay Cierges, Belle-Vue Farm, and finally
Hill 230, the high point of the whole Ourcq line. Like the Round Top
at Gettysburg, it dominated the whole position, and if it went, the
position went with it.

It was the last day of July. If the Rainbow had almost nothing
left but its nerve, the 32d was fresh. They took Cierges and lay in
position to go on to Belle-Vue Farm and Hill 230 the next day.
On August 1 they did it. The men went in "yelling like Indians,"
and when it was over, "Here about the farm dead were strewn
everywhere. Rain was falling and the fingertips of the dead were
creased in little wrinkles from the water. Many faces there were
familiar to me; it was depressing. At a corner of the farm a German machine gunner sat in a pit with his hands still gripping the
handles of his Maxim. He wore glasses and had been a short man.
Now he was shorter than before for a shell fragment had sliced off
the whole upper two inches of his skull leaving it startlingly flat. A
peculiar thing about it was that his spectacles were undisturbed."[10]

That night the Germans pulled back to the Vesle. The salient was
ended, but they had managed to get the great majority of their
men and gear out, and run up an appalling American casualty list.
The men in the line knew, even if no one else did, that unsup-
ported infantry attacks were not going to win this war. When the
Fourth Division went in to replace the Rainbow, the Iowans figured
their regiment was down to 30 per cent of normal strength. The
Rainbow's New York regiment stumbled back through the bloody
fields around Meurcy Farm. Here Wild Bill Donovan had been
called "the bravest of the brave" by the men who fought next to him
because he was always out in front; here Sergeant Joyce Kilmer, the
poet, had died, killed by a sniper. Almost too weary to see, they
went back, but when they passed the bodies still lying near the Farm,
Father Francis P. Duffy, their chaplain, heard sobbing in the ranks.

If the Ourcq had been rough, the Vesle was going to be rougher.
In the first place, it was a real river, not much wider than the Ourcq

to be sure, but a good deal deeper and swifter. From the heights on its south bank the Americans had to come down open country into the valley, make their way across the marsh along the river edge, then do what they could to get across the water and up the heights on the far side. It was almost a mile from the hills on the south to the hills on the north and the Germans had used the five days since the fighting on the Ourcq started to infest the position with artillery cruelly registered in on every fold in the ground that might be useful to the advancing Americans. Command was about to learn a lesson they had started to learn on the Ourcq: dead men can't advance.

Through August 3 the Fourth and the Thirty-second Divisions pushed forward to the Vesle through a storm that turned bad roads into impossible ones. The struggling artillery horses simply couldn't get the guns forward, even with the cannoneers heaving on the wheels until the engineers came up and managed to get the worst of the mudholes filled with rocks, stumps, and anything else available. Corps—ever optimistic—told the Fourth, going into battle as a complete division for the first time, to go right on to the north bank of the Vesle. The men struggled ahead, debating whether the rain or the German shells were falling harder, got thoroughly lost in the teeming dark, and finally settled down short of the south bank until dawn could come and they could find out where in hell they were.

On the fourth, the rain kept up and appeared to act as a positive tonic on the German artillerymen. The Fourth kept trying to move down the open slopes to the river and every time they tried it their formations were knocked about like pins in a bowling alley. On their right the Thirty-second was doing a little better. The 127th Infantry got into Fismes, got kicked back into the marshes south of the town by a counterattack, and when their colonel, Russell Langdon, counted heads he found he didn't have a regiment any more. By putting everybody into one unit, though, he managed to get up a battalion-sized outfit. Back they went into Fismes, and just at nightfall they were all the way up to the river—albeit with a disconcerting number of German snipers and machine gunners in their rear who clobbered the unwary through the night.

Through the fifth and most of the sixth the artillery caught up with the infantry and went to work on the German guns. They could have been firing Chanel No. 5 for all the good it seemed to do. The conclusion should not be drawn that the German field artillery was so much better than the American. They simply knew the ground south of the river, they knew every spot useful for troops or gun emplacements, and they could fire on them blind, by the map. The Americans were firing into unknown territory, with only an occasional muzzle flash glimpsed by the spotters for guidance. Air reconnaisance could have helped fill the gap, but the only planes in sight were German.

Then at four-thirty in the afternoon the Fourth attacked. The 1st Battalion of the 58th Infantry actually got across the river and kept moving, "stumbling over the shell-sown field, muddy with falling dirt, clothes torn by shell fragments, trying not to see their fallen comrades as they passed, the men gained the railroad, where a number of prisoners and eight machine guns were captured . . . the embankment rocked with the impact of large shells. Machine-gun bullets ricocheted off the rails, striking fire as they passed."[11] Marvelously, with artillery and machine guns from Bazoches and Château du Diable digging into their flanks, they made it all the way to the Soissons-Reims road and dug in under the shell-torn poplar trees. They were absolutely exposed, there was no support for them north of the river, but they managed to hold through the night while the Germans made it bright with star shells to keep help from coming up. All that night and the next day the engineers sweated to get a bridge across the Vesle. "As fast as [the bridges] were laid down they were destroyed by enemy artillery. Again and again, sweating, panting, the attempt was made. Trees were finally chopped down and lashed together with wire to form temporary bridges. . . . The enemy artillery fire concentrated on the river was too heavy. Upon all sides geysers of earth sprang up and vanished. A direct hit on a bridge section tossed [engineer troops] high in the air, twisting and turning in horrible limp shapes until they struck the ground."[12]

Some 350 men from the 47th Infantry did get across, many of them by wading or swimming, and made it to the railroad embankment just east of Bazoches. That gave the Fourth two disconnected bridgeheads. They could be supplied only in driblets and what was to become of the men in them was anybody's guess. This was a front that was eventually going to be known as "that hellhole on the Vesle," and it was working hard to earn its title.

On the right that day the Pennsylvanians had come back into the line to replace the Thirty-second and a brigade from the Third was thrown in east of them. Back at command they said the Vesle action was no longer an offensive, but simply sector warfare. The semantics weren't going to mean much to the men in the line.

On the eighth the Pennsylvanians fought their way across the river and into Fismette and held it, if a town can be said to be held when the enemy still occupies one corner of it and sends raids roaring through the streets nightly. Next day—the ninth—the Fourth fought its way into Bazoches, was blown out again by a strafing air raid, but managed to hold a line along the railroad embankment. Back to this line they pulled the 1st Battalion of the 58th which was beginning to feel lonesome north on the highway all by itself. During the next few days the Seventy-seventh—a draftee division, mostly New Yorkers—came in for the Fourth and the Pennsylvanians spread out a little to take the ground where the brigade from the Third had been. The men settled down in the steaming, stinking August river bottom to put as much pressure on the enemy as they could without making a real offensive out of it.

On the nineteenth Mangin started a new drive eastward from Soissons and though that made it obvious that the Germans couldn't hold the Vesle line much longer, no one seemed to have told the Germans about it. All they did was get their artillery going full blast again, as though expecting a new attack. The Americans did drive into Bazoches and up around the Château du Diable, a small country home, but the Germans had a going-away present before pulling back to the Aisne. Before dawn on August 27 they came streaming down off the high ground to push the Seventy-seventh out of Bazoches and slaughter two companies of the Pennsylvanians in Fismettes. Cut off from help by a barrage along the river, the outnumbered infantrymen died where they stood while hand grenades flew like confetti at a wedding.

Mangin was still driving in from the east, though; the Vesle line had to give. As August drew to a close, the Butcher found himself held up in front of Juvigny; bethinking himself of the American divisions he had had at Soissons, he put in for another one and got the Thirty-second, now calling itself "Les Terribles" after capturing Fismes. It led with its Michigan brigade on August 28, made good progress in the morning across open ground toward Juvigny until German artillery stopped the advance and they had to lie there the rest of the day with the guns slugging them. Next day they tried again and got nowhere. Come the thirtieth and the Wisconsin brigade went in, moved up with a French division attacking brilliantly on its right, and captured Juvigny so thoroughly that it was hours before any of its personnel filtered back to tell the German command the town was lost. Next morning Mangin—true to form—attacked again behind a triple barrage that withered the German defenses, and there seemed to be no holding him. Three days later the men down on the Vesle got the word that the Germans really were pulling back. The infantry started forward, found only rear guards, and left the hellhole on the Vesle behind them.

The operation that had begun with the First and Second divisions struggling up through the rain to attack at Soissons was over. The Château-Thierry salient was gone, and if the Germans still fought superbly there were signs that they were hurting for man power. The French were attacking, the divisions for Pershing's long-sought American army were now ready, and the British—whom the Germans had counted too badly battered in the spring to mount another offensive this year—were attacking east of Amiens and moving well. Foch looked ahead to a fall of attacks all along the front, giving the enemy more action than he had the men to handle and, finally, a knockout blow in the spring of 1919.

Happy Birthday, Dear General

On August 10 General John J. Pershing formally took command of the American First Army. We were now an army, not separate divisions, and that single-minded man immediately proceeded to prepare for the attack he had first conceived more than a year earlier. The sector was to be the old Toul area, far to the east, quiet since the early part of the war, the first training ground of many of the American divisions. Here it was that the First Division had fired the first shot, here that the Yankee Division had taken a whipping during the German raid on Seicheprey back when the Yankee was young and foolish.

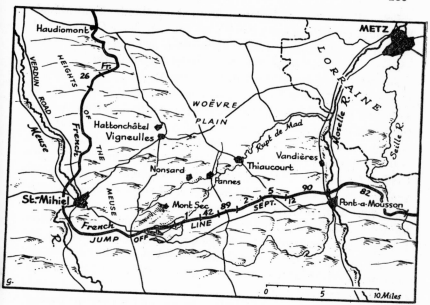

SAINT-MIHIEL: The line of battle around the salient where an entire American army went into action for the first time

The old plan had called for breaking the Saint-Mihiel salient, then driving north for Metz with its railroads and mines. Foch wanted to make a drive farther west, the best Pershing could get was permission to do a job on the salient and even about that there would be further argument. As late as August 30 Foch paid a visit for the purpose of suggesting limiting the Saint-Mihiel push and moving some of the American divisions west to operate with the French. When he went so far as to insist on it, Pershing—as tough a customer as Marine Colonel Catlin called him "a man of inflexible determination"—went ramrod and replied, "Marshal Foch, you may insist all you please, but I decline absolutely to agree to your plan. While our army will fight wherever you may decide, it will not fight except as an independent American army."[13] That settled it, but the drive on Metz had gone out the window in the bargaining. After the salient went, the bulk of the Americans were to hustle back west to fight in the Argonne.

From all over France they were brought together for Saint-Mihiel. What lay before them was a damp plain into which the Germans had pushed a position about twenty miles deep and some thirty miles across at its widest point. The tip at Saint-Mihiel marked the best enemy effort to get over the hills along the Meuse River and in behind Verdun. They had never been able to break through, Verdun itself had held, and the salient had become a fixed feature on the front. Along its southern face Pershing aligned, from left to right, the veteran First and Rainbow plus the Eighty-ninth, a Midwest draft outfit. Together they made up the United States 4th Corps with General Dickman, who'd commanded Third Division back in the long ago days of the German spring offensive, as corps commander. On their right was 1st Corps with Second Division in as a stiffener and the Fifth, Ninetieth and Eighty-second, all fresh, filling out the line. For corps commander they had Major General Hunter Liggett, who'd had it down on the Ourcq and figured the job there could have been done with less bloodshed if the Frenchman Degoutte hadn't overruled him so often.

Around the tip were two French divisions and up north the United States 5th Corps—the Twenty-sixth (Yankee) Division and the French Fifteenth—under General George Cameron. Behind them all were seven divisions in reserve, including the Third, Fourth and the Thirty-third which had gone on from Hamel to get one whole regiment into a British attack and do a good job at Gressaire Wood.

Note that the job turned on what the 4th and 5th Corps were able to do. The French at the tip were simply to peck ahead and trouble the enemy; the 1st Corps with its green outfits was a shoulder, but the 4th and the 5th had to drive straight on with their southern flanks open if the show was to move.

If the men were American, the hardware was borrowed. Pershing noted that out of 3,010 pieces of artillery brought up for the attack, exactly none were of American manufacture. A fractious American colonel named Billy Mitchell commanded the Air Force, but the bulk of the planes and pilots were French and British. There were 267 light tanks, all French, but a little better than half of them did have American crews. Pershing had hoped for more tanks, including some heavies, but they weren't to be had, so plans were made accordingly. First, the bombardment was to be a short one—four hours—not the kind that went on for days and gave the enemy time to bring up reserves. Second, there was the problem of what to do about all the barbed wire in front of the German positions. There weren't enough tanks to clear it out. The French had tried leveling it with artillery and found their infantry still got cut up trying to fight through the remnants. Pershing decided to leave it alone and spend his guns on the German artillery and machine-gun positions. If they could be knocked out, the infantry could take its time and get through with wire cutters provided for the occasion. The number of clippers he had in mind weren't available through regular channels and the Ninetieth Division—a Texas and Oklahoma outfit which had been raised on barbed wire—had its supply officers roaming the towns of central France buying the cutters at retail when they could find them.

In the early days of September the men tiptoed up, the guns were handled as though part of a smuggling operation, and there was much leaving about of phony letters suggesting that an attack was about to occur in three other places. It all fooled nobody. The Paris papers predicted an American attack, the German papers did the same, and the Swiss—precise souls—named the time and place. Inside the salient German General Fuchs sat nervously with 75,000 men against 216,000 Americans and 48,000 French. To make that unhappy man unhappier, none of his divisions were first-rate and the Austro-Hungarian First Division was downright unreliable. If Fuchs saw some of the letters his men wrote home, they must have made him feel like the Duke of Wellington, who said that he didn't know whether his troops frightened the enemy, but they certainly frightened him.

"For here it rains day in and day out. We are lying outdoors here under the open heavens. We never get dry and the things we have on our bodies will certainly rot. You have no idea how bad we feel. We get such bad food, worse than a dog, and the men have no more courage."

"We are expecting every day an American attack and when the bombardment starts we will get it from three sides. . . .What have we done that the whole world has designs on our lives? If the Americans attack we will be in Metz in two days."

"The men are so embittered that they have no interest in anything

and they only want the war to end, no matter how. We are certainly
only the slaves of our government."

"I am so nervous that at the sound of every shell I fall to my knees
and trembling overcomes me. I never used to do that."[14]

The shells started falling at 1:00 A.M. on September 12. The American infantry lay in their jump-off positions, and it was raining again.
The boys in the First and Second divisions began to wonder whether
this business of rain just before a big attack wasn't getting to be a
bad habit. For the First, though, the displeasure with the weather
was assuaged by the pasting Mont Sec was getting from the guns.
Mont Sec was the highest ground around; the Germans had filled it
with tunnels and guns until it was a fortress. The First figured that
Mont Sec was going to be tougher than Soissons; one of the boys in
the 18th Infantry Regiment noted dryly, "The infantrymen in the
front lines generally enjoyed the display of bursting shells." It looked
so good that some of the men figured they'd be more comfortable
advancing than lying there in the muck and cries of "Let's go!"
started along the line.

At 5:00 A.M. they went. What happened next has since been called
the "stroll at Saint-Mihiel." In truth, the whole job was going to cost
7,000 casualties and to the men who suffered them it was no stroll,
but considering that the First Division alone had taken that many at
Soissons, it seems fair to say that this time everything went right.

German artillery reaction was light. We controlled the air; the
fliers were able to put the artillery on German guns that had survived the bombardment. The infantry cut their way through the wire
or simply jumped over it; a French observer reported that Americans
were better for this sort of work because they had longer legs. The
dreaded machine guns opened, but they were thin and halfhearted.
In front of the First and the Rainbow a dinky stream named the Rupt
de Mad had been swollen to eight feet wide and six feet deep by
the rains; it should have been a real heartbreaker, but even here the
infantry got across more wet than bloody.

There were some sharp little fights as a few machine gunners went
down in the best stubborn German tradition, but nothing more. First
cautiously dropped off a battalion to patrol Mont Sec; again, no
holocaust. "Prisoners began to come back in droves. We had to press
forward so fast we could not keep track of them, but gave them a

kick in the back and sent them on their way." On the Eighty-ninth Division's front a sergeant named Harry Adams sent the last two shots in his pistol winging after a German disappearing into a dugout, then yelled for the man to come out and surrender. The man came, and 299 more Germans came out right behind him, hands up. "... Assembling them under the menace of his empty pistol, [Adams] convoyed them safely to the rear, startling his platoon commander ... into the conviction that it was a German counterattack which threatened."[15]

By midafternoon things looked so good that an American cavalry patrol was sent forward, but the machine guns were too much for them and they turned around, fortunately before they were slaughtered as the French horsemen had been at Soissons. As evening came, the southern force was on a line running through Nonsard, Pannes, and Thiaucourt and still going forward. The Yankee Division, coming down from the north, had had some trouble breaking through the crust, but was moving beautifully. At dark the First was into the Bois de Vigneulles, but there was still a ten-kilometer hole between the First and the Yankee Divisions for the fleeing Germans to slip through. Pershing got on the phone himself to tell the 5th Corps to keep the Yankee Division moving all night. The word went down the line and the Yankee Division put its 102d Infantry forward, not in attack formation, but in a marching column, and started for Vigneulles and Hattonchâtel. Their general, Clarence Edwards, told them to get there before the First did and they made it. By 3 A.M. they were in both towns, capturing an entire German ammunition train on the way. About six in the morning patrols from the First came to link up and the Saint-Mihiel salient was finished, some 14,500 prisoners and 443 guns captured. It was September 13, which date just happened to be General John J. Pershing's birthday, and he noted in his diary that it was "a very happy one."

For the next three days they adjusted the lines northward, finally settled on a front from Haudiomont to Vandières, and bemoaned the fact that Foch wouldn't let them keep right on going to Metz. The Supreme Commander, however, wanted them for a drive between the Meuse River and the Argonne Forest and they had just ten days to get there and get themselves organized. It was going to be as tough as Saint-Mihiel had been easy; the biggest American fight of the war.

Chapter Six

"I SHALL BE READY WHEN FUELED"

THE NAVY'S WAR

IN late March, 1917, the steamship *New York* left the States bound for England, and before she was many days at sea a security-minded steward noticed that a passenger named Mr. V. J. Richardson was using a pair of pajamas marked with the initials J. V. B. This suggested to the steward that Mr. Richardson was at least a pajama thief and perhaps something more sinister, so he trotted along to the *New York's* skipper with his find. That gentleman mustered whatever histrionic ability he had to show the proper concern. He alone knew that Mr. Richardson was indeed a phony, in fact Commander J. V. Babcock, United States Navy. The commander's traveling companion, Mr. S. W. Davidson—a man of suspiciously military bearing regardless of costume—was Admiral William Sowden Sims, president of the United States Naval War College. Note that both sailors were new at cloak-and-dagger work and had simply reversed their first initials, scarcely the slickest ruse in the world.

Nothing dates Wilson's decision to go to war more certainly than his reaction to a March 23 cable from Ambassador Page in London. Page had said, "I cannot too strongly recommend that our Government send here immediately an admiral of our own Navy . . . he would have all doors opened to him and a sort of special staff appointed to give him the results and methods of the whole British naval work since the war began."[1]

Wilson agreed, and Sims got the call. For one thing, he had been born in Canada and to make him doubly acceptable to the British had delivered a celebrated speech in London in 1910 in which he'd declared, "If the time ever comes when the British Empire is seriously menaced by an external enemy it is my opinion that you may count upon every man, every dollar, every drop of blood of your kindred across the sea." At the time the Germans had protested and Sims drew a stiff reprimand from President Taft, but that was all to the good now. Finally, we were going to need someone in London who could hold up our end in an argument and here Sims had a reputation. No one had forgotten that, as a junior officer, he had raised a gorgeous row with his superiors over deficiencies in naval gunnery, gone over their heads to Teddy Roosevelt and won his point.

As though to give the admiral a taste of the real thing, the *New York* bumped into a mine going into Liverpool, wound up with a hole big enough for a horse and wagon blown in her side, and had to transfer her passengers to the S.S. *Tynwald* to get them ashore. There a special train waited to take Sims to London and a mess of disheartening facts.

Very simply the submarine was winning the sea war, and it was just a matter of time, and not much time either, before England was starved into surrender. The public hadn't been told and the American Government hadn't been told, but since unrestricted sub warfare had resumed losses had been 536,000 tons in February, 603,000 tons in March, and an appalling 900,000 tons in April. Construction could not keep pace with losses; at anything like the April rate of sinkings the British merchant marine, and hence Britain, would be finished by fall.

"It looks as though the Germans were winning the war," said Sims.

"They will win, unless we can stop these losses—and stop them soon," said First Sea Lord Admiral Jellicoe.

"Is there no solution for the problem?" asked Sims.

"Absolutely none that we can see now," said Jellicoe.[2]

On April 14 Sims cabled the bad news to Navy Secretary Daniels and urged him to get every American destroyer available and anything else that could be fitted out for anti-submarine work over to Europe at flank speed. Daniels had come to much the same conclusion after talking to British admirals in Washington and the same day the order went out to Destroyer Division 8, "Fit out for long and distant service."

Captain J. K. Taussig, commander Destroyer Division 8, was at home in Norfolk that night, one foot in the family automobile on the way to a dance, when the telephone rang and they gave him the word. Taussig went back to the car and headed for his ships. At dawn the next morning the six destroyers—tin cans they call them in the fleet and these were four-pipers, so called for their four smokestacks—were running, with their crews of 100 men each, north to take on stores in the New York and Boston Navy yards. Taussig didn't know where he was headed so he took on stores to meet any emergency; when they sortied from Boston ten days later the ships were displacing 1,400 tons each instead of their rated 1,100. There were sealed orders to be opened fifty miles at sea; Taussig kept his patience until midnight, figured he wasn't more than four or five miles short of fifty, and opened the envelope: they were to proceed to Queenstown, Ireland, and report to the senior British naval officer present for anti-submarine duty.

A destroyer is nothing but a knife edge crammed with machinery below and guns and torpedoes topside. When the seas are coming from ahead, she bucks and twists like no bronco that ever lived, and water pounds down on the bridge until a man would think he was sailing under Niagara Falls. Put the sea on the beam and she'll roll forty, fifty, sixty degrees, hang there as if she were never coming back, then snap up and repeat the horror on the other side. Midway over the six ran into a gale that lasted six days and "all hands ate off their laps, that is those who ate at all did."

Then it cleared, and the British destroyer *Mary Rose*, sent out to bring them in, made the signal, "Welcome to the American colors." Taussig in the *Wadsworth* sent back, 'Thank you, we are glad of your company," and then—tentatively, the new boy on the block—"Shouldn't we be zigzagging?" *Mary Rose*, wily veteran, shrugged. "It is safer to zigzag, but it is a terrible nuisance."

Later a British artist would paint the six of them—*Wadsworth, Conyngham, Porter, McDougal, Davis,* and *Wainwright*—steaming into Queenstown in column and call it "The Return of the Mayflower." It was on Friday, May 4, brilliantly sunny, and "The Stars and Stripes were broken out on public buildings, on private houses, and on nearly all the water craft in the harbor; the populace armed with American flags began to gather on the shore; and the local dignitaries donned their official robes to welcome the new friends from overseas." The Germans had prepared a welcome, too—a submarine had laid mines at the harbor entrance during the night—but the minesweepers had figured that possibility and swept them up.

The dignitaries made their speeches, a newsreel cameraman

specially detailed by the British Government ground out the footage designed to lift sagging British morale, and then Taussig and his commanders started up the steep hill crowned by the Cathedral of St. Cloman's and Admiralty House. There waited the new boss, Admiral Sir Lewis Bayly. According to legend, Bayly asked first, "When will you be ready to go to sea?" and Taussig set a standard for every destroyerman who would ever come afterward by snapping back, "We are ready now, sir."

Legend has it pretty nearly right. An officer who was there recalls that Captain E. R. G. R. Evans, the British liaison officer, "introduced Taussig to Bayly as the commander of the division and when the latter failed to make any reference pleasant or otherwise to the coming of our vessels I was astounded. After acknowledging the introduction, Bayly's first words were these, 'Captain Taussig, at what time will your vessels be ready for sea?' Taussig replied, 'I shall be ready when fueled.' The admiral then asked, 'Do you require any repairs?' Taussig answered, 'No sir.' The admiral's third and last question was, 'Do you require any stores?' Taussig replied, 'No, sir.' The admiral concluded the interview with, 'You will take four days' rest. Good morning.'"[3]

On the face of it, Bayly sounds like the coldest of all British cold fish, but Taussig already had in hand a letter delivered at the dock:

Dear Commander Taussig:

I hope that you and the other five officers in command of the United States Destroyers in your flotilla will come and dine here tonight, Friday, at 7:45, and that you and three others will remain to sleep here so as to get a good rest after your long journey. Allow me to welcome you and to thank you for coming.

Yours sincerely,
LEWIS BAYLY

Dine in undress; no speeches

The chill over the first meeting had nothing to do with Taussig or Americans; Bayly simply considered newsreel cameramen an abomination. He'd been ordered to let them in, but kept his back resolutely toward them and concluded matters as quickly as possible.

As the sea war was being fought in May, 1917, the German submarine had only two disadvantages and neither of them was serious. First, sub skippers got terribly lonely. They assuaged this by jabber-

ing away with each other and the Fatherland over radios carefully
monitored by English radio direction finders. Accordingly, the Admiralty had a very good idea of how many subs were at sea and, in
a general sort of way, where they were. The second problem was a
bit more serious. Torpedoes were expensive and a sub couldn't carry
many of them. The skippers preferred to sink merchantmen by sur-
facing and doing the job with gunfire. They were slightly more vul-
nerable on the surface, but not much. They almost always got in the
first shot, often they outranged the freighters' guns. Destroyers could
do a job on them—they had more guns and better-trained crews than
the freighters, they could ram at high speed, they could drop depth
charges if the sub submerged—they could do all these things, if they
could find the submarine. Under the British system, however, each destroyer was assigned a square of ocean in the danger zone and expected to look out for merchantmen and hunt subs within it. Since
the squares ran to about nine hundred square miles, it was no great
problem for the submarine to avoid his enemy.

At his headquarters in London Sims reasoned thus: why hunt the
sub when he could be made to hunt you? If merchantmen traveled
together in convoys, they could be surrounded by a screen of destroyers—the sub must come to the destroyer or forgo his prey altogether. Let it be said that this was not a newly minted, totally original notion with Sims. The English had convoyed during the
Napoleonic troubles and earlier and the Admiralty had considered it
in this war. The objections were a shortage of destroyers and merchant skippers who swore up and down they couldn't hold convoy
formation in the dark.

Sims represented a solution to the first problem—American destroyer divisions were arriving at Queenstown at the rate of one a
week, building a force which would total 35 tin cans by July 5 or more
than double the number the British had ever been able to put into the
area. Sims felt there were enough. "Such influence as I possessed at
this time . . . I threw with the group of British officers which was
advocating the convoy." Prime Minister David Lloyd George liked
the idea—"civilians in general were more kindly disposed to the convoy than seamen, because they were less familiar with the nautical
and shipping difficulties which it involved"—and in mid-May an
experimental convoy ran from Gibraltar to England without a loss.

As for the merchant skippers, Sims found "they suddenly discovered that they could do practically everything which . . . they had declared they were unable to do."[4]

Thus the pattern was set—most of the destroyer work was going to be convoy rather than individual patrolling. While the system was being organized for general use, the tin cans at Queenstown were learning their business. Bayly sent them out for the first time on May 8. The *McDougal* was hardly clear of the harbor before she mistook a buoy for a periscope and blazed away with all guns, setting a record according to observers for "misses per gun per minute." The *Wadsworth's* first periscope turned out to be a stick, and she went to general quarters half-a-dozen more times that day before her officers and men became accustomed to the littered wartime sea. They steamed "through miles and miles of this stuff, barrels, boxes, crates, lumber, wreckage, etc. Now and then there would be a big patch of oil spreading out for a mile or more marking the place where some tanker had gone down. Open boats, usually empty, and now and then gruesome dead horses would float by. Then there would come an SOS call from some ship beyond our station or some patrol vessel would report picking up the survivors from such-and-such a vessel."[5] Even in the relatively mild spring weather it was tough duty; five days out and three in port worked out to be about the limit of the men's endurance over any protracted period.

In port the officers could go to the yacht club for relaxation or accept invitations for tea at Sir Lewis'—that gentleman proving notably less frosty on closer acquaintance and the affairs further brightened by his niece and hostess, Miss Violet Voysey. Miss Voysey could have given the Queenstown saga a storybook ending by marrying an American; she did not, however, do so.

At first an enlisted man was able to go up to Cork and have himself some fun, but then trouble started. Part of it stemmed from the conflict between Americans and members of the pro-German Sinn Fein movement; the rest stemmed from the considerably more basic matter of women. The sailors had more money than the Irish boys, which meant that they got most of the girls. There was some minor skirmishing, then a sailor knocked down an Irishman who'd been abusing his date; the man's head hit the curb and he died. A civil court acquitted the sailor, but the whole matter was promptly opened up again by a sermon in which Americans were accused of harboring and executing the most dire designs on Irish girls. Liberty parties started going ashore with weapons hidden under their blouses. Cork was declared off limits. To replace it, an enlisted men's club was set up on the Queenstown base with an entertainment program that must have been pretty thin gruel for the men, but doubtless very soothing for such of their mothers as happened to read a typical program as published in a book of the period.

Overture, Battle Song of Freedom — The Orchestra
Dustin Farnum in Five-Reel Feature — Davy Crockett
Selection, My Sunshine Jane — The Orchestra
                    Conjurer Lance Corporal Hortopp
Scotch Reel — Members of the Black Watch
Singing — By All Hands
Bursting into Society — One Reel
National Anthems — The Orchestra[6]

Back in the States, the first big test of the convoy system was shaping up. The German Navy had promised its people that the Americans would never be able to get their troops to France. In New York that rather fussy-looking admiral, Albert Gleaves, who went about with a pince-nez hanging down the front of his uniform, was getting ready to dispute the point. As commander of Convoy Operations in the Atlantic, he had at hand two Navy transports, a converted German freighter, and some hastily chartered American steamers. In all, enough for about six thousand men. They were supposed to go off to France on June 9, but what with building in bunks for the troops, getting lifesaving equipment aboard, and what not, it was the fourteenth before everything was ready.

In the gray pre-dawn, minesweepers went down Ambrose channel to make sure no submarine had laid mines during the night. Then the expedition got under way. There were four groups, two of four ships, two of three ships, each with its own escort of either three or four destroyers and a cruiser. Gleaves had pounded a set of rules into them until they were as familiar with them "as with the Lord's Prayer": no lights at night, throw nothing overboard to leave a trail for subs, zigzag constantly, keep radio transmissions to a minimum, don't belch smoke all over the sky to attract attention.

For 1,500 miles, in perfect weather, they steamed as though headed for the Azores. So far, a hundred false alarms, but no submarines. Then a sharp turn to port and a course as though for Scotland. Along this leg the tanker *Maumee* appears as if by magic and refuels the destroyers which are going to go all the way. The little ones, the short-legged boys without enough fuel capacity to make it from here, and the old coal burners, turn and head for home—this is the limit of their cruising radius. Smart or lucky, the Germans hit them just right—some destroyers have turned back, the Queenstown cans haven't joined up yet—and on June 22 four torpedoes rip through the convoy. German luck has run out, though. All of them are close, but no cigar. The ships reply with gunfire which isn't even close and go on their way feeling like real fighting men. There was another brush on the twenty-sixth—the destroyer *Cummings* actually saw a U-boat, dropped a depth charge, and brought up oil and debris—and then they were off Saint-Nazaire, home free. Unfortunately, there was a delay in picking up pilots and Gleaves sweated big drops while they anchored in the roadstead overnight. Next morning they went ashore, all 6,000 of them, and the German Navy would have to think up another story.

Before it was over, 2,000,000 American troops would come over in American convoys without a single loss of life owing to enemy action. As one man said of the first one, "All we lost was one horse—and that was a mule."

The convoy system was working, the first troops were across, and back home the Navy was about to win one of the key victories of the war with a weapon no more impressive than the electric welding rod. To get enough troops across meant finding ships and no one was quite sure where they were coming from. The British were stretched to the limit, the American merchant marine wasn't up to the job by itself, the shipbuilding program was under way, but results were months in the future. Marvelously, however, there were no less than 104 ships in American ports to be had for the taking—German ships which had run in to hide from the British Navy and been taken over by the United States the day war was declared. No less than 20 of them could be converted to troop carriers. There remained only one small difficulty. Ever since unrestricted submarine warfare had been resumed on February 1, 1917, the Germans had been industriously disabling the ships by breaking up their engines. Teutonic thoroughness had apparently devised a master plan for the job: almost all the damage was done by smashing the engine cylinders. The Germans calculated that it would take a deal of time to manufacture new engines—some of the cylinders were nine feet in diameter—and the Shipping Board agreed with them. It remained for the New York Navy Yard to suggest that there was no need for manufacturing new engines, that the old cylinders could be repaired by electric welding. It was a revolutionary idea. Until then insurance companies wouldn't even insure a ship if she carried a repaired cylinder. The job started on July 11 and on September 8 the *Friedrich der Grosse*, an 11,000 tonner now known as the *Huron*, made her first trip as a troop carrier. In all the 20 were to carry half a million men across, a quarter of the entire American Expeditionary Force.

Sooner or later the subs were bound to strike back at the little ships that had ruined the submarine blockade, and on October 15, 1917, it finally happened. The *Cassin*—a Queenstown veteran—had left Queenstown harbor at dawn and was running east, engaging in target practice, when, as recalled by an officer aboard her, "just after we had finished lunch and while we were sitting around the wardroom, the officer of the deck, Lieutenant Angroll, reported sighting a submarine two points on the port bow about three miles away. The captain rushed to the bridge and I followed. 'Fritz' had submerged so we changed course and ran toward that point. The lookout in the foretop had first seen the Hun, and both the quartermaster and Mr. Angroll looked at her cruising on the surface. When we got to about where we thought she had submerged, we changed course again and at that moment (1:58 P.M.) the captain shouted, 'We've been torpedoed! There it is!' I saw the torpedo making tremendous speed toward us directly amidships on the port side. Without hesitation the captain gave, 'Hard left! Emergency full speed ahead!' and so I am here to write about it. 'General quarters' was sounded at once. I started down the ladder after Lieutenant McClaren to my station. I could still see the thing coming, and it was an even bet whether or not it would hit or miss, when *blam!* and there was no doubt. It had struck about fifteen feet from the stern on the port side. Before I could get to the fourth stack there was a second violent explosion which proved to be the depth charges."[7]

Gunner's Mate Osmund Ingram had seen the torpedo coming, had seen it was going to hit aft, knew that if the depth charges were knocked overboard water pressure would set them off, further damaging the ship and killing any men who might have been thrown into the water. Even though it looked as though he and the torpedo were going to get there at the same time, he galloped aft to get the safety forks into the charges They did arrive together, and Gunner's Mate Ingram vanished in the explosion that blew 30 feet of stern off the *Cassin*. Later they broke the rule that destroyers must be named for officers, named a new one the *Ingram,* and Secretary of the Navy Josephus Daniels observed, "There is no rank in sacrifice or honors."

There were nine wounded and a deal of flooding aft, but the next day they managed to get the *Cassin* in tow and into port, and in due time built a new stern on her and sent her back to the war.

Just a month later the score was evened. It was November 17 when six American destroyers, including the *Fanning* and the *Nicholson,* and two British ships got under way from Queenstown with a westbound convoy of eight merchantmen to be taken to the edge of the danger zone and there exchanged for an inbound group. It was an overcast day, but the sea was calm. The destroyers spent a routine time getting their charges into formation and it was nearing four in the afternoon when the *Fanning* came steaming along the rear of the convoy waiting impatiently for merchantman *René*, the last straggler, to get into position. It was ten minutes past four when one of the bridge lookouts, Coxswain David Loomis, sang out, "Periscope!" Officer of the Deck Lieutenant Walter Henry wasted no time waiting for his skipper to get on deck, but bent on turns for 20 knots, turned to port as hard as he could, and headed for the enemy. The periscope was gone before he got there, so he dropped a depth charge and the water boiled and erupted astern as the *Fanning* turned to attack again.

To their sorrow, there was no sign of damage inflicted—no oil came, no bits of deck grating, nothing to indicate that the submarine hadn't gotten off scot free. The *Nicholson,* handled with equal dispatch, ran over the spot and dropped another ash can, but for fifteen long minutes nothing happened.

Below a great deal was happening. Kapitan Leutnant Gustav Amberger, at first delighted to find that his ship had sprung no leaks, was now horrified to discover that the concussion had wrecked his motors, jammed his diving planes, and broken his oil leads. He had exactly two choices: to lie on the bottom until his air gave out or blow ballast and surface. He blew ballast.

Up she came before the astonished destroyermen, her stern breaking water at a 30-degree angle. The *Fanning* let go with her deck guns, the *Nicholson* followed suit, and chucked another depth charge over for good measure. Then out of the conning tower popped Amberger, hands high, crying "*Kamerad*." After him came his three officers and his 35 men and the air was full of "*Kamerads*." The Americans were so busy wondering whether it wasn't all a trap that no one noticed two German seamen slip back below. They opened the sea cocks to scuttle the ship and while the *Fanning* and the *Nicholson* watched, the *U-58* slid slowly out from under her officers and men and sank. *Fanning* was closest. The men started to swim toward her. They made it, except for one Franz Glinder who was floundering so badly that Chief Pharmacist's Mate Harwell and Coxswain Conner leaped from the *Fanning* and pulled him aboard. Save for the good it did their consciences, they could have saved themselves the ducking; Glinder died on deck.

The *Fanning* put out dry clothes, coffee, and cigarettes all around (Amberger would write later, "The Americans were much nicer and more obliging than expected."), and headed for Queenstown, her collection of warm, dry German prisoners singing happily.

It was the first kill for an American destroyer, and, as things turned out, the only certain one during the war. Lewis Bayly came aboard to congratulate all hands; to make his pleasure even more clear he attended evening entertainment at the enlisted men's club, something the Americans had been trying to get him to do for six months. Their lordships at the Admiralty sent a nice wire in high-toned English and Sims sent one in destroyer English which ended, "Go out and do it again."

The subs were going to get in one more punch against the cans. It would take one of their best men to do the job, Hans Rose, and *U-53*, the same combination that had given the east coast of America fits back in 1916 when they sailed into Newport. This time Rose was working off the western end of the English Channel when he upped periscope and saw a lone destroyer. The range was two miles, but Rose decided to gamble a single torpedo on it.

The can was the four-stacker *Jacob Jones*. She and the *Nicholson* had taken a convoy to France and were running back to Queenstown when the *Jones* asked for and received permission to drop behind for target practice. She was headed home again when they spotted the torpedo boring in on the starboard side. Officer of the Deck Lieutenant Kalk came left to try to parallel the track, didn't quite make it, and they caught it aft. As the stern went down, it was the *Cassin* all over again—depth charges going off at their set depth, this time smashing the whaleboat, killing the men in it, killing more men struggling in the water, blowing what was left of the stern to kingdom come. Skipper Bagley tried to get off an SOS and found he had no radio left. In ten minutes she went down, stern first, bow straight up like a monument for seconds before it slid under. Seaman Barger was still aboard her, desperately trying to get one of the boats loose when she went under, but somehow he managed to swim clear. In the freezing water they had one boat, the rest were rafts. Lieutenant Kalk swam from raft to raft to care for his men, until he died of exposure. In the distance they saw *U-53* surface, pick up a couple of men who had floated away from the main body, and then submerge again. The men in the boat and on the three rafts knew perfectly well that they weren't going to last long adrift in the December seas.

They didn't know it at the time, but it was Rose who saved their lives. Even though it meant giving away his own position, he got off an SOS for them, giving longitude and latitude and the fact that there were men to be rescued. Sims said later, "It is perhaps not surprising that Rose is one of the few German U-boat commanders with whom Allied naval officers would be willing today to shake hands."

Even with the assist from Rose, it was a near thing. More men died of exposure during the night. The rafts drifted away from the boat, then—a bit of luck—a merchantman stumbled on the boat and used her wireless to ask for more rescue craft. It was morning when the sloop *Camellia*, which had heard Rose's SOS, found the last 25 survivors. In all, 64 men and two officers died—about two thirds of the ship's company—but sinkings were down to less than half the fatal April rate and the submarines were no longer winning the war.

If the German Navy was having very little luck with the troop and supply convoys moving to France, it managed a bit better against the empties heading home for a fresh load. The westward-bound vessels

were escorted, but common sense dictated that a transport empty
was worth less than a transport full of troops; if destroyers were short,
the empties traveled with a thinner screen. On October 17, 1917, the
Antilles, a 6,878-ton steamer converted for troop carrying, took a
torpedo in the port side with such force that a lookout was thrown
clean out of the crow's-nest and killed in the fall to the deck. Navy
Radio Operator Ausburne rushed to the radio shack, pushed Merchant Marine Operator McMahon out, locked himself in, and stayed
over his key tapping out the SOS until the *Antilles* went down with
him six and a half minutes later. In all, 67 men died and 167 lived to
be carried back to the new naval base at Brest whence they once more
started for home on the *Finland,* a 12,229-tonner.

The *Finland's* convoy had a fair escort—three converted yachts,
four destroyers—but she was scarcely clear of the harbor when she
got it. The men off the *Antilles* were already jumpy, the *Finland's*
merchant crew wasn't feeling any better for what the *Antilles* men
had told them. The result was a wild rush for the boats with abandon-
ship drill forgotten. Worse, the engine and fireroom gangs left their
posts in a panic. A good black gang deserves a bushel basket full of
medals when a ship is taking hits: they must do their duty without
knowing what's going on, with the certainty that if the ship goes most
of them are trapped. Officers with guns in hand got them below
again; marvelously they discovered that the *Finland* had enough life
left to get back into Brest under her own steam. The Navy, though,
had had a bellyful of merchant mariners; the order went out for all
troop transports to be Navy manned from stem to stern.

On the cargo ships it continued to be armed-guard duty—navy gun
crews, usually under a petty officer—sailing with a merchant marine
that wasn't always entirely glad to see them. It was rough duty. One
armed-guard outfit found "an insufficient supply of provisions was
carried which on the outward trip resulted in no fresh meat after the
eighth day. While lying at a French port, we had no breakfast or
dinner. Coming home, the fresh provisions were gone after three days
at sea and we had to eat the emergency rations in the lifeboats. On
the day we reached port there was nothing left in the ship except tea.

"On both outward and return voyages the lights from ports and
doors were continually exposed while passing through the danger
zone. I protested to the captain, but no steps were taken to stop it.

While nearing the English coast the Morse lights and whistles were used, in spite of my protests, and the captain also refused to zigzag. . . .

"During an encounter with an enemy submarine either the captain or the first officer gave the signal to abandon ship about ten seconds after the enemy was sighted. The firemen came on deck, the engines were stopped, and there was a rush for the boats. The captain ordered the engineers below and requested that I send one of my men to see the order obeyed. . . . [The captain had apparently decided his "abandon ship" order had been premature.]

"The chief engineer was ordered by the captain to go below and get the ship under way. He did not obey this order, and I therefore covered him with my pistol and threatened to shoot him if he did not immediately get the ship under way. He obeyed my order."[8]

Like the destroyers, the armed guard discouraged more submarines than it damaged, but the net result was the same: the ships got through. One fight can stand as typical of hundreds the gunners made during the war. The *Norlina,* with an armed-guard crew under Chief Boatswain's Mate Gullickson, was headed home from England when a torpedo struck her on the port side. The ship was hastily abandoned by most of the crew; only Gullickson and three of her officers remained aboard long enough to realize that it had been a dud torpedo that had struck and bounced off without exploding. Back came the gunners, back came the crew, and back came the submarine determined to finish the job. The wireless operator on *Norlina* reported the fight that followed: "When about six hundred yards off our starboard quarter, a shell from our forward gun hit her and she submerged. Again she appeared, and our after gun hit her and blew away her periscope. Another shot from our forward gun fell right on top of her. There was a shower of black specks rising high in the air and a light blue smoke arising from the stern of the submarine. Our crew . . . gave a hearty American cheer when the submarine disappeared. The *Norlina* fired nineteen shots in all. One of the gunners said afterward we ought to have given them two more and made it twenty-one shots, the presidential salute."[9]

Item: *Norlina* was empty, lightly ballasted, and rolling heavily. Item: if Gullickson's boys got three hits out of 19 rounds under these conditions, he had himself one hell of a set of gunners. Item: it doesn't really matter. They got enough hits or enough near misses to convince the sub that hanging around was unhealthy. The *Norlina* kept going.

There were still some big ships to be lost from the lightly screened convoys headed for the States. In May of 1918 *U-90*, Captain Remy, put three torpedoes into the *President Lincoln*, one of the converted German liners. She was almost out of the danger zone at the time and her escorts had already been called off to take in a troop convoy. Remy cruised around among the survivors in the boats, looking for officers to take prisoners. In one he spotted Ensign Black, with whom he'd gone to college in the States, and he called over, "We don't want you, Black."

A petty officer remembered later that the crew took it all lightly, yelling, "Liberty party shoving off," as they went over the side. Throughout the night the boats and rafts, tied together, stayed afloat. "The boys started to sing all the popular songs such as 'Good-by, Broadway; Hello, France,' 'Over There,' 'Keep the Home Fires Burning.'" It was past midnight when destroyers *Warrington* and *Smith* came steaming up to the rescue.

The *Covington*, another former German, was the next to get it, and a coxswain on the *Rijndam*, a Dutch ship commandeered by the United States, began to feel eerie. *Rijndam* had also been present when the *Lincoln* was hit and the youngster remembered "there was another big boom and another shower of water and splinters and bits of boats—and over and above all flew the body of a sailor high in the air. It's going to be a long time before I can get that thing out of my mind—that tremendous shower of spray and wreckage and 'way above everything that poor smashed kid, his white suit standing out against the blue sky." Now it was *Covington* and "It was a funny thing about those two ships. Each had tied up to Number 2 buoy inside of the breakwater at Brest just before she started on her last trip. And each was on her sixth round trip as a transport. So on our next trip the old *Rijndam* had to draw Number 2 buoy. Naturally, we felt that it was all up, with wreaths on the grave and Uncle Joe and Aunt Mary coming 600 miles to Newark for the funeral."[10]

There was still one big sinking to come, the largest the Navy had during the war. In the spring of 1918 the German Navy decided that long-range U-boats working off the American coast might cause enough trouble to draw destroyers back from Europe. The ruse didn't work—no one had the slightest intention of stripping the troop transports to protect coastwise shipping—but the visitors did some mine laying and into one of these mines ran the U.S.S. *San Diego*, a 13,680-ton armored cruiser with 8-inch guns, on the morning of July 19. She was running off the south shore of Long Island: her skipper tried to beach her, but both engines had been knocked out. Instead, they had to go into the water when she began to go down twenty minutes later. For once the depth charges didn't go off, the safety forks had been put in place, and out of 1,184 men they lost only six.

Nineteen seventeen was coming to an end, and if the winter already showed signs of what it was to become—the coldest, nastiest, iciest winter the Atlantic had seen in years—the Navy was still able to feel a little smug. The crisis at sea had passed. The destroyers out of Queenstown and Brest were getting the convoys through. Five American battleships—*New York, Wyoming, Delaware, Florida,* and *Arkansas* —were with the British Grand Fleet in the North Sea, keeping the German surface fleet bottled up. Three more battle wagons—*Oklahoma, Nevada,* and *Utah*—lay at Bantry Bay in southwest Ireland ready to chase any surface raider who might sneak out. The little subchasers that were going to plug the last holes in the anti-submarine screen were beginning to arrive and a vast project was afoot to lay a mine field right across the North Sea, thus keeping the subs from getting out at all. There was still work to be done, but one seaman's recollections of Christmas that year are a fair clue to what the atmosphere must have been. The converted yacht on which he served was lucky enough to be at the bustling base at Brest for the occasion. In the morning they had to coal ship, the dirtiest job in the world.

The coal came alongside on a lighter and all hands turned to; half of them on the lighter shoveling the stuff into baskets, the rest lugging the baskets to the bunkers and dumping them. At the beginning it was hard to keep footing on the rubbly mountain of coal, but the baskets didn't have to be passed so far. Later, a man could get a firmer footing on the deck of the lighter, but the baskets had farther to go. It being Christmas, though, the ship's Victrola was brought to the bridge, a seaman detailed to keep it wound, and if there were no Christmas-carol records to inspire the coal-dust blackened crew there were at least the popular songs of the day.

Once coaled, the ship and the men had to be cleaned, the coal dust

got into everything. They finished in time to go to the English Christmas service at Chapelle St. Joseph. In the afternoon someone smug-
gled champagne aboard, enough to make everyone feel festive and
inspire an impromptu football game on the dock. Afterward everybody cleaned up for the second time that day and came back aboard
for Christmas dinner with French kids from the neighborhood as
guests.

The little subchasers that began to arrive that frozen winter were
among the least likely ships of the war. Made of wood, only 110 feet
in length, they were so short of facilities that the standard way of
doing laundry aboard them was to tow the dirty clothes astern. There
wasn't room for a fore-and-aft passage below decks; a man had to
come out the forward hatch, grab a lifeline, and fight his way back
to the after hatch. It would have been tough duty for veteran seamen
and the subchasers carried the most amateur sailors since Wynken,
Blynken, and Nod went to sea in a wooden shoe. They had one
advantage: the new listening devices. These tubes, lowered from the
ship's bottom, could pick up the sound of a submarine's engines. The
operator, by working his tube in the direction where the noise was
the loudest, could get a fair bearing on the sub. Three subchasers
working together and reporting their bearings to a single plotting
station could get a very good position on the sub, thus:

and rush in to attack with depth charges.

Sims ordered thirty-six of the new boys under a round, combative captain, C. P. ("Juggy") Nelson, to the Greek island of Corfu. His notion was that they should blockade the Adriatic by a vigorous patrol at its southern end where the Strait of Otranto narrows to a mere 40 miles. Thus German and Austrian submarines would be stuck in the Adriatic, no bother to Allied shipping in the Mediterranean. It was July, 1918, when Juggy's boys made Corfu—after sailing 6,000 miles from New London, Connecticut—and two weeks later Austrian sailors had already discovered that the listening tubes gave them more action than they cared for and refused to run the blockade. It was quite a job of work for a flotilla where a typical engine-room crew consisted of one former taxi driver, one former diemaker, and one former tractor mechanic.

At the northern end of the great sea front a more elaborate blockade was in the works. Since the beginning of the war it had been obvious to almost everyone that if one mine field could be laid across the English Channel at its narrowest point opposite Calais and another from Scotland over to Norway, the submarine would be bottled up in the North Sea where she might cruise to her heart's content without finding much important shipping to molest. On the map it looked perfect, and the Admiralty heard a lot of harsh things said about its failure to get on with the job. In truth, the scheme had two bugs. The little English Channel field could be laid, but the mines didn't hold well, the field never lasted long enough to bother the subs much. As for the big field up north, there simply weren't enough mines of any kind to make a field 250 miles long.

Then an American civilian named Ralph Browne came up with a new gizmo. The old mine was a floating chunk of explosive that went bang! whenever a ship ran into it. Obviously one needed a great many mines to lay them thickly enough for this collision to have any great chance of occurring. Browne's new mine had a long snake of copper cable coming out of it and all a ship needed to do was touch the snake at any point to start an electrical circuit going and make the bang. One mine would now do where four were needed previously and the great North Sea mine field became possible.

At Norfolk a plant was thrown up to melt the TNT and pour it into the mine casings, 300 pounds to the mine. Across the sea the American Mine-laying Squadron set up shop at Inverness and Invergordon in the Highlands, using a couple of idle distilleries as housing for the men. It was June 7, 1918—one in the morning—when the first expedition stood out to sea, destroyers running ahead to form an anti-submarine screen and a squadron of cruisers and battle wagons lying off to guard against surface raiders.[11]

The squadron worked in line abreast, the first ship to lay running the red Baker to the truck as the first mine went over, then letting a steady stream go from the launching station, one every eleven and a half seconds. When her supply of 600 or so mines was almost exhausted, she gave the next ship to lay a standby, then made the signal: "Begin mine laying at once, I have suspended," as the last one went over. The mines rolled to the stern for launching on little railroad tracks, and the grim monotony of the operation was broken only by an occasional blast—one mine in every twenty-five or thirty—as a faulty firing mechanism detonated the mine when it went into the water.

Before the job was over, the Americans had made fifteen expeditions and a smaller British outfit eleven, and between them they had put 70,000 mines down. They formed a barrage 230 miles long and between 15 and 35 miles wide. A sub could get through, but at the very least it meant up to three hours surfaced or six hours submerged of sweating it out. No one knows how many submarines failed to get through. Best guesses run to around six or eight; the usually extremely conservative Admiralty credited the barrage with a total of 23 U-boats sunk or damaged. At Wilhelmshaven submarines followed the example of the Austrians and refused to take their ships to sea. A good month before it all ended the submarines had nearly become a thing of the past.

There was one show left. The Austrians were getting a lot of mileage out of the port of Durazzo, just north of the Strait of Otranto, and in late September the British and Italians decided to go smash it up. Each detailed three light cruisers for the job. Since there were subs in Durazzo, the British asked Juggy Nelson for some chasers to keep them from making trouble. Juggy sent twelve and led the parade himself in No. 95. While first the Italians and then the British ruined Durazzo, the chasers skipped between the geysers thrown up by shore batteries until No. 129, skippered by a reserve ensign named Jacoby, found herself a sub and went for it. Two more chasers—No. 215 and

No. 128—headed over to help out, spotted another periscope, and opened fire with their deck guns. The sub dodged through the fire and past them, both chasers made good use of their small turning circles to spin on their heels and go after her again with depth charges. Jacoby was favoring his sub with the same depth-charge treatment and pretty soon debris, oil, and metal plates started to fly up with the explosions. The college boys gave a victory whoop, escorted the cruisers home, and grinned over the well done from the British commander, "Their conduct was beyond praise. They thoroughly enjoyed themselves."

That was the Navy's war. It wasn't a fancy war. There were no big actions, just the drudgery of convoy work, the drudgery of the Otranto blockade in hellishly uncomfortable little ships, the drudgery of dropping all those mines into the North Sea. It was nothing to the big show that was coming scarcely twenty years later, but some of the same men would be around—Bull Halsey, for instance, had a can for a while and Raymond Spruance was on the battleship *Pennsylvania*. Admiral Ernest King, Chief of Naval Operations in the Second World War, was a captain, Chief of Staff, Atlantic Fleet.

Even in a relatively quiet war, though, there are the permanent dangers of the sea, and just one more story is worth repeating. It so impressed Admiral Gleaves that he printed it in full when he came to write his own story of the war. It concerns a trade school—Annapolis—lieutenant (j.g.) named R. P. Whitemarsh who was sailing as the Navy's representative on a chartered British steamer named *Dwinsk* when she was torpedoed and sunk in the Atlantic. Whitemarsh found himself in a badly leaking boat, its sails rotten, and with only a little water and nothing to eat but sea biscuit. The other boats sailed away and after six days Whitemarsh was with starving men in an unseaworthy boat and a bad blow coming up.

"A line was made fast to the mast to indicate the direction of the wind and I gave the helm to Seaman Fallon. He lay on his back in the stern sheets and steered while the boat was making five or six knots through the water. At 5:00 P.M. the gale was raging furiously with a heavy sea running. At 6:00 P.M. Fallon, drenched repeatedly, had a cramp and Cadet Currie took his place. . . . He had not been at the helm five minutes before he saw a heavy cross sea coming down upon us. Unfortunately he released the tiller and obeyed the impulse to throw up his hands to keep off the water. The sea dropped in over the starboard quarter and washed him overboard, at the same time filling the boat to the gunwale.

"I straightened the boat out and all hands turned to with hats, buckets, and shoes to clear the boat of water and man the oars. The attempt to back the boat to pick up Currie only resulted in getting her into the trough. Currie was swimming toward us but not a third as fast as we were drifting. To save the lives of those remaining in the boat, we had to abandon the attempt to rescue Currie.

"A little later another sea dropped down on top of the boat and knocked everyone about, swamping the boat again. Pritchard, helmsman at this time, was suddenly stricken, and when the boat was again freed of water, he lay down in the bottom. I took the tiller and stood up in the boat in order to see the waves and feel the wind to better advantage. The men sat down in the bottom to improve the stability and three of them appointed themselves my protectors by hanging onto my feet and knees.

". . . The wind coming from the west dying down a little. My arms were aching after eleven hours at the helm and after a sea anchor had been rigged by lashing together two oars, the Frenchman relieved me. The wind moderated during the day, but the swell was high.

"In speaking of the storm that day, Gregory, who had followed the sea for forty years, declared he had never seen anything like it. If, by having to endure the storm of that night again, the world would give him every luxury known to man for the rest of his life, he said he would refuse.

". . . Monday, Tuesday, and Wednesday passed with light, variable winds and calms. These days taxed the courage of the men the greatest. They all knew we were in the Gulf Stream and drifting farther away from land every hour. When some of the crew who had practically abandoned hope began to sing familiar hymns, including 'Nearer, My God, to Thee,' I made them stop, and the American seaman Richards and I sang 'Homeward Bound' and other cheerful popular hits.

"The food ration was cut to two thirds of a biscuit a day with a quarter of a pint of water. The second engineer officer, Pattison, became guardian of the hatchet and whenever this weapon went forward to sharpen pegs or open tins, he would follow unostentatiously after and bring it aft again. He expected a raid on the food and water supply, but his fears were unfounded.

"The spirit in the boat was excellent. Helpfulness and brotherly care were very evident in sharing clothing and sleeping places and in assisting one another at work. Two of the weakest were excused from work. Those on lookout details had their eyes infected until they were temporarily blind. . . . The first man to sight the steamer that would pick us up was to have the biggest dinner money could buy when we landed.

"But the men were depressed in spite of it all. The sun would bake them mercilessly and later cold rains would chill them to the bone. One man made an attempt to drink salt water and another thought it would be better to go over the side and end it all. Wednesday afternoon rain began to fall heavily. After washing the salt out of the sail, all hands drank their fill of water and caught an additional four gallons.

"By midnight the wind from E.S.E. was blowing a gale with high seas and continuous rain. When we took a couple of seas the sail was shortened, but we made the most of the opportunity to run in. The crew was drenched with spray, but the time for compromise was past.

"Friday morning at nine-thirty Collins jumped up and began waving his arms. He had sighted a steamer to the eastward heading toward us. The sail was left up until the helm and the men of our boat could be clearly seen and then we rowed alongside."

They had been ten days in the boat. Next day the 19 who survived wrote out the following, signed it, and took it to Whitemarsh:

"We, the undersigned survivors of the torpedoed steamship *Dwinsk,* wish to show our undying appreciation of the conduct of Lt. (j.g.) R. P. Whitemarsh, US Navy, who under the most trying and perilous conditions set an example of courage and bravery beyond all praise, and we feel that his conduct and devotion to duty when face to face with destruction in a raging storm in an open boat when most of us believed that the end had come, carried us through until the storm passed and later, after many days in this boat, when all hope of rescue seemed small, he was always cheerful and hopeful, and encouraged us to further efforts."

Thus always in wars at sea.

Chapter Seven

"THIS IS THE MOST DANGEROUS BRANCH OF THE SERVICE"

THE AIR WAR

Go back to April 20, 1916—almost a full year before America entered the war—and find French Captain Georges Thenault arriving at the airdrome near the Vosges Mountains in eastern France, with a strange crew in tow. The men with him are seven pilots, the nucleus of a new escadrille, and they are Americans. This is the first American unit to fight in the war. Note their names—Norman Prince, Bill Thaw, Victor Chapman, Kiffin Rockwell, Jim McConnell, Elliot Cowdin, and Bert Hall. Only one, Hall, will come through truly whole: Chapman, Rockwell, and McConnell will be shot down, Prince killed in a crash, Thaw wounded, Cowdin retired because of ill health.

For the moment they were known as the American Escadrille; later there'd be a search for a snappier title and they would fight the new name into the books for keeps—the Lafayette Escadrille. Originally, the notion of an American volunteer flying group had come from Norman Prince. A young man of means from Prides Crossing, up near Boston, Massachusetts, he'd traveled in France before the war and taken some flying-boat lessons back in the States. In Paris he didn't find the French particularly interested—they already had more volunters for the air service than they could handle. An American doctor named Edmund Gros saw the propaganda value of the idea, though, and sold it to the authorities. Interested Americans were signed up, dodging the citizenship problem by enlisting through the Foreign Legion, which didn't ask for an oath of allegiance. Most of them were glory boys; one wrote home, "This is the most dangerous branch of the service, but if anything does happen to me, you all surely can feel better than if I was sent to pieces by a shell or put out by a bullet in the infantry where there are seventy-five out of one hundred possibilities of your never hearing of it."[1]

It may seem strange that, assuming one is going to get killed, it makes a hoot of difference whether one gets it in the air or on the ground. Indeed the same sort of mind might ask why does a man go enlisting in a French shooting war when he doesn't have to? For that matter, why go up in airplanes at all? It was only thirteen years since the Wright brothers had made their first flight and only nine since the United States War Department had ordered its first military aircraft. The specifications called for a paragon that could hurtle along at 40 miles an hour and keep two people up in the air for at least sixty minutes. The Wrights managed to build it, but on one of its first demonstration flights Orville crashed from 75 feet, killing early birdman Lieutenant Thomas Selfridge and injuring himself. It came as almost a relief to the graybeards in the War Department who didn't really care for the new weapon anyway. It seemed a menace to cavalry, to which many of them were deeply devoted. Congress didn't think much better of it; it was 1911 before they voted even a tiny appropriation for aviation as such. By that time the air arm, functioning as part of the Signal Corps, had mushroomed to no less than five planes, three balloons, and six pilots. A Lieutenant B. D. Foulois had logged 52 hours in the air and a Lieutenant Henry "Hap" Arnold, who'd command the whole show one war later, had logged 29.

In fact, when the war began in 1914 there was hardly a country in the world which wasn't doing more with the airplane than the United States. This is how it stacked up:

	Planes	Pilots	Appropriations
France	260	191	$7,400,000
Russia	100	28	$5,000,000
Germany	46	52	$5,000,000
England	29	88	$3,000,000
Italy	26	35	$2,100,000
Japan	14	8	$1,000,000
United States	6	14	$ 125,000

The world had gone to war with a collection of planes of which no conservative-minded citizen would want any part. Research had pushed them up to a thundering 80 miles an hour, but their wings had a chilling tendency to fall off and they went into spins with lethal regularity. In the beginning many of them were "pushers"—that is, the propeller and engine were in back of the pilot. This simplified certain problems of controlling the plane, but if something went wrong on a landing the engine was apt to tear loose, go plowing ahead on momentum, and mash whatever happened to be left of the pilot.

As though flying these crates didn't keep the casualty lists high enough, a Dutchman named Tony Fokker, working for Germany, figured out a way to arm them. Previous to Fokker no one had doped out a reliable system to keep a machine gun mounted ahead of the pilot from gnawing its own propeller down to a nub as it fired. Pilots satisfied their blood lust by shooting rifles at each other as they passed in the air. Fokker worked out a synchronizing gear that allowed the machine gun to fire only when a blade of the propeller was not in front of it, and the air war was on in earnest.

Although the two-seater training plane in which the instructor sat in one cockpit and the student in the other was already in use, a good many of the Escadrille boys got their wings in a series of Blériots which the novice handled solo from the start. The first of these was a little horror called the *Penguin,* so called because a three-cylinder engine and a five-foot wingspread kept it from rising off the ground. In it the student taxied up and down the field, learning to drive in a straight line in spite of *Penguin's* built-in desire to go in circles. This accomplished, he was allowed a more powerful Blériot which would actually leave the ground. In this he was supposed to crow-hop up and down the field, rising to three or four feet and then landing again. In the beginning the landing consisted simply of cutting off the motor and letting the ship come down with a thump. Then ". . . by degrees we take the machine higher and higher in straight flights up and down a big field. All these flights are straight, the machine being brought to the ground at each end of the field and turned by hand."

In theory, the instructor told the student when he was far enough along to fly the plane around the field, performing a series of gentle turns—*virages*—to do so. In practice the student was apt to overshoot the field and perform his first *virages* simply because it was that or stay up in the air for the rest of his life. And a turn in a Blériot was not to be underestimated; one of the men who tried it explained, "Being of light construction the plane had plenty of give in the air. Frequently, making a tight bank, I have looked back and seen the tail whipping around after me, bending in a perfect arc."

For protection the student had his seat belt and a safety helmet "... it weighed just short of a ton, it came in two sizes, too small and too large." Thus equipped, one novice—by no means a prodigy—managed to rack up three calamities in one day. Once he turned over, but hung safely by his belt until rescued. Once he flipped up on his nose while landing—this time the overworked belt broke and he was flipped forward against the upper wing to score a black eye and a cut. Finally, he got himself thoroughly confused and landed in an empty field instead of the airdrome.

Having learned to fly—or perhaps, more properly—to crash and walk away from it, the pilot moved on to cross-country work where the trick was to get lost near a château, preferably belonging to a family with daughters, where stray Americans were treated with extraordinary kindness.

The final step was combat flying, acrobatics and the like, and the first and most heart stopping of these maneuvers was to put the plane into a spin—a *vrille*—and then get out of it. Not only was a *vrille* useful in combat as a means of pretending to be hit when one was not, but a *vrille* was the first inclination of any plane when something went wrong in the air and he who could not get out of one was in a bad way. Thus, as seen by a young American:

"He did one and then attempted another, but when his machine stopped spinning around he continued to come directly toward the ground, nose first, with his motor running full speed. Down, down he came, faster on account of his engine than a big boulder would fall. For a second it seemed that he would land right on top of me, but I was too struck by the terribleness of it to run and in an instant the machine had crashed into the earth about one hundred yards off. The grass must have been six inches high and after the crash we could not see one piece of the debris projecting. . . . The engine of the airplane had been buried far in the ground. There was nothing left of the man at all—just some clothes and pieces of flesh."[2]

With such as this on his mind, a young pilot went up less than lightheartedly. "The lieutenant said, 'Start your *vrille* at 1,000 meters [3,000 feet]. I made up my mind that the instant the altimeter registered 1,000 I would do it. I was scared stiff, but when I hit 1,000 I cut my motor, pulled the stick, jammed my stick and feet way over. The machine hung motionless, then fell with a sickening sensation and started to spin with the fuselage as an axis. To come out you must put the controls in the middle. That brings you out in a nose dive, then you haul back the stick, put on the motor, and are off. Well, I did all these things. When the altimeter reads 900 you come out. The machine drops so fast that it beats the meter. So I really fell 300 meters spinning like a top. When I came out and found I was alive and breathing, I grinned and shouted for joy."[3]

Checked out and rejoicing in a corporal's stripes, the pilot was off for the front. The French air service was not precisely rank crazy; a good pilot eventually made sergeant, one who was good and lucky enough to keep on living might go all the way to lieutenant. At first they were shepherded over the lines by veterans and one of the Escadrille's youngsters tried to put words to the wonder of the first time out—below "a series of brown, woodworm-like tracings on the ground—the trenches. My attention was drawn elsewhere almost immediately, however. Two balls of black smoke had suddenly appeared close to one of the machines ahead of me and with the same disconcerting abruptness similar balls began to dot the sky above, below, and on all sides of me. We were being shot at with shrapnel. It is interesting to watch the flash of the bursting shells and the attendant smoke puffs—black, white, or yellow, depending on the kind of shrapnel used. The roar of the motors drowned the noise of the explosions. Strangely enough my feelings about it were wholly impersonal."[4]

The process of transferring American fliers from other units to beef up the Escadrille went on; they hadn't been in business more than a few days when there came the greatest of them all. Raoul Gervais Lufbery was his name and, in truth, he was American only in an offhand way. His French father had transplanted himself to Waterbury, Connecticut, when Raoul was a kid, but the boy returned to France to be brought up by relatives. To the end of his days his English suggested a man talking while favoring a badly swollen jaw. He came to the Escadrille no kid like the rest of them, but a man in his mid-thirties, short—just five foot six—stocky and bull-necked. Most of them came from monied homes; Luf came from nowhere, a former sailor, former soldier with the United States Army in the Philippines, a mechanic. Out in French Indo-China he'd run into a Frenchman named Marc Pourpe who was crazy enough to think commercial aviation had some future in that part of the world. Came the war and Luf went along to France with Pourpe as his mechanic until the older man, whom he regarded almost as a father, was killed. Then Luf decided to fly himself; it was a break for the boys in the Escadrille that at first he was terrible at it, a virtual washout. If he'd been one of your born fly-by-the-seat-of-your-pants naturals he'd never have had to learn the hard way, and learning the hard way had a lot to do with making him a steadying influence on the Escadrille and a mentor of the youngsters who came later with the regular American Air Service.

The techniques of aerial combat were essentially simple. In the first place, one wanted to be high in spite of the fact that above 12,000 feet it was freezing even in the Teddy-bear flying suits. Height gave a pilot a better view of the air battlefield and when it came to an attack, he'd be diving and gaining speed rather than climbing and losing it and perhaps stalling his engine out. Since a single-seat ship, with its fixed guns in front of the pilot, could fire in only one direction—dead ahead—pursuit planes were attacked, obviously, from the rear and above. Two-seaters, however, had a sting in the tail. In addition to the forward machine guns, the observer who occupied the rear cockpit had one of his own on a ring that could be swiveled through a full circle. Accordingly, two-seaters were to be attacked from the rear, but from below—since the observer would then have to shoot his own tail off to get at his tormentor. Not that observers were beyond some such shenanigans: one astonished pursuit pilot found himself peppered from a plane whose belly was turned toward him. The observer had simply pointed his gun into his own cockpit and was shooting through the floor.

At the beginning of the war it had been single pilot against single pilot, but the pattern had changed considerably. The basic unit was now the squadron with 20 or more planes and it often flew all together, each man helping to cover his neighbor. As a result, mass dogfights that involved a hundred planes or more and delighted the poor damned infantry in the mud below were becoming common. Above squadron there was a superior organization called wing or group—the former was the British designation, the latter French— which was becoming increasingly important as larger numbers of planes were used to support a particular attack. The notion of massed air power to bomb and strafe as an assault weapon was still in its infancy, but by 1918 the Germans would use 900 planes in their spring offensive and the Americans 1,500 for the drive at Saint-Mihiel. In 1916, though, the single combatant was still an important man. After flying his assigned patrols, a pilot was free to go out again alone and get himself shot at if his commanding officer had no objections.

The new American Escadrille made some kills, took some minor wounds, and then got hit hard for the first time. Corporal Clyde Balsley was out on a four-plane patrol, got jumped by a larger German outfit, had his guns jam, and "I swung in every direction, went through a cloud. Bullets followed. Black patches on my wing. I sideslipped from that one and rolled over on my back. I was in another line of fire. The linen tore with the bursts. I was about 12,000 feet up and while I was completely on my back, something struck me—like the kick of a mule. I had a sensation like my leg was shot away and put my hand down to learn if it was still there. . . . My safety belt held or the blow would have knocked me overboard. I cut the motor. My legs were paralyzed. Feet strapped to the rudder bar, my rudder went out of control. . . . I fell into a tight spin. Around and down, around and down, it was all over.

"Soon I should hit the ground . . . that would be all. How strange that I, the I that had seemed undying, should hit the ground like all the rest. I remember the first man I had picked up. I should look like that. I remembered when I had picked up Captain Jolain. I had cried. Would anyone cry for me? . . . My mind cleared and I tried to push my right leg back into action. I pushed with all my strength. My feet strapped to the rudder bar straightened it up. The ship was coming out. . . ."[5]

Incredibly, he landed the plane. In the hospital, they expected him to die, but he lived, and one afternoon Victor Chapman put a bag of oranges in his ship and flew off to see him. Fokkers got Chapman. The first of the original seven was dead.

Kiffin Rockwell went next—another Fokker did the job—and then Norman Prince crashed in, "feeling for the ground" on a night landing, and died in the hospital. Jim McConnell was the last of the original gang to get shot down and they found a letter he'd left for precisely that occasion:

"My burial is of no import. Make it as easy as possible for yourselves. I have no religion and do not care for any service. If the omission would embarrass you I presume I could stand the performance. Good luck to the rest of you. God damn Germany and *vive la France*."

Replacements came, and the Escadrille went on with men such as Didier Masson, a Californian who'd been the entire Mexican air force just a few years earlier, and James Norman Hall, who'd team up later with another flier named Charles Nordhoff to write the history of the Escadrille, and later, *Mutiny on the Bounty*. At the field they made a mascot of a lion cub named Whiskey—later supplemented by another named Soda—and, in addition to more routine guests, sometimes had Germans for callers. Bombing wasn't much in those days, but still enough to unsettle a man:

"When the motors tell you they are almost overhead it is time to lay low in a trench. The bombs are usually dropped quite close together in groups of four to eight perhaps. They of course fall in the line along which the course of the machine carries them. Suppose the first one falls say three or four hundred yards from you and the next a hundred yards closer. It is not hard to judge whether you are approximately on that line or not. . . . When they come within a couple of hundred yards you can hear them whistle for several seconds before they strike and they all sound uncomfortably close. You just squat there in a trench, listening to the oncoming hiss, and wondering whether the next one is going to only fall in the trench with you or square in the middle of your back. If it comes good and close, there is a blinding flash, a deafening explosion, dirt flies all over you, and the ground rocks under your feet."[6]

A bomb good and close qualified a man for membership in the Should-Be-Dead Club—an organization that also took in characters who landed planes that no man should have been able to land considering the number of holes shot in them and pilots who succeeded in extricating themselves from meetings with unseemly numbers of Fokkers over the lines.

Their main business, of course, was shooting down German aircraft and they got to be good at it. The Escadrille wound up with 199 confirmed kills and they probably dropped that many more which were not confirmed since French rules called for two independent witnesses before a kill could qualify. That meant that planes dropped behind German lines rarely got into the record. One man remembered it this way:

"Finally I caught sight of two German machines flying far within their own lines and perhaps 1,000 feet below us. . . . As we started after the Boches, it was impossible to always keep in the sun and they caught sight of us and started back into their lines . . . one fell in behind the other so that it was possible to attack him as though his comrade were not there.

"I went after this fellow as I would a single-seater, diving on his back instead of going under his tail. . . . I am afraid I started shooting too soon. . . . However, I think I must have had the great good luck to hit the pilot with one of my first shots for the Hun just kept flying along in a perfectly straight line without maneuvering at all, giving one the easiest target imaginable. I could see my bullets hitting the machine and going all around the pilot's seat and no man in his senses would fly straight ahead with this going on. When within about forty yards I suddenly saw the machine gunner let go of his gun, throw up his arms, and flop down out of sight in the body of the machine, so it was a two-seater after all.

"About that time a lot of white smoke started coming out of the Hun's motor. Then he began to climb until he was at such a steep angle that the motor could not pull the machine up any farther and it seemed to hang almost stationary for a few seconds. You have seen a duck when it is mortally shot climb straight up for a while, flutter a second or so, and then fold its wings and fall. This Boche reminded me for all the world of such a bird. He slipped sideways on one wing and then plunged vertically. . . .

"This was a rube way to go after a two-seater, for although it gives you a splendid shot, the machine gunner has an even better one."[7]

One of them, quoted in a history of the Escadrille, found himself envying a mate who'd made a kill and found it hard to understand himself. Until that moment he'd considered himself one of the mildest of men.

America came in and there was no part of the armed forces on which more hopes were built by the public than the air. To the young men, the Escadrille fliers were legendary fighters, and along with the legends from the front were a fair share of yarns about relaxation in Paris with champagne and other diversions typical of the locale. To others, it seemed "the quickest and least onerous method of defeating Germany," and the air enthusiasts, used to having to fight for every nickel, didn't do themselves any good by pushing that notion when they went before Congress to testify on the Aviation Act. Representative Fiorello La Guardia, who'd wind up flying Caproni bombers himself on the Italian front, heard them out and said he didn't agree "with what is being said about this war being won with the airplanes we provide today. This war will be won in a much more cruel and less spectacular fashion."

He was right. To begin with, the whole Air Service consisted of 131 officers and 1,087 men. They had something less than 250 airplanes, all of them vastly antiquated by Western Front standards. There were two fields—one on land borrowed from an aviation company outside San Diego, California, and the other in central Long Island. The first outfits to go to new Kelly Field in Texas had to start life as birdmen by installing a sewer system. Until the job was done, washing was done at pumps, the ratio of pumps being one for each 2,500 men. The tarantulas and scorpions were so bad that a man learned to shake his shoes out each morning before he put his feet into them. One Texas outfit had itself all organized as the 15th Aero Squadron until they discovered that, in the confusion, someone had already organized a 15th out in California. The Texans got themselves redesignated the 20th. They trained in two-seaters, the instructor communicating with the pupil through a primitive intercom made of a hose with a dime-store funnel stuck in either end. The instructor occupied the dangerous front seat. Vernon Castle—half of the dance team of Vernon and Irene Castle—had been flying with the British and was sent back to teach. A student crashed him in and killed him.

Little items on the deaths of student pilots became almost a daily feature of the papers, and the wonder of it was that there weren't more: the men came strictly as beginners. In one outfit there was a theater operator, four salesmen, three lawyers, two journalists, five engineers, a pianist, a banker, a cotton planter, an auto race driver, a broker, and a mining man.

To make pilots out of such material, they were first sent to one of the cadet ground schools established at eight universities around the country. After twelve weeks they were ready for primary flight training at fields like Kelly where they sprouted wings by working out on the most famous American plane of the war—the JN-4 trainer, the Jenny. Those who passed were shipped overseas to get their advanced training at American fields in France. In all, we managed to produce the very creditable total of 10,000 pilots. Getting them something to fly, though, turned out to be another matter.

We were hardly in the war than the French sent over a memo saying that it would be most helpful if America could provide 5,000 pilots and, starting in January, 1918, 2,000 planes and 4,000 motors a month. This was pure hogwash—the whole Allied air force had only 5,528 planes in it at the time—but the public thought it was just the right challenge to American mass production, know-how, and what-not, and figured to see clouds of our machines darkening the Western Front skies in no time at all. The public was in for its biggest disappointment of the war.

First, there was the question of what sort of planes were to be built. Clearly there was no time to design brand-new planes; a commission was sent scurrying through Europe to select the best models for American production. At the end of July, 1917, it made its report— the British DeHavilland 4 would be produced as an observation plane and day bomber, the British Bristol and the French Spad as fighters, and the Italian Caproni as a night bomber. The problem can be stated right off: assuming that these were the best designs available as of July, what would be the situation by the time a nation with no aircraft industry to speak of got tooled up, produced the planes, and shipped them to the front? The answer, given to the remarkable rate of progress in Europe, was predictable: the planes would be out of date.

To try to lick the problem it was decided that, though we would build foreign designs, they would be improved by powering them with a new, advanced American motor, new from the ground up. Indeed, this decision had been made even before the airplane was selected. At the end of May two engineers—J. G. Vincent of Packard and E. J. Hall of Hall-Scott—had locked themselves in Washington's Willard Hotel. On June 4 they emerged with plans for the Liberty engine. A pilot model had been produced by July 3. The public was suitably impressed.

Instead, however, of beginning to pop off production lines in the manner of Ford cars, the engine program fluttered, sputtered, and stalled. It *was* a good engine, but tooling up for it and ironing out the bugs in an assembly-line model simply took time. It was December before Packard got its first two assembly-line models off and by that time they were obsolescent; instead of an eight-cylinder model we now needed a twelve. That meant redesign, and the whole process started all over again. Packard counted no less than 1,022 changes made in its production design between September, 1917, and February, 1918. In all, the program which was going to be pouring out 4,000 engines a month by January, 1918, produced a scanty 1,110 in the entire period up to May 25, 1918. By that time the public was no longer under any illusions about darkening any skies.

The plane program got off to a bustling start when a Bristol fighter arrived in the States in August and Aviation Section officers set about redesigning it to take the Liberty engine. Unfortunately, the redesign so increased the weight of the plane that the first models produced here crashed and the whole program was canceled. Scratch the Bristol.

The Spad and Caproni programs never got that far. No Spad ever was produced; it died in a welter of telegrams about whether or not single-seat fighters were really worth while. The Caproni, our original selection for night bombing, was reconsidered against the British Handley-Page, and the war was over before anyone made a real decision about which to build.

Calamitously, the one plane we really did get into production was the DeHavilland 4. It was already out of date by the summer of 1917, but there was one authentic DH 4 on hand to copy. It was charged later that the Bureau of Aircraft Production felt it damn well had to get some kind of plane produced even if it wasn't a very good one.

With redesigning for the Liberty engine and sundry other problems, it was February, 1918, before nine DH 4's were produced and May before they got into mass production. For the men overseas, even that was too soon. The planes were shipped to France to be shot out of the sky in such profusion that pilots called them "flaming coffins." In all, about 950 of them got to the front, and that was the total result of our efforts to darken the skies of Europe.

By the winter of 1918 Congress was beginning to suspect that all was not well with airplane production, but it remained for George Creel to put the fat squarely in the fire. This time Mr. Creel was causing his trouble all by himself. The great adventurer in advertising got out a statement about American battle planes being en route to the front in France. It was an occasion of much joy; hence there was much misery when it turned out that involved were not planes, but a plane—and it was not en route to France, but en route from a factory to a nearby field for testing. In addition, Creel released some pictures with captions that might lead the simple-minded to think that these were American battle planes in France. It turned out that they were training planes in the States.

Questions were asked in Congress, and in March rumors of a secret report made by Gutzon Borglum directly to Woodrow Wilson began to leak out. It included the charge that Army Colonel Deeds had actually been guilty of favoring old business connections in the aircraft procurement program.

Aircraft production was actually very little more fouled up than the rest of the munitions schedule—particularly considering the disadvantages under which it had started—but the hopes had been so high that the reaction was doubly bitter. Nothing would do but a special investigation under the impeccable Charles Evans Hughes which came up with the suggestion that Deeds get a court-martial for "acting as confidential adviser of his former business associate." The War Department decided it didn't want to be bothered with the court-martial, but it did separate production and operations into the Bureau of Aircraft Production and the Division of Military Aeronautics. It was a better setup, but by that time the war was almost over.

All it proved was that you couldn't start an aircraft industry from scratch—and besides, we were green at organizing an industrial war anyway. After all, the Liberty ship program didn't do a great deal better. Significantly, the one experienced aircraft firm we had did make itself a little bit of a record. The Curtiss Aircraft Company had been turning out 100 planes a month for the British and drew the job of turning out training planes. By April, 1918, they'd produced 2,837 JN-4D's—the immortal Jenny.

Training in the States completed, the new pilots were shipped to France and England to work out in battle planes. In England, they didn't care for the food. One outfit reported, "Once a week we had rabbit, supposedly to improve the ration, but as these were cold-storage rabbits, packed in Australia in 1911, few of us ate them."[8] Another outfit departed for the front with the deathless words of a dental officer ringing in its ears. "Men, I am about to address you for the last time. I want you to promise me—in fact, I am putting you on your honor—you will keep your teeth clean. I have here a toothbrush just the same as you will find in your kit. You are to brush your teeth night and morning, like this . . . up and down, not sideways."[9]

The 95th Aero Squadron was the first actually up in the lines, but they were sent without any gunnery training or, indeed, even any guns on their Nieuports. Undaunted, they flew a patrol without guns and caught hell from Lufbery who, with some other Escadrille men, had transferred to the American service. They listened respectfully, for "in that youthful branch of the service he was the only tradition we had."

Back went the 95th for its gunnery practice and in came the 94th, with its "Hat in the Ring" insignia and Pershing's former chauffeur, now known as Lieutenant Eddie Rickenbacker. He had been Richenbacher, but Americanized the name when war came. Like Luf, he was a little older than the rest of them—twenty-eight—and he had ten years of the toughest kind of motorcar racing behind him. Credit Luf with a good eye for men: the first two he selected to take out on patrol were Douglas Campbell, who would be our first ace, and Rick, who would be our greatest.

Out they went in the Nieuports—they weren't so good as the new Spads, but the French weren't wasting their best ships on American pilots—and Rick's first reaction was that it was pretty lonely up there. Luf swung back by him once and he felt better. Then, at 15,000 feet, he became aware of the great cold, then a rising nausea portending airsickness. He fought back the sickness, tightened up as anti-aircraft bursts—Archies—bounced his plane around the sky, and then rode out his two-hour patrol faintly disappointed at not even seeing an enemy plane. When they got back, Luf pointed out that four Germans had passed ahead of them and another gone by below—the boys didn't have "vision of the air" yet. Rick felt a little more martial when he discovered that the Archies had chewed three holes in his ship.

The 95th—with its kicking-mule insignia—came back from target practice. That gave us two whole squadrons operating together and we could get down to business. The pilots, a youthful lot much given to singing "Hurrah for the Next Man to Die," promptly inaugurated a series of fines:

Downing an enemy plane—five bottles of champagne
Getting downed yourself—three bottles of champagne
Crack up on landing—one bottle of champagne

The lot was saved up until a party seemed called for—an event which could be occasioned by something as simple as swapping another squadron one Spad, one Nieuport, and two mechanics for one pilot. One alert young man sought to confuse the enemy by having a tail gunner painted on the rear of his fuselage. It worked; a German attacked from below instead of above and shot the alert one in the seat of the pants.

Then, on Sunday, April 14, the American Air Service got their first two kills. Lieutenant Alan Winslow who got one of them remembered that "At eight forty-five I was called to the phone, told by the information officer . . . that two German planes were about 2,000 meters above the city which is only a mile or so from here. . . . We were rushed down to our machines in sidecars and in another minute were in the air.

"Doug [Douglas Campbell] started ahead of me. . . . I gave him about forty-five seconds' start and then left myself, climbing steeply in a left-hand spiral in order to save time. . . . I had not made a complete turn when straight above and ahead of me in the mist of the early morning and not more than 100 yards away I saw a plane coming toward me with huge black crosses on its wings and tail. I was so furious to see a Hun directly over our aviation field that I swore out loud and violently opened fire. At the same time, to avoid my bullets, he slipped into a left-hand *renversement* and came down firing at me. I climbed, however, in a right-hand spiral and slipped off, coming down directly behind him and on his tail. Again I violently opened fire. . . . I fired 20 to 30 rounds at him and could see my tracers entering his machine. Then, in another moment, his plane went straight down in an uncontrolled nose dive, his engine out of commission. I followed in a straight dive, firing all the way. At about six feet above the ground he tried to regain control of his machine but could not, and crashed to earth."[10]

Campbell got the other one and by the end of May had run his score up to five to qualify as our first ace. His fifth was scored against a Rumpler—a two-seater—and the German observer hosed him with machine-gun fire until his belt was empty, then stood in the cockpit with his arms folded while the plane went in. At the end of June both the 94th and the 95th were moved over to support the fighting along the Marne and two new squadrons, the 27th and the 147th, joined up. Across from them were some of the best outfits in the German Air Force, including one pursuit squadron commanded by the great pilot Ernst Udet. Behind them was a notable loss—Lufbery was gone. In May he had attacked a two-seater, veered away—apparently with jammed guns—and then his plane went into a dive, afire. Close to the ground Luf fell or jumped. Some thought he had hoped to land in a nearby stream and somehow survive. Others remembered that he had drummed it into the youngsters always to stick with the ship, not to jump near the ground, and guessed that he had simply been climbing back on the fuselage, away from the flames, when he fell. In any event, he was gone, and there would never be another one like him. The men who knew him best always said that they never really knew him. There would be as good pilots later, but there was no substitute for the man who had never known a father and yet had managed to be something like one to a lot of badly frightened young men.

On the Marne the 95th set up a bar—The Château 95—which was famous the length of the front, and there was a hospital with real American nurses nearby. There was also a marked upturn in pregnant though unmarried girls in the area. The fatherless results were christened with names such as Foch and Pershing. The Fokkers, though, started to make themselves felt. The 27th sent out a six-plane patrol and lost five of them. Teddy Roosevelt's son Quentin—brave, but green and reckless—was shot down and killed. Alan Winslow went down and finished the war as a prisoner. Four new pilots came up and three were gone within three weeks. It didn't always come out so badly—one man was seen in a dogfight, did not return, and a fellow pilot wrote, "The next day we mournfully placed him among the heroes. Granvall was elected to pack up his effects and to console and stifle the sobs of the blacksmith's daughter who was distraught with sorrow. 'Si brave, si gentil,' she wailed. Charlie had just divided the most popular of Jim's belongings and was making an official inventory of what remained, the blacksmith's family was beginning to get dry-eyed again, when the prodigal son returned. . . ."

By this time the French had enough Spads to be able to let the

Americans have some. No one mourned the Nieuport. If one dived it vigorously, one wing—usually the right—was apt to crumple. Even if one coddled it, there was something wrong with the way the covering was attached to the leading edge of the wing and it was not unusual for a wing to start shedding its fabric. One pilot—obviously presidential timber for the Should-Be-Dead Club—twice landed ships with his upper wing nude as a skeleton.

Of course a parachute would have saved a man from having to land a dangerous plane, it would have saved Lufbery's life. Amazingly, parachutes were not in use. Although an American—Captain Berry—had made the first successful experiments in jumping from a plane as early as 1912, parachutes were not issued to pilots. Crews of observation balloons used them with great success; they were the only way down once an enemy plane set the bag on fire. The pilots themselves considered the device unwieldy, there was some official opinion holding that it would tempt pilots to abandon their planes too readily. Perhaps officialdom should have promoted them harder, but it's only fair to point out that the flier never warmed to the idea, although German pilots used them successfully at the end of the war. It was 1919 before a chute was adopted as standard United States airplane equipment and even then it took a 1922 order making the use of parachutes compulsory to get them into general service.

While the pilots were making a score over the lines, another sort of fight was starting back at headquarters. In March, 1917, a Major William Mitchell had wangled himself six months' leave and gone over to Europe to see what was going on. Something of a maverick, this Mitchell—son of a wealthy family, he'd enlisted at the beginning of the Spanish-American War and stayed on to become a career officer. He'd made his reputation in the communications end of the Signal Corps; the word on him was that he was too impatient for garrison duty, but a good driver on tough jobs like stringing a telegraph line in Alaska.

He hadn't been an original air force pioneer, but by 1916 the air war in Europe had shown him enough so that he went out and learned to fly. He'd no more than arrived in Europe, of course, than America came in and he was kept on to become chief of Air Service, First Army, when veteran airman General Foulois came over to be commander of the air service. Mitchell was capable at getting things organized, but at this stage his most marked innovation was an informality of dress for which the air was going to go on being famous right through the Second World War. In an army that favored tight jackets with a stand-up choker collar, Mitchell suddenly emerged with a jacket floppy as an oversized sports coat, a soft-collared shirt with necktie, and pants of a particularly noxious hue that eventually became known as "Air Force pink." Since Pershing didn't court-martial him on the instant, it can be concluded that he thought a great deal of the young man.

Veteran airman Foulois didn't suit Pershing. He was moved down to the First Army, a paper organization, Mitchell down to the 1st Corps, and an engineer brigadier general named Mason Patrick brought in to run things. It was Pershing's notion—and a not totally unsound one—that a good administrator was a good administrator even if he had no previous experience in aviation. Patrick did a good job; if some of his conceptions lagged behind Mitchell's, so did those of 99 per cent of all officers in the French, British, and American armies.

Mitchell had sought out British General Hugh Trenchard, the greatest air leader the war produced. Trenchard believed two things: first, that the business of the airplane was not the gallant but essentially negative business of shooting down enemy planes, but large formations of bombers, flying into the enemy's country and destroying his railroads, cities, and factories. Second, he believed this could best be done with an air force independent of the Army and Navy.

Today it seems elementary, but at the time only Trenchard and the Italian aviation theorist Douhet really understood it. By 1918 Trenchard had pursuaded the British to let him have an independent bombing force. It never amounted to much, but in a manner of speaking the Second World War was won right there. Hermann Goering, who flew for the Kaiser, and then went on to build Hitler's Luftwaffe, thought he understood, but he built a force good only for smashing field armies and opening holes for the *Panzers*. When he came to the Battle of Britain, he had no proper heavy bomber. The only people who did were the British—with "Boom" Trenchard still at the helm—and the Americans who'd learned from him.

Mitchell's part in all this would come later. For the moment he must have been happy at the 1st Corps down on the Ourcq, because its commander, Hunter Liggett—run to fat, but with none of it above the neck—was a ground commander who appreciated the future of air. Then he was back at the First Army—readying for Saint-Mihiel. He and Foulois didn't get along and Foulois selflessly decided that Mitchell was the better man to run the show and asked for a transfer. That left Mitchell in command of 1,500 planes for the Saint-Mihiel push. His plans showed Trenchard's teaching—plenty of power against the enemy rear and communications to smash things up and trap the army in the field. In fact, the German resistance folded and the flying weather was rotten, but planes got off 3,300 sorties anyway. Among others, Rickenbacker and Reed Chambers skipped under the low clouds to stall a German artillery column by machine gunning its horses. The plan had been a good one; clearly Mitchell knew what to do with his tools. A few days later he was already plumping for a paratroop operation which even his greatest admirers concede was a bit advanced for the equipment at hand.

In July the 27th Squadron got a new pilot and almost immediately started disliking him. His name was Frank Luke, a tall blond kid from Arizona who held off in a sullen, bashful silence or talked too much. If he said anything, it was apt to be a suggestion that he was a better pilot than any of them. Then he came up with the report that he'd shot a Boche off Squadron Skipper Major Harold Hartney's tail while on patrol. There was no confirmation on it; the squadron put him down as a liar.

Before it was all over Hartney would call him "the most extraordinary flier ever produced by the American army" and Rickenbacker said he was "the greatest fighting pilot of the war." For the moment, though, he hung off more sullen than ever, then on September 12 started running up the record that would come to 15 balloons and 6 planes destroyed in seventeen days.

The German observation balloon—the *Drachen*—must have looked an easy mark to an outsider. It just hung there—run up from the ground on a cable, and it carried no weapons. Below it, though, anti-aircraft guns clustered and over it German pursuit planes hovered. From its basket observers could spot artillery fire or report on troop movements. Here was a target the infantry could understand. They were looking right down the infantry's throat and the fliers were always under pressure to get them out of there.

On September 12 Luke burned his first one and promptly landed at the nearest American balloon station to get affidavits signed by the men who'd seen it go down. He was sick of being called a liar. His outfit still wasn't impressed, and Hartney was even considering having him transferred. Then, on the fourteenth, Luke went up again. With him went Lieutenant Joe Wehner, the only buddy he had, a kid of German ancestry who'd been chivvied by security offiecrs until he, too, felt like an outcast in his own service. Luke burned two more, and Wehner knocked two Fokkers out of the enemy air cover. The 27th began to think differently.

On the morning of the fifteenth they did it again—two bags for Luke, two Fokkers for Wehner—and came back to announce they were going to take two more that evening. Hartney invited Billy Mitchell over to watch the show. Promptly at six fifty-eight Luke got a balloon over Spincourt—in easy sight of his own airdrome—and then dropped another. He and Wehner landed with the light gone and their ships full of holes. On the sixteenth they added another pair.

The luck couldn't hold and on the eighteenth it broke. Luke got two more, then six Fokkers jumped them. Wehner was turning to fight them off when a seventh, which had held back high, came down and blasted him. Luke got two Fokkers before he could fight his way clear and get an observation plane on the way home. There he waited, heartbroken, for Wehner to come in, grieving for his friend and muttering, "I'm glad it wasn't me. My mother doesn't know I'm at the front yet." Hartney sent him up to Paris on leave, but he came back early and got a Fokker on the twenty-sixth.

He must have known he'd follow Wehner before long. At night he shot craps with outrageous luck and then, devout Catholic, dumped it all into the collection plate at the village church on Sunday. Working with Lieutenant Ivan Roberts, he got another balloon, but the Fokkers got Roberts. Hartney realized that Luke was too dangerous to work with anyone. He took him off regular patrols. On the twenty-ninth, Luke went up alone and never came back. After the war the citizens of the little village of Murvaux signed a statement in which they said that on that date an American aviator had within their sight downed three balloons and two Fokkers, been shot out of the air, and continued to fight on the ground until German infantry killed him. There was no sure identification, but given the date, the location, and the performance, it almost had to be Frank Luke, the balloon buster.

The war came down into its final weeks and the infant air service fought over the Meuse-Argonne and over the British front. Rickenbacker was working up to his 22 kills. As fliers go, he was pretty much the antithesis of Luke. He was squadron skipper of the Hat in the Ring now, but still found time to check his engines himself and have his crew sort through his machine-gun bullets for malformed shells which might jam his gun. In the air he was cautious; it was Rick who made his boys circle the field three times before landing. He'd noticed that coming down from 15,000 feet fogged a man's brains; better to stay in the air a minute or two longer and then land with a clear head.

A few of our bomber pilots got into action against enemy supply dumps and railroads. Some flew the poky DH 4's; one outfit sent out a flight of seven only to lose five and have a sixth come home with a dead observer aboard. Small wonder that there was little enthusiasm for extra excursions such as dropping propaganda leaflets. One truck driver—the period slang for a bomber pilot—noted about the propaganda: "The charming picture of the deserter's reception in France made me feel like deserting to France myself, but I was there already . . . No one wanted to make a special trip over the lines so the bundles built up and the cook started breakfast fires with them."

Before it was all over, some 650 American airmen had seen action and they'd claim a total of 781 enemy planes and 73 balloons knocked down. To get at the real significance of the thing, the story has to go on a little farther—into the twenties. For one, in a war where very few individuals got the folks back home very excited, the Rickenbackers, the Lufberys, and the Lukes fired up a lot of kids who promptly started making model planes with rubber-band motors and devouring pulp magazines such as *War Aces*. Some of them would grow up to be wild-blue-yonder types of the next war.

More important, exposure to Trenchard and the experience at Saint-Mihiel had Billy Mitchell all fired up about an independent air force. By 1921 he had whooped up air power to a point where he was given a crack at bombing the old German dreadnought *Ostfriesland* which had to be destroyed under the terms of the peace treaty anyway. He sank it with one-ton bombs dropped from six Martin bombers and a beautiful row started. Mitchell wanted coast defense turned over to him, Admiral Sims—retired—announced that the battleship was a thing of the past, and the Navy was in an understandably savage temper. Before Mitchell was through he'd pushed his notion so hard and in language so intemperate—he spoke of the "almost treasonable administration of the national defense by the Navy and War Departments"—that they had to court-martial him. He pulled a five-year suspension and, considering his tone of voice, he deserved it. All the services, by that time, were wrestling with midget peacetime appropriations and nobody was getting what he wanted as quickly as he wanted it.

Withal, though, it helped. It helped the young Navy men who were pushing for a carrier force, it helped the assault-minded big bomber men in what was now the Army Air Corps, and right in the middle of the row the post of assistant secretary of war for air was created. Consider what we took into the war and then reflect that by 1932 the corps had 1,300 officers and 13,000 men. The infant of 1917 had grown up; when we needed it again there was going to be something ready.

Chapter Eight

"KEEP THE HOME FIRES BURNING"

BACK HOME: 1918

BACK in the States the Fourth of July had come around again. The year before, the First Division had sent a promissory regiment up to Paris and the promise was all we had to offer. Gresham, Enright, and Hay had had four months to live before they became our first combat dead.

This year, though, we had nearly a million men in France and they were fighting and winning. Back home the production mess showed signs of straightening out. And the country itself had changed, perhaps never so much in any previous single year of our history.

The American woman had taken a giant step. She'd come streaming out of the kitchen to work in factories and shipyards. Some of it was because of necessity, the need to bring in a pay check now that the man of the house had gone to war or because the wartime inflation was forcing prices up faster than family income. Some of it was because of patriotism—even women who obviously didn't need the money were going into volunteer work. More than either, though, it was a welling up of the demand that had been coming for years that women be accepted as adult, first-class citizens capable of voting, leading their own sex lives, and generally taking a grown-up part in the life of the country.

Some of the more adventurous sisters even went to France as nurses, Red Cross girls, or YMCA workers. One artilleryman who was fortunate enough to pull a few days' leave at the American leave area around Aix-les-Bains in southeast France remembered that the nicest part of the whole junket was the appearance of real American girls at a YMCA dance. There weren't enough to go around so each soldier was given a red, white, or blue ribbon, and participated according to the color of the flag displayed during any particular number.

Woman wasn't the only second-class citizen trying to step up. The Negro, whose lot hadn't changed much since the Civil War, heard about the wages in northern factories and came up from the South a-running. One of the earliest Lafayette Escadrille men was astonished to find that his first flight instructor was an American Negro who'd come over on his own and had made sergeant with the French. Then the American draft began transplanting Negroes by the thousands. In France most of them worked as labor troops—unloading ships and building roads—but they got a look at another kind of life, one without much color line drawn, and, since even labor troops need corporals and sergeants, some of them got a taste of authority and the responsibility that goes with it.

Even if the war didn't change the lot of the Negro a great deal, it changed our national image of him. The old picture of the comical darky who sang minstrel songs as if he had a mouth full of mush vanished for good, and we were left with a much more troubling vision of the black citizen who wanted education and some sort of standard of living and who clearly was going to make demands about them.

And we were growing out of being a hick country. Men who would never have gone farther than the county seat in a lifetime moved around the country during their training and then saw France and sometimes England, too. A song writer asked how we were going to keep them down on the farm after they'd seen Paree, and indeed we couldn't. The artistic and adventurous young were going to flock there after the war and even the staidest would come home with barbarously pronounced French tidbits like "mercy bo-coo" added to his speech and a taste for *vin rouge*. If nothing else, American boys were serving in places no one had ever heard of, and people started to look at maps who'd never looked at maps before in their lives.

There was a heady sense of power in the country that summer. We had gone to Europe, we were turning the tide, we were the healthy giant among the exhausted older nations of the world. Just how we were going to use all this power wasn't quite clear. To the jingo, the obvious answer was a drive to Berlin with the victory crowned by a public hanging of the Kaiser. To Wilson, with his Fourteen Points, it was more complicated, but even he had not put before the country the degree to which we were permanently involved in Europe whether we wanted to be or not. No one was explaining the basic conclusions to be drawn from what was going on: the world was smaller and the airplane would make it smaller still. If we could put an army in Europe, someone in Europe could presumably put an army in the United States. A debating society such as the League might be the answer, but one only had to look at the Russian Revolution to know that in at least some situations the debating-society idea didn't work. It was the lesson we might have learned in Mexico—there are some people who just don't know how to conduct a nice, orderly revolution.

For the moment we enjoyed feeling strong and didn't think too much about the fact that the shrinking planet was going to squeeze all these disorderly revolutions right in on our doorstep.

The Fourth-of-July festivities for 1918 began at 12:01 A.M. The Shipping Board aimed to launch 100 ships that day; out in Superior, Wisconsin, a shipyard anxious to be in first slid a new steamer into the water just after midnight. It was still dark in New York City when the first of the 75,000 who were to march up Fifth Avenue in the Fourth-of-July parade began to assemble around the Washington Square starting area. Day broke warm and clear; at 8:30 A.M. they started up the Avenue. The theme of the first half of the procession was The Nation at War. Soldiers and sailors marched, there was a 20-foot battleship mounted on a truck chassis and on another a real Navy gun crew went through loading drill on a real Navy gun. From a Salvation Army float doughnuts were tossed to the crowd and overhead the unheard-of total of 20 airplanes flew past in formation. Drifting slowly after them came a dirigible, dropping copies of "The Star-Spangled Banner" to the throngs beneath. On the steps of the Public Library a reproduction of the front had been set up: eight sculpted doughboys defended their trench against the attacking Boche while real machine guns spat electric sparks to simulate firing.

The second half of the parade was the Nationalities Section, and on this much thought and some grief had been expended. The notion was to have each nationality group in the United States represented, including the original inhabitant, the American Indian. Early in the proceedings, though, it became apparent that while all the nationalities were united in a desire to wallop Germany, some of them still harbored assorted old-country feuds against each other. Most of the feuds had been headed off by a decree that no group was to wear national costumes, thus keeping old-country reminders to a minimum. Even so, as the line of march was forming, the Italians found themselves marching behind the Hungarians and would have none of it. The Irish contingent was hastily inserted between them and peace restored.

At the very head of the Nationalities Section came a Mr. Chadiali, announced as New York's only Zoroastrian Parsee. Mr. Chadiali marched with his little boy (it is impossible to figure out from contemporary accounts why the little boy was not also a Zoroastrian Parsee) and bore a banner inscribed "America always." After him the groups came in alphabetical order, the Armenians leading the way, devoid of national costume, but with a float dramatizing their past difficulties with the Turks.

In all, it was a ten-hour affair—nor was it the only affair of the day. Over in Paris the Avenue de Trocadero was renamed the Avenue du President Wilson and a reporter roaming the city found an old lady sewing herself an American flag to display while a little girl cut out the necessary stars from a paper pattern. Elsewhere in France the Thirty-third Division was contributing two companies to the Australian assault at Hamel and a number of other men not in the assigned companies managed to sneak along and get into the fight.

In London the King and Queen attended an Army-Navy baseball game, watching in some confusion as Navy won, 2 to 1. In the evening Mr. Winston Churchill addressed an assemblage of Americans; some of the color and phrasing that were to rally a nation twenty-odd years later was already apparent: "Deep in the hearts of the people of these islands is the desire to be truly reconciled to their kindred across the Atlantic, to blot out the reproaches and redeem the blunders of a bygone age and dwell once more in spirit with them." From the other side of the world the Japanese sent an equally chummy birthday note: "We trust you, we love you, and if you will let us we will walk at your side in loyal good fellowship down all the coming years."

Down in Washington George Creel also wanted to emphasize how the country was made from the unity of many nationalities. He arranged for representatives of thirty-three groups to sail down the Potomac with President Wilson on the presidential yacht, the *May-*

flower, for a ceremony at George Washington's grave at Mount Vernon. They assembled around the tomb, overhung with purple wisteria, and while John McCormack sang "The Battle Hymn of the Republic" (accompanied by a piano hidden in the trees) each laid a wreath. Wilson spoke, calling for victory, and summarizing in a general way his Fourteen Points.

The national holiday came to a close. There had been a few mishaps—the French contingent in the New York parade was miffed because someone forgot to assign it a band, the Shipping Board launched only 95 ships, not 100—but on the whole it had gone well. Even the casualty list from the front was small; Pershing reported 15 killed in action or dead of wounds and 26 wounded. In Germany the Kaiser was considering what was to be done about his Foreign Secretary Kuhlmann, who had made an unfortunate speech suggesting that a German military victory was no longer possible.

The country had come back strongly from the frustration of the winter before when the industrial plant had been blundered into a standstill.

Come March, though, and the great German drive had swept forward in France to distract the public from the home front. The first anniversary of our entrance into the war was to mark the beginning of the Third Liberty Loan drive, and though the sweep in Europe was the best possible argument for the new $3,000,000,000 loan, a tremendous hoopla campaign was organized behind it. Some of it was official, some just private fervor. One could buy for one's Victrola, for instance, a record containing eight wartime hits—"Keep the Home Fires Burning," "Over There," "I May Be Gone a Long, Long Time," "Pack Up Your Troubles," "It's a Long Way to Berlin, but We'll Get There," "Where Do We Go from Here," "Good-by, Broadway, Hello, France," and "I Don't Know Where I'm Going, but I'm on My Way." Alternatively one could get Al Jolson singing "A Lump of Sugar—A Girl That Mr. Hoover Ought to Know," or a sentimental gem rendered by Harry Bun called "A Baby's Prayer at Twilight." It was advertised with a drawing of a child and its mommy gawping at a photograph of a man (presumably Daddy) in uniform. On the flip side, Mr. Bun offered "My Beautiful Alsace-Lorraine," a notion about on a par with doing a ballad about Carbondale, Pennsylvania.

As the loan drive started some poor devil of a newspaperman at the New York *Times* was summoned by his editor (with whom he was obviously in bad standing) and told that for the duration of the drive he would produce each day one bright, snappy slogan in favor of buying bonds to appear at the top of the paper's page one. The name of this hero is forgotten by even the oldest inhabitants of the *Times'* newsroom; he started off, however, with a punchy "Liberty Bonds or German Bondage," then followed with "Come Across or the Kaiser Will," and "He Buys Twice Who Buys Quickly."

Out in Collinsville, Illinois, some locals gave a more direct demonstration of their patriotism by laying hands on one Robert Prager, suspected of talking socialist nonsense, and lynching him. A jury acquitted them in forty-five minutes.

Back in New York the sloganeer reeled off "Bombard the Boche with Bonds," "The Soldier Gives—You Must Lend," and "Buy Over Here to Win Over There." His next effort suggests that he was beginning to feel the strain: "Buy Bonds and Take the Helm from Wilhelm."

Inspired by Illinois, some Oklahomans put a rope around the neck of Henry Rheimer, who didn't display an American flag, and had him strung up when the police "persuaded" the mob to cut him down.

The loan was going well; the $3,000,000,000 would obviously be subscribed and it began to look as if four might be raised. Inspired by the response, the newsman laid into the Kaiser: "Lend a Hand to Uncle Sam or Bend a Knee to the Kaiser," "Back the United States or Back Down to the Kaiser," "A Bond Slacker Is a Kaiser Backer." The drive went over the top. In all, more than eighteen million people bought more than four billion dollars' worth of bonds and the only casualty was George Creel, who was rapidly becoming accident prone.

During the drive Creel spoke in New York to inspire purchasers and had he left it at that, he would have been all right. Instead, he consented to answer questions and someone asked him what he thought of "the heart of Congress." Never one to let common sense stand in the way of a good line, Creel whipped back, "I have not been slumming in years."

Speaker of the House Cannon summed it up for Congress by observing that Creel "ought to be taken by the nape of the neck and the slack of the pants and thrown into space." In a slanging bee Creel would have had no trouble defending himself. He was a man capable of characterizing Senator Lodge's mind as "like the soil of New England—highly cultivated, but naturally sterile. An exceedingly dull man and a very vain one—deadly combination." As for Senator Reed, Creel noted that in his newspaper days ". . . there was not a week in which I did not try to hold him up to the contempt and ridicule that were deserved by his character and abilities."

Unfortunately for Creel, Congress had something to fight with besides billingsgate. It was budget time, and although Creel suddenly spoke softly to everyone and couldn't have been politer, he wound up with his appropriation slashed.

Over there the First Division had won at Cantigny and the Marines had started working their way through Belleau Wood. Back here Mr. John MacGregor of Brooklyn slugged his wife and then offered as defense that she was acting like the Kaiser. States began passing anti-loafing laws in the belief that if a man wasn't in the service he ought to be doing something useful in a war plant. Up in Providence, Rhode Island, the police caught a man whose only activity was going fishing. The court gave him six months. It was amazing, though, what a man could do and still be considered to be making a contribution. Senator Calder of New York arose before a convention of the National Association of Piano Merchants of America and informed them that they were "an essential industry. . . . It is necessary for our fighting men to have music on the battlefields." This conjures up the fascinating picture of Piano Merchants charging along behind the infantry trundling a piano between them. General Crowder, however, decided it was time to be a little more precise about just who was essential. He issued a list of non-essential occupations and to the delight of the men in France it included baseball players. The men overseas had never been quite able to understand why a man fit to play the game wasn't fit enough to fight Germans. World's heavyweight champion Jack Dempsey went to work in a shipyard.

On Broadway Ziegfeld offered a new *Follies* which included Will Rogers, Ann Pennington, the beauteous Lillian Lorraine, W. C. Fields doing his juggling act, and Eddie Cantor in a sketch about a terrified young man taking the tests to become an aviation cadet. The real hit of the year, though, opened a little later without Ziegfeld girls or indeed any genuine girls at all. The show was called *Yip, Yip, Yaphank*, and the only pulchritude in it was afforded by doughboys dressed up in skirts. Originally it had been nothing but a camp show gotten up at Camp Yaphank on Long Island. Much of it was pretty standard soldier humor; what made it popular enough to be brought to New York was a single number in which a sergeant named Irving Berlin came out and sang a song he'd composed called "Oh, How I Hate to Get Up in the Morning." It was the greatest song hit of the war; come another war and another soldier show more than twenty years later and Berlin would again stop the show by coming out to deliver his diatribe against buglers.

The movies also had some patriotic offerings, all bad. They included *Outwitting the Hun, The Claws of the Hun,* and an epic stinker called *To Hell with the Kaiser* in which an energetic American girl killed the German Crown Prince and captured Wilhelm. One critic felt that even patriotism didn't demand that he like this one and pronounced it "a travesty."

Casualty lists began taking up a full page in the papers as the fighting along the Ourcq and the Vesle got dirty. One New York church rallied to this grim reality by banning the throwing of rice at weddings to conserve food. In the shipyards Edward Hurley came up with a gimmick that promised to have more practical results. Since the time it took to complete a ship depended in large part on how fast the rivets that held it together could be driven, Hurley started encouraging riveting contests. The first claimant to the title was Finner Schock of Baltimore, who drove 658 in eight hours. In no time Charles Woldwise had beaten him with 1,202 in the same period. Gradually the record crept up to 1,624, and then Schock won the title back with 2,720 in nine hours. Papers began offering cash prizes and to the best of Hurley's knowledge the final championship went to one Tom Horn of California, who drove 5,620 in nine hours.

The country had been hearing about an influenza epidemic in Germany and later in Spain. Interest in it centered, naturally enough, on what damage it might do to the German war effort until—in August—a few Spanish ships began arriving at East Coast ports with cases of flu aboard. Even then no one except public health officials paid much attention; it would be another month before the entire nation would be watching the flu almost as intently as it was watching the fighting in France. For the moment the civilian was more concerned with uncomfortably high prices. The theme began to appear in ads—"As Our Marines Rout the Huns—So Monroe Clothes Rout High Prices"—and, more important, appeared as the basis of laborer's complaints which broke out into strikes. In defense plants the tendency was to give them raises and pass the cost along to the Government. When that couldn't be done, the strikes got bitter and the threat of the draft was held over the heads of the workmen. Wilson himself used it to get Bridgeport, Connecticut, machinists back on the job.

While the draft had been notably fair-minded about the various sorts of conscientious objectors who turned up in its nets, there were a few very conscientious objectors who wouldn't even go along to the extent of coming in to explain why they didn't want to participate. Thus out near Heber Springs, Arkansas, some mountain folk of this breed holed up in old Tom Adkisson's house and wouldn't come down in the valley to register. Sheriff Duke of Cleburne County took four men one July morning and went out to bring them in. It was just dawn when Duke called on them to surrender; for an answer he got a spatter of fire from 15 or 20 hidden riflemen, and Porter Hazlewood, one of the posse, went down mortally wounded. Duke withdrew to return about noon with a posse of 25 men. Something like a pitched battle took place, complicated by the fact that one of the mountaineers, a Mrs. Ida Simmons, a small woman with an enormous shock of brilliant red hair, stood between the lines waving her arms and alternately shouting good old hymns and cursing the invaders. Even so, one of the posse caught old Tom ducking past a gap in his board fence and knocked him sprawling with a shot. The draft resisters, Tom included, filtered through the posse and vanished into the woods.

As a feature writer in the Arkansas *Gazette* had the decency to point out at the time, they were fundamentally perfectly good people, but this draft business was more than they could understand. They comprehended very little beyond the rim of their own hills, they had a distaste for law officers anyway (as the *Gazette* writer pointed out many of them had gotten into the hills with officialdom hot on their trails in the first place), and they were much influenced by a disowned offshoot of the Baptist faith taught by one

Preacher Russell in a tract called *The Unfinished Mystery*. Old Tom Adkisson was a particularly devout Russellite and based his draft stand on its claim that killing was wrong. Apparently he did not feel that the injunction extended to law officers. Russellism or no, probably the best statement of their position was made by a woman called Old Mother Blakeley who had three sons—Jim, Jess, and Lum—involved in the fracas. "Men, hit's wrong to kill," she told the posse. "I know they tell terrible things on them German soldiers, but they hain't got over here yit an' hit'll be plenty o' time fer to fight when they jump on us in our own kentry."

Of course the governor of Arkansas couldn't see it that way and turned out the Home Guard and a machine-gun company to run them down. For a week the soldiers trailed through the hills, finding no one, but destroying stores of food and ammunition. In the end, the resisters came in themselves, weary of being chased, and the last man to surrender was old Tom—wounded, but grim and game and announcing that the whole business was his responsibility.

None of the excuses that can be made for the mountain men can be made for Grover Cleveland Bergdoll, America's most artful draft dodger, and in his day the best hated man in the country. Part heir to a Philadelphia brewery fortune, Bergdoll had distinguished himself prewar by flunking out of the University of Pennsylvania, flying a plane in a time when very few people did, and making a considerable reputation as an automobile racer. Since he drove off the track in very much the way he did on it, he picked up a plethora of traffic violations and at one point did three months in jail for driving without a license. To at least one member of the family it seemed even then that Grover was whacky; an older brother tried to have him dealt out of the family fortune on grounds of incompetence. His mother, however, adored the handsome young man.

Although Bergdoll had offered his services to the German Air Force in 1914, he showed no enthusiasm for any branch of the United States service. He did register for the draft, then asked an exemption on the grounds that he owned a farm, but was turned down. After that he simply ignored draft mail and when the final notice arrived, he and his brother Erwin vanished. He stayed vanished until January, 1920, in spite of a habit of sending post cards to the Government and dropping into Philadelphia once in a while to see his mother. It was on one of these visits in 1920 that federal agents and police followed a tip and went to the house. Mrs. Bergdoll appeared at the front door with a .38 revolver in one hand and a blackjack in the other. A second group of agents slipped in the back door and found Grover tucked under a window seat in a second-floor bedroom. He was hustled off to Governors Island, court-martialed, and sentenced to five years at hard labor. Considering that he had been the object of a national manhunt for a year and a half, he might have been said to have made an ample nuisance of himself, but the case was actually just beginning.

About six weeks later one of the succession of lawyers Mrs. Bergdoll had provided for her boy presented himself to the Army with a request that Grover be let out briefly under armed guard in order to go to Maryland and dig up $150,000 worth of gold he claimed to have buried there. Incredibly, the Army granted the request. Escorted by Sergeants John O'Hare and Calvin York, Bergdoll headed for Philadelphia by train; on arrival they were met by the family car which promptly broke down, causing the whole party to repair to the Bergdoll mansion for the night. The next afternoon, while Bergdoll was entertaining the sergeants with recitations from Shakespeare, the telephone rang and he stepped into the next room to answer it. A few minutes later the phone rang again, and a sudden sickening light broke over Sergeant O'Hare. He stepped into the next room and found it empty. Bergdoll, with the family chauffeur, was driving to Canada. Once there he would go on to England and finally Germany.

In spite of two attempts to return Bergdoll to American jurisdiction by kidnaping him, interest in the artful dodger died down; he was even able to sneak back into the country in 1927 and 1935 for visits. Then, with war coming on in Europe, he asked for a pardon in order to come home permanently. Refused the pardon, he came home, stood trial, and was sentenced to ten years. In 1942 he asked to be let out in order to enlist. The Army refused, but in 1944 pardoned him for good behavior. The Pentagon prayerfully requested the Justice Department to kill any and all other charges against him; the Army wanted the case closed once and for all. They were overoptimistic—in 1950 Bergdoll's oldest son Albert was arrested for draft dodging, and pleaded guilty.

Chapter Nine

THE LONG GREEN LINE

As autumn came on, the home front still felt good. Austria was putting out peace feelers. We had a million and a half men in France, and a real American army had won at Saint-Mihiel. The Bulgarians were coming apart under blows from French General Franchet d'Esperey and were obviously not long for this war. In Palestine British General Sir Edmund Allenby added a tactical classic to the history books at Megiddo, when he pinned the Turkish line with infantry, then sent his Australian cavalrymen crashing through the Turkish right flank. It was the last great cavalry charge in history. The Aussies went booming north, then buttonhooked to walk all over the enemy communications and destroy the Turk as a fighting force. A man reading omens for the Western Front, though, might well have paid heed to one thing: the Turks had been beefed up with some German machine gunners and though there weren't enough of them to make any difference in the result of the battle, they never broke. The Turks fled, the British raced north after them and here and there hit a machine gunner, still on his gun, holding where he had been ordered to hold until he was overwhelmed.

Obviously, the Germans were going to die hard, but the suspicion began to grow that they might just be finished off before winter if the pressure could be kept on. Foch ordered the British to keep going in the north, aiming for Cambrai, and at the other end of the German position, now one huge salient, put in a French attack west of the Argonne Forest, an American attack east of it. Both had Sedan as a general sort of objective. If any of the attacks got through, the Hindenburg line would be broken and the railroad line that ran all the way from Metz up to Valenciennes disrupted. That railroad was Germany's chief reliance for supply and troop movements; once it went, every German in France was in acute danger of remaining there permanently.

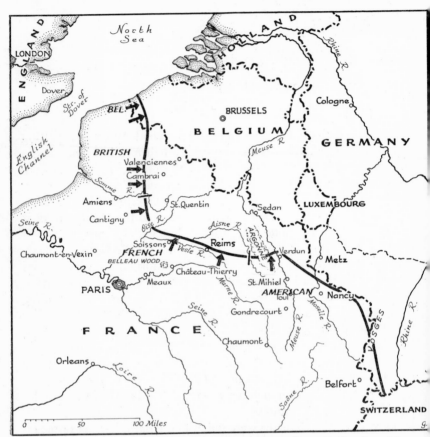

THE END BEGINS: The front as it was in September, 1918, when Marshal Foch launched his final great assaults

The Americans and French were to jump off September 26—which meant there simply wasn't enough time to bring up the veteran divisions who'd done the driving at Saint-Mihiel. To do a job on difficult, heavily fortified terrain, Pershing scraped together what he could, but when he got them all in line the result looked painfully like amateur night.

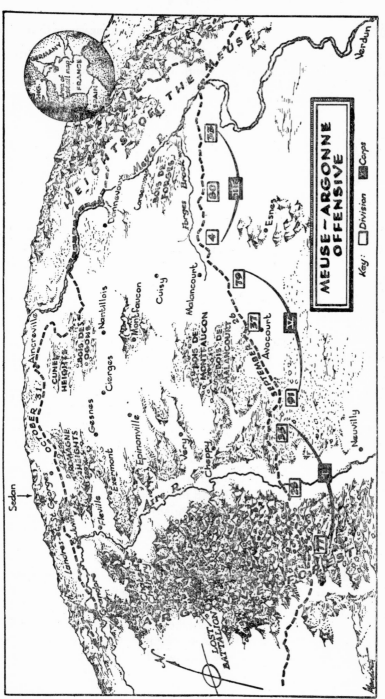

The Meuse-Argonne Drive, Part I: The battle line as it looked at the beginning of the greatest American fight of the war

On the left, he had Liggett's 1st Corps—our most experienced corps organization now, but this time without any really tried-in-the-fire divisions. The Seventy-seventh had had a month's position warfare down on the Vesle, but this was a New York draft division, full of the city's slum kids, and there were those who asked whether it was the ideal outfit to fight in the Argonne thickets. Fortunately, the Vesle losses had been made good with some westerners who at least knew a tree when they saw one. On their right was the Twenty-eighth Division and it had done well enough in the fighting up from the Marne and the Vesle. Now, though, they had a problem that would have vexed even the veterans of the First or Second divisions: advancing up the Aire River Valley, they had to keep one flank in touch with the New Yorkers in the Argonne, who obviously would be moving more slowly, and the other flank in touch with the Thirty-fifth Division on their right, which was supposed to move even faster. Not that anyone knew for sure how the Thirty-fifth would do—they were National Guardsmen from Kansas and Missouri, with no real battle experience to date.

The center belonged to Major General George Cameron's 5th Corps and when poor Cameron looked over what they gave him, he may well have wondered how he was going to make out before they learned their trade. The Ninety-first Division was a magnificent collection of oversized young men from the Pacific slope, experience nil. The Thirty-seventh was an Ohio outfit, experienced only in a very quiet sector. The Seventy-ninth was Pennsylvania draftees, experience nil.

On the right Major General Robert Bullard's 3rd Corps was going into action for the first time. It had the Fourth Division, blooded on the Vesle, plus the Eightieth, a Blue Ridge outfit, and the Thirty-third from Illinois. Both the latter divisions were innocents except for a little line time with the British.

Back home the battle got to be called the Battle of the Argonne Forest, but in truth the First Army was attacking on a twenty-mile front that ran from the Argonne over to the Meuse River. Only the Seventy-seventh Division was actually going to do any fighting in the forest and no one really expected them to take it. French advances west of the forest and American to the east were to make it untenable, so the Germans would have to withdraw. The real fighting was going to be up what amounted to two valleys east of the Forest. One was formed by the heights of the Argonne dropping down into the valley of the Aire River, then rising again to some hills that culminated in the high point at Montfaucon where the Crown Prince used to do his observing back in the days when the Germans were driving on Verdun. East of Montfaucon the ground fell off again to the Meuse River, but right across that river were heights to gladden the heart of German artillerymen who could sit on them and look menacingly down on the flank of the American advance.

Thus, while the First, the Second, the Rainbow, and the rest of the varsity got itself reorganized, the second team made ready to go up against the Hindenburg line with enemy artillery on both its flanks and the certainty that its own artillery was going to have the devil of a time keeping up with it once it got moving. This was ground that the French and the Germans had fought over. It has been called shell pitted, churned up, a waste. None of the expressions quite do it justice. It was a sea of shell holes in which even the shell holes had shell holes. There were no roads and the very material to build them would have to come up over roads which didn't exist.

An artillery outfit thought that just getting to the Argonne on time was the hardest job they did during the war. They hiked over from the Vesle for nine days, a lot of it in rain, and the men were so worn out they slept on the horses—or did until some disgusted driver cried out, "All men off wagons, horses aboard, drivers in the shafts, forward march!" There was an autumn nip in the air as they plugged ahead, hiding in the woods by day, marching at night. The French in the line were to remain there until the last possible moment; American officers who went forward to look things over did so in French uniforms, and over the telephone net installed for the American Army no word of English was allowed to pass.

As the dark fell on the evening of September 25 the men slid forward to their jump-off positions. It was artillery first, swinging into prearranged battery positions, then the infantry, stripped down for fighting. Each man had 250 rounds of rifle ammunition, two cans of corned beef, and six boxes of hard bread as iron rations, and supplemented as often as not by a loaf of bread carried impaled on the bayonet at the end of the rifle. In the quart canteens the wiser heads carried water, the unwise *vin rouge* or *blanc*. A veteran could have told them that the wine turned a man's stomach and made him vomit when the going got bad, but there weren't many veterans in the outfits feeling their way up to the white tapes that marked the jump-off line. What a man could carry to shoot with and eat was going to make a great difference in the next few days, because once the line started forward no one knew how long it would take to move supplies across the waste land in front of them.

No two divisions are quite alike, and along the line little signs of character were cropping out as the watches ticked down to barrage time. The Fourth Division—thinking stoically ahead as good regulars should—already had its engineers building a brand-new road forward, the better to supply itself once it started to move. The Thirty-third was contemplating Forges brook and swamp in front of its position. The French said no one could get across the bog, but the Thirty-third was supposed to do it. Showing remarkable savvy for a green outfit, they had their engineers waiting to go forward under the barrage and throw light bridges over the mess to keep the doughboys dry.

Over in the Thirty-fifth Division, the men were angry. The Kansas and Missouri National Guardsmen had been at war with the Army since training days back in the States; the issue: National Guard officers. Since we've had a Guard there has been a certain regular Army suspicion that a lot of Guard officers are political appointees and no damn good in war. There is some truth in this notion. There is also a Guard suspicion that the regulars have a prejudice against Guard officers and will replace them whenever they can. There is also some truth in this notion. The Thirty-fifth had lost a lot of its Guard officers, it felt many of them were good men and it felt that its artillery brigade commander—regular Brigadier General Lucien Berry—was simply a spy sent down to bedevil Guardsmen. Now, on the eve of battle, the much-loved commander of its Kansas infantry brigade was relieved, and the change was going to be felt.

Years later Harry S. Truman, who was a lieutenant in one of the division's Missouri batteries, would say of the trouble, "Of course, there always has been difficulty between the regulars and the National Guard and reserve officers. That started with George Washington's administration and has gone on throughout the history of the country. I do not think it is a particularly bad idea because it causes the

National Guard and reservists into always being better than the people who try to high-hat them and that has usually worked out all right."

This time, though, it wasn't going to work out. The men were going to fight magnificently, but they were not going to be handled as a division properly pulled together at the top ought to be.[1]

The infantry was still moving forward when the big guns of corps and army artillery opened half an hour before midnight. Many of the men had never been so near heavies before; they went on with hands over their ears as the muzzle blasts and gusts of hot wind shook them. At two-thirty on the morning of the twenty-sixth divisional artillery joined in all along the line, nearly 4,000 guns were firing, and "The night turned lurid, then murky as the smoke settled lower. Red flares stabbed the blackness, faded out, and were repeated. The intonations, first distinct, became merged into an earsplitting drumming. . . . The night moaned and whined and shrieked to the terrible fusillade." In front of the Thirty-third the engineers slipped down to throw their duck boards across the swamp, mortars began pumping out smoke shells to make a smoke screen along the jump-off line, and at five-thirty the First Army went over the top.

The bombardment had left a lot of smoke along the line, the smoke shells had made it thicker, and just to finish the job there was a good thick mist on the ground that morning. On high ground there was still visibility, but on low ground a man suddenly found himself walking alone in a cotton-batting world almost as soon as he left the trenches. For a credit, it protected the infantry from the German machine gunners. For a debit, it broke the formations all to pieces as men stumbled cursing into shell holes half filled with water from the rains. Liaison was lost, exposed flanks were flapping about in the muck like so much wash on a line, support troops pushed forward into the assault waves, and if the barrage hadn't made mincemeat out of the lightly held forward German positions, the whole show might have folded then and there.

Instead, it went well. The Thirty-third whipped across Forges brook on its bridges, then turned neatly right to take over the bank of the Meuse. Next to them the Eightieth plunged straight ahead to get on the bend of the Meuse north of Dannevoux. Between them they made the right flank of the attack secure from Germans who might be tempted to cross the river. Of course, nothing they could do could prevent artillery from being fired across.

The Fourth Division got one of the big breaks of the day, then had the rewards taken away at the last moment. Still thinking ahead like old pros, they'd put men who could travel by compass with each of the assault companies. As a result, when the sun finally broke through, the Fourth's boys were not scattered all over the battlefield, but still in good order and roaring ahead. By twelve-thirty they were all the way into Nantillois, a mile past Montfaucon. Later, Pershing thought they could have been allowed to turn left and grab the all-important Montfaucon high ground, but at the time the corps thought they were getting too far out in front and made them stop and sit down for five hours. The Fourth turned the air blue, but by the time they had permission to go again German support had come up and the great chance was lost.

Of course, the Fourth hadn't been assigned to take Montfaucon; that was the Seventy-ninth's job, and they got off as if they were going to do it in good style until they hit the Bois de Malancourt and the open fields north of it. Here the 313th Infantry was held up; the tanks supposed to support it were bogged down in the waste of No-Man's Land and it was coming on dark before the 313th got up to the Bois de Cuisy from which it was to attack Montfaucon. Its artillery was far behind and nobody except Cameron back at corps thought it could get into Montfaucon that night. But Cameron said go, so Colonel Claude Sweezey had his boys start across the long, open plain that led to the Montfaucon heights. For support they had five light French tanks. Their last battalion commander was killed, the tanks complained of the darkness and pulled out just as they got across the plain, but in spite of all "Baltimore's Own" kept going ahead and one company actually got into the outskirts of the village before the order came to withdraw, the men went back through the night to the Cuisy Woods, and the First Army had its first setback on the day's work.

On the Seventy-ninth's left, the Thirty-seventh started off with the Bois de Montfaucon ahead of them, and if they could get through it, a chance to try for the village itself from the other side. The artillery had done a good job on the woods: "Only a few dugouts had escaped destruction. . . . One body was that of a comparatively elderly man. He lay with his head cushioned upon his arm, with wide-open eyes staring glassily toward the road. As some of the men passed, they imagined that the eyelids of the German slowly closed and opened, but a closer examination proved him to be quite dead. In a ditch near a former machine-gun emplacement, bodies in field gray lay in a tangled heap, evidently the result of a shell. One of the dead presented a horrible sight, with his head swollen to abnormal proportions from a dreadful wound in his jaw. Another, a sergeant evidently hit squarely by the shell, had a charred mass of burned uniform and flesh where his legs should have been. The third lay in a pool of blood with the top of his head completely blown off. Nearby a horse, minus a head and neck, completed the gruesome picture."[2] The casualties were not to remain one-sided. The Thirty-seventh came out the north side of the Bois de Montfaucon, started down the slope to the dry stream bed from which the ground began to climb toward Montfaucon itself, and as soon as they started upward, fire from the hill cut them to pieces. Back to the woods they went, re-formed, came on again with two tanks as a pitiful armored force, and once again they were blasted. Without artillery the job couldn't be done; the problem of moving anything but men across No-Man's Land was beginning to assert itself.

The Ninety-first, doing very well indeed for new boys, made it all the way to the southern outskirts of Epinonville, which meant that Montfaucon was now by-passed on both sides and didn't figure to hold out long. The Missourians and Kansans of the angry Thirty-fifth moved out into some of the thickest fog along the entire front; the fight had scarcely started when its units were wandering around in the murk without any particular notion of where their fellows were. Eventually, the sun burned through, and the 138th Infantry found itself in front of Cheppy, a smashed-up village full of German machine gunners. There they lay for three hours, pinned down, until a dozen tanks came up and escorted them forward in style. By nightfall the division was up south of Very—a creditable day's work—but the confusion in the fog and the unsettled officer situation were making themselves felt. Battalions were complaining that it was hard to reach the regiment, regiments complained that no one could find the brigade. What the army calls liaison was starting to break down; when that happens, men and units start to feel lonely and see ghosts.

Way over on the left, the Pennsylvanians slipped up along the edge of the Argonne and spent the day in high spirits because one of their brigade commanders—a regular who they felt took a dim view of the National Guard—lost track of one of his regiments and was worked over thoroughly by Major General Charles Muir, the division commander. Next door the New Yorkers of the Seventy-seventh started forward through thickets which would have vexed Daniel Boone—the Argonne is not one of your manicured-type French forests —and found digging out the machine gunners about as tough as getting raspberry seeds out of your teeth. Their big scene was still a few days off, with the Lost Battalion about to become the most famous unit in the Army.

On the second day the lines edged forward a little, but the only big get was Montfaucon on the hogback in the center. The Seventy-ninth Division decided that Colonel Sweezey's 313th Infantry still had enough to get up the hill even after the pasting they'd taken the evening before. This time there were some French light tanks to help out with the German machine gunners; by eleven forty-five in the morning Sweezey sent a carrier pigeon back with the word that the Baltimore boys had the town.

There had been a cold rain for most of the first two days and on the third it kept right on raining. Artillery couldn't get up. The men on the line were soaked and hungry; across from them the Germans were clearly bringing up more men and guns. A colonel of the Thirty-seventh Division was told to push his men ahead and replied that "he'd be damned if he would move his hungry and exhausted troops forward another inch.... We spent the balance of the afternoon doing nothing, but getting wetter and hungrier and wincing a little harder at the crash of each new shell, of which there were now plenty." Clearly the first big rush had about spent itself. Even the brass was getting a taste of it. The Fourth Division's Major General John Hines surveyed the damp cement floor of the only available dugout, then went outside, lay down on a pile of cordwood, and spent the night there in the rain.

Sunday the twenty-ninth was the end of it, and while what hap-

pened to the Thirty-fifth Division wasn't quite typical, it illustrates
how badly things had started to come apart. Its commanding general, Traub, went forward in the cold, damp dawn for a look around
and found his men so badly disorganized that he fired off a message saying they had "lost their punch." The division historian at-
tributed it all to "the United States Army system which replaces
National Guard officers, however competent, with regular army
officers, however incompetent." In truth, they'd gone into battle with
no experience and woefully short of officers, whatever their background. The two infantry brigades, for example, were commanded
not by brigadier generals, but by colonels. Command was splintered
by the regular-National Guard feud and some of the Guard's criti-
cisms about General Berry were turning out to be only too well
founded. By the morning of the twenty-ninth, Traub, no firebrand,
had complained to corps so often about Berry that corps gave Traub
permission to relieve him.

Dawn came and the little groups of men along the front prepared
for one last attack. They were no longer a division—or even a brigade
or a regiment. The breakup that had begun in the fog on the first
day was now complete; between bad communications and inexperienced officers, liaison was almost totally lost. Their artillery was
far behind them—rounds fired from the 75's for the first three days
tell the story:

> September 26   —37,033 rounds
> September 27   — 1,090 rounds
> September 28   — 2,624 rounds

Even two small groups getting ready to attack Exermont were too
shaken up to get coordinated. The first try—by 125 men—simply
vanished in the German machine-gun and artillery fire. The second
try was made about 6:30 A.M. by Major James Rieger and what
was left of his battalion. A Baptist deacon in peacetime, Rieger led
his men out, through the rain that had started again, across an open
field, then down the hill and toward the creek that lay in front of
Exermont. There was no artillery support for them and the fire from
in front was so fierce that the men moved "as if they were walking

forward through a driving hailstorm . . . they turned their faces to lee-ward and, leaning forward against the blast, pushed forward with the point of the shoulder offered to the gale." Miraculously, they got into the village and for the moment held it.

Another regiment tried to get up with them; a few men got through but most fell back before the enemy fire. By noon Traub was asking corps that the whole division be withdrawn. At Exermont the Ger-mans were hitting Rieger from three sides; various officers, unable to get word from the top, began putting out orders to retire. Where the men were under command—as Rieger's were—they fell back stubbornly, holding the attacking Germans at bay. Where men were isolated, some sense of being surrounded set in and the retirement was made with a rush to the rear. About a mile back of the high tide the division's engineers had laid out a new line, the retreating men were thrown into it regardless of unit as they drifted back, and there they held through the night and the next day.

The men had fought as bravely as men could—they took more than eight thousand casualties. Individually their officers had fought gal-lantly, but as a division the Thirty-fifth—feud-ridden and raw—simply needed to be reorganized before it could go any farther. Back at First Army headquarters the realization was growing that the long, green line which had started the Meuse-Argonne fighting had done all it could; it was time to put some veterans in before making another push. Up from the rear came the First Division to relieve the Thirty-fifth, the Third to relieve the Seventy-ninth, and the Thirty-second, of Juvigny fame, to replace the Thirty-seventh. The men they relieved had nothing to apologize for; since the battle had started the line had moved through two German defense lines and advanced some six miles. The French had said they couldn't take Montfaucon that winter.

While the new outfits got into position, the front was quiet, but New York City's Seventy-seventh Division kept plugging away in the Argonne. The boys—described by their own Major General Robert Alexander as "a group of hardy frontiersmen from the Bowery and the Lower East Side"—were having their trouble in the thickets. Supposedly French advances to the west and American advances to the east would make the Argonne so uncomfortable for the Germans that they'd withdraw. This was not in fact happening, and the

Seventy-seventh's General Alexander was a driver with no taste for sitting around and waiting.

On October 1 Alexander—a thunderous chewer-outer—chewed out his brigadiers; the brigadiers gnashed the colonels at regiment, and the colonels walked hobnailed up and down the backs of their battalion commanders. The word was attack again on the morning of October 2. At 0830 the men moved out, and leading the advance of the 308th Infantry was the 1st Battalion, Major Charles Whittlesey commanding. A New Englander by birth and a New York lawyer by profession, Whittlesey was feeling a little frail that morning. The day before his men had pushed far enough for the Germans to get in behind them; they'd been cut off from the rest of the outfit and it had been an unsettling experience.[3]

So they walked out, and in a few days they were going to be famous. Try to picture them: New Yorkers, with some westerners in for replacements, moving through a heavy wood, a shell falling once in a while and taking a man or two with it, but nothing really stiff yet. On the right was their own 307th Infantry—not that anyone could see it in the woods, but knowing it was there gave you a good feeling, a sense of going in with your own people. On the left were the French—and until recently there had been American Negroes brigaded with them. We fought segregated in those days—and through most of the next war—and no one wanted to face up to the problem even to the extent of using black and white units next to each other. The Negroes had been turned over to the French. By education and experience they had few men who could make officers, few to make noncoms; they were fighting beside men whose language they couldn't speak. There is no blinking the fact: when it got tough, they broke. Years later the Army would discover in Korea that the Negro was a hell of a fighter when he got an even break; but that would be years later. This morning—October 2, 1918—Whittlesey's boys went in knowing that the second-class citizens on the left had collapsed and, of course, the French always moved slowly.

They hit a valley running straight north from them and the sides were a cinch to be full of machine guns; men moving up the bottom had about as much chance as Custer's troopers at Little Big Horn. Whittlesey looked it over and decided to go up the hill to the left, then changed his mind and asked permission to go up the hill to the right, and received it. The regiment's 2d Battalion under Captain George McMurtry had closed up behind them while they waited. The two forces started up a draw on Hill 198.

A lot of Germans had been pulled eastward that day to fill in the front; Whittlesey's men had stumbled on a hole left open in the German line. Over Hill 198 they went, down the slope to Charlevaux Brook, and across a wooden footbridge with long-range machine guns taking a whack at them as they advanced. They were in the bottom of a valley with a steep rocky bank ahead rising to an old Roman road running east and west. What with the bank before them and the trees on either side, no one could see much, but something told Whittlesey that it was the same old story; he was way out in front and it was time to see whether he had any communications left.

It was coming on night as he pushed two men out to the left; one hit Germans and wound up a prisoner, the other came back to report that there was no help thataway. A messenger to the rear did get back. The division saw they had a break-through that ought to be supported and told a battalion of the 307th to go up and help. The support got lost in the dark—one company finally came through the next morning to add to the 575 men Whittlesey still had left.

Somewhere around six the next morning the Germans slipped in behind them and chopped up the men at the runner posts which were supposed to supply liaison through the tangle of trees. Inside the pocket Whittlesey was still sending messengers to the rear and the men were digging in—funk holes was the inelegant doughboys' name for their shelters. The holes were ready just in time. Around nine-thirty a *Minenwerfer* began dumping shells all over the position. Worse, some of the machine-gun fire accompanying it clearly came from the rear. By noon, between the firing and scouts and patrols reporting Germans in every direction, Whittlesey knew he was surrounded.

That afternoon the men could hear German voices ordering an attack, then a hail of potato-masher grenades came through the trees. The officers held the men in their holes; the potato mashing went on for ten minutes before the Germans, getting cocky, moved in closer. They were in as nice and neat a line as anyone could keep in the trees when the Americans opened fire and the attack dissolved.

Night came on, and now the men in the pocket were down to a total of 520.

Come October 4, and right after lunch—a collation consisting of a few crackers the men had left and were eating a half at a time—the division decided it couldn't get infantry through and that artillery support was the word. In the pocket the men could hear the shells coming, watched a few shorts fall south of them, and then dived in terror as the misdirected barrage plastered them. Whittlesey went for one of his last two carrier pigeons to get a message back and stop the slaughter. Omer Richards, his pigeon man, exhausted and with the ground shaking from shell-fire shock around him, let the first pigeon get out of the crate and escape. They were down to one bird— a male name Cher Ami. This message was clipped to his leg:

> We are along the road parallel 276.4.
> Our own artillery is dropping a barrage directly on us.
> For heaven's sake, stop it.

Cher Ami flipped into the air, then perched in a tree as though nothing was going on while the men shouted and pelted him with rocks and sticks. Finally getting the word, he took off. It was four o'clock when he made the pigeon loft back at division and he just barely made it: an eye was gone, the breastbone smashed, and one leg shot away. Before the message got over to the gunners, they were already lifting the barrage, figuring they'd done Whittlesey all the good they could for the moment. The men in the pocket had been pounded for just short of four hours.

Dawn came on the fourth day, and if it had rained a lot during the night, it had at least kept the water hole filled. The muddy hole was inside the perimeter, but German snipers made it a bad place to be. Still, the water had to be gotten; a man can go a long time without food, but without water he goes mad. An Italian from New York's Bowery named Zip Cepeglia got to be the acknowledged master of getting down and getting the liquid back. Food was almost gone; Richards, the pigeon man, was eating bird seed since the pigeons wouldn't need it any more.

By midmorning the artillery had a chance to try to square the account for the day before. An American pilot was flying along the front, and if he couldn't find the pocket, he did see a German concentration just north of them about to attack. He dropped the flare signal calling for fire, and this time the gunners got it right and blew the attack apart. It cheered the men and they had enough left to beat off an attack themselves in the afternoon, but they were faint from hunger.

Through October 6 the 275 men who were left lay in their holes, keeping below the machine-gun fire, and eating the last scraps of food. In one hole they were licking out the last specks of salt and pepper in the bottom of a condiment can. Planes flew over and dropped real food, but it fell outside the perimeter, to the delight and nourishment of the surrounding Germans.

They didn't know it, but they had it made. A couple of hundred men dug in on a hillside in the Argonne weren't the whole front. To both the left and the right of them things had been happening. Those two old pros, the First and Second Divisions, had gone back in and thrown a left, then a right punch which was tearing the whole German line loose from its moorings. If the enemy was going to get to Whittlesey's starved ragamuffins they had to do it now or never, because the time was coming to pull out. But inside the pocket they didn't know. Instead, early on the morning of the seventh Whittlesey started Private Abe Krotoshinsky toward the rear in a forlorn hope of getting a message through. Krotoshinsky took two men with him; by midmorning they were back, one wounded, with the word that Krotoshinsky was probably dead.

If it was hard to get out, one man did succeed in getting in. Private Lowell Hollingshead had squirmed out after some of that food the planes had dropped. The Germans got him, gave him a cigarette and a bowl of soup, then sent him back in with a note for Whittlesey. It was a polite little request that the Americans surrender and even said, "We are appealing to your humane sentiments to stop." It was a great chance for Whittlesey to get a line into the history books—something like John Paul Jones' "I have not yet begun to fight" or Tony MacAulliffe's "Nuts!" at Bastogne—but the major was a conservative New England type not given to phrasemaking. Or perhaps he was just too damn tired. In any event, he simply grinned and then ordered the men to pull in the two white panels put out for the airplanes to spot, before the Boche drew any faulty conclusions from them. The Germans reconsidered the "humane sentiments" and put in a flame-thrower attack that lasted until dark.

Just as the cold October dark was falling, Abe Krotoshinsky, alive, after all, was down behind a tree, catching his breath for another dash south through the woods. Suddenly he heard voices, then words—English words—and he was inside the American lines. He was a little, pale guy, not one you'd pick to stand up under a physical beating, but he gulped down a cup of coffee, grabbed a can of corned beef to eat on the way, and started walking back north to lead the relief to the pocket.

He might just as well have gotten himself some rest. At almost the same time Company B of the 307th was pushing north, pressing the retreating Germans so as to get through to Whittlesey. Their Lieutenant Tillman fell into a shell hole in the darkness, found it inhabited, and in due time discovered that the inhabitant was an American. They took the lieutenant to Whittlesey, a few minutes later Krotoshinsky came up with his gang, and the Lost Battalion—which always after preferred to call itself simply the Surrounded Battalion—was relieved. There were 194 men left who didn't have to be sent to a hospital. General Alexander came in person the next morning and someone asked if he wanted Whittlesey brought to him. "By no means," said the general, "I'll go to him," and so saying walked down the road to tell the major he was now a lieutenant colonel.

It wasn't a terribly important fight, nothing like John Buford's dismounted cavalrymen, say, holding off A. P. Hill's corps on the morning of the first day at Gettysburg, but what they did no one could have done any better. The country has never forgotten it, and the men who did the fighting never forgot it. One in particular never forgot: Whittlesey. They gave him the Congressional Medal of Honor and made much of him, but something ate at him. No one ever figured out exactly what it was, perhaps he felt that that terrible artillery barrage that had killed his own men was somehow his fault. In any event, in 1921 he sailed for a vacation in Cuba. On the first night out he went up on deck and threw himself over the rail.

Chapter Ten

"THE WAR THUS COMES TO AN END"

ON TO 11 A.M., NOVEMBER 11, 1918

FOR a nation that hadn't been in the habit of mixing into other nations' business the late summer of 1918 brought another shock. Not only were we involved in a war in western Europe, but Americans read in the papers that our troops were going ashore in such unlikely spots as Archangel in northern Russia and in Siberia. The ordinary citizen had only the vaguest notion of what these forays were all about, and small wonder, because neither did Washington. As for Archangel, the British had peddled the notion that if troops were landed there, the Bolsheviks would flee in confusion, and somehow a new eastern front to torment the Germans could be established.

In truth, the British were not especially optimistic about a new eastern front, but they did think the Red Revolution might be whipped and the Whites restored. The eastern front was simply frosting on the cake to get around Woodrow Wilson, who'd said he was against any armed intervention in Russia's affairs.

The Siberian matter was even more complicated. The American army was dispatching two regiments to Vladivostok under a dutiful, conscientious major general named William Graves, and he had a memo from Wilson himself which set forth his task. In cooperation with small British and Japanese units, he was supposed to keep the Siberian railroads open until Czechoslovakian forces could be evacuated through Vladivostok.

What the Czechs were doing in Siberia is a story in itself, a minor epic of the war. Anxious to form their own nation, they had fought with the Russians against the Austro-Hungarians, and when the Czarist army went under, the Czech Legion wanted to go right on fighting. Moreover, the would-be government of would-be Czechoslovakia was anxious to keep the force in being as something to bargain with at the peace table. Accordingly, the Czechs were to march

RUSSIAN ADVENTURE: American troops were landed at Archangel and Vladivostok to set up a new eastern front and protect the Trans-Siberian Railroad

to Vladivostok, move to Europe by ship, and continue the fight on the Western Front. It would have been a difficult maneuver in a revolution-torn country, at best, and it became more complicated when the Reds decided that they preferred the Czechs disarmed. The Czech Legion—some 60,000 men in all—shook off their disarmers and promptly began a fighting retreat along the line of the Siberian railway.

Nor were the Czechs the only outsiders in Siberia nor our only reason for being there. No one had mentioned it to poor Graves, but the State Department was worried sick that while the Reds and the Whites were bleeding one another to death, the Japanese were going to take over Siberia. The Japs, in fact, had precisely this in mind, and when Graves arrived he noted—though he was a man slow to think badly of others—that the Japs did have a great many more troops than the token forces he'd been led to expect. Finally, the British were on the scene laboring, as at Archangel, under the delusion that the Bolsheviks were a rabble capable of being dispersed by a show of force. They were busily arming the Whites and giving them British uniforms. A good many peasants, hard up for clothes, joined the

Whites long enough to get a nice warm British overcoat and then deserted to the Reds. To head the White array, the British were supporting a dim-witted Russian admiral named Kolchak who proved a constant disappointment to them.

The Japanese also had a pair of puppet candidates in the works—two cutthroats named Kalmikoff and Semenoff. These two led groups little better than robber bands. Officially, they were supposed to be raising troops for the White forces, but their methods were so brutal that they probably did the Reds more good than otherwise. Even the kindly Graves observed: "I . . . met for the first time the notorious murderer, robber, and cutthroat Kalmikoff. He was the worst scoundrel I ever saw or heard of and I seriously doubt . . . if a crime could be found that Kalmikoff had not committed."[1] Graves found Semenoff slightly less odious on the grounds that he committed no murders personally, but simply ordered others to perform them.

Into this stewpot of intrigue tramped the two American regiments. They scattered inland to guard the Trans-Siberian railroad, had far more unpleasantness with the Japanese—who wanted arms shipments to go to their personal favorites—than with the Bolsheviks, and the last of them didn't get home until 1920. Their box score shows that the Czechs got out of Siberia safely and the Japanese did not get the area, but the Bolsheviks did. The additional regiment sent to Archangel saw a good deal more fighting and suffered a total of 2,000 casualties from all causes, including disease, before they were withdrawn in 1919.

As far as the outcome of the war on the Western Front was concerned, these few thousand men couldn't have been more out of it if they'd stayed home in the States, but the expeditions were going to be terribly important to what came later. For one thing, our relations with the new Russia were off to a bad start and in the years to come the Reds would get a lot of propaganda mileage out of our intervention in this affair. More important, it made people back home nervous. We were clearly going to win the war in Europe, but now our troops had been engaged against the Bolsheviks, and it was worrisome. A shadow began to fall across the victory that hadn't even come yet.

That peace was coming was clear enough. On October 1, Bulgaria left the war, then on the sixth came the Austrian note asking for peace terms, and on the seventh the first German wireless message: "The German Government requests the President of the United States . . . to take steps for the restoration of peace, to notify all belligerents of this request and invite them to delegate plenipotentiaries for the purpose of taking up negotiations. . . . The German Government accepts, as a basis for the peace negotiations, the program laid down by the President of the United States in his message to Congress of January 8, 1918." They referred, of course, to the Fourteen Points.

The Germans had seen it coming since August 8 when three French corps, one Canadian, one Australian, and one British, had smashed into their lines all along the front with enough tanks behind the punch to keep it moving. German Major General Erich Ludendorff, a man of superb military sense and very little of any other kind, knew weight when he saw it and called it "the black day" of the war for the German Army. Even the Kaiser concluded that a time would have to be chosen soon to open peace negotiations. If he really hoped to negotiate, he was mistaken. Wilson didn't dignify the note with a personal reply, but fired back an answer through Secretary of State Lansing telling the Germans they'd have to withdraw their troops from all foreign soil if they wanted an armistice. Just as promptly France, Britain, and Italy got off a memo to Wilson in which they declared that they wanted no part of an armistice in which the German Army kept its arms.

As though to lend force to the Allied message, a German submarine sank the British steamer *Leinster* in the Irish Sea with a loss of 450 lives. Accordingly, when the Germans sent a second note to say they accepted Wilson's terms, he whipped out a far stiffer answer, mentioning the *Leinster* sinking, and making it good and clear that the Allies felt they had the military situation well in hand. If Germany wanted an armistice, she could lay down her arms.

Back at Foch's headquarters, in October, the situation did look in hand. The Germans were falling back on the French and British fronts and Pershing was preparing a new push in the Argonne. To the men moving up to do the pushing, the situation didn't look quite so rosy. The First Division was going up and though to a query about what corps they belonged to they could still shout back, "We don't belong to any corps—we go to the corps that needs us most."—they were moving into a fresh battlefield with new graves and dead horses along the road. The division historian noted that their mood was "grim resolution." As a member of the Rainbow said of the same spectacle when they went into the line a little later, "The numerous dead did not add to . . . morale."

It was to be a varsity affair this time. On the right of the line were the Fourth and the Eightieth divisions which had been in the drive since it started. Then came the Third—the heroes of the Marne—and next the Thirty-second which had done well for Mangin at Juvigny. On the left, the First plus the Twenty-eighth and Seventy-seventh were holding down their old stands in and around the Argonne Forest itself. Thus this time there could be no excuses. These were some of the best we had, and if they couldn't go through, then the American army might really be as poor as the Germans liked to claim it was.

The Meuse-Argonne front was no longer quite the whole show. Elsewhere on the front the Twenty-seventh Division and the Thirtieth had been lent out to the British. On September 29 they jumped off south of Cambrai and punched a neat hole in the Hindenburg line where the Germans were hoping to hold on until winter closed down the front. Farther south, just to the west of the Argonne Forest, the French attack was stalled by a nasty piece of high ground called Blanc Mont. Having promised the French American help for the sector, Pershing did not short change them; he sent the Second Division.

Up went the Second, over the limestone countryside that gives Blanc Mont its name, and found the sector so lively that the very trenches from which they were supposed to jump off were still hiding German snipers. Ahead lay an open plain with a woods, the Bois de la Vipère, in the center, and beyond, Blanc Mont. When the Mont fell, the whole German position west of the Argonne would go, the scheme for pinching out the forest itself would work, and, incidentally, the Lost Battalion, still trapped at that time, could be relieved.

Long, long ago—four months back at Belleau Wood—the Second Division would have wasted time on the Bois de la Vipère and the German artillery would have cut them up while they wasted it. They were wiser now; the Second's Marines would attack left of the Bois, the infantry regiments on the right, and they'd converge once they got past it instead of fighting through the thickets. At dawn of October 3 they jumped off—the attack orders got up to the line so late that one battalion commander never did read his until after he reached the objective. The artillery preparation was fierce and short. And there were French tanks to help clean out the machine guns.

Forward they went, through the barbed wire with pieces of Frenchmen in blue still tangled in it from old attacks. French divisions on either side couldn't get moving, machine-gun fire began to pour in from the flanks as well as from ahead. Lejeune, commanding the Second, was so mad he offered to resign. Some men went down, shot in the back, but the rest drove past the Bois de la Vipère, came together, and went up the hill. About noon they were on Blanc Mont to stay, although the Germans contested the decision in a series of stiff counterattacks. The American Thirty-sixth Division came up to help out, and the two of them pushed on toward the village of Saint-Étienne before the Second Division was pulled out of the line to replace its 5,000 casualties and report back to American First Army.

It was five-twenty-five in the morning of October 4 when the second big Meuse-Argonne push started, and it had hardly left its jump-off line when the veterans knew they were in trouble. The Germans had strengthened their line during the lull. From across the Meuse artillery flogged the Fourth Division so badly that those excellent soldiers were not able to hold even the small gains they made. The Eightieth made it to the Bois des Ogons, but along the rest of the line it looked as though no one was going to make any headway. The artillery fire from the front and the flanks was just too heavy. For an infantryman, artillery fire has a specific meaning. When it starts to fall, he drops to the ground, but as it comes down, even if it doesn't kill him, the concussion lifts him up and then slams him back down again. No matter how good a man he is, he may wet his pants or mess them and, according to his belief, cry, pray, or die on the spot of a heart attack.

Like the Second, though, the First had learned something from all the blood it had shed, and the lesson for today was: small groups of men scurrying forward under the control of noncoms or junior officers do much better against machine guns and artillery than large groups of men advancing in fairly regular lines. Infiltration is the technical expression, and the Germans had been using it since the spring, but it needs the coolest kind of veterans to make it go, and up until now we simply hadn't had the men to do it. If anyone could do it, though, the First could, and when artillery smashed up the first mass attack, handfuls of men kept going. By dark the 16th Infantry had slithered its way as far as Fléville, making a three-mile-long finger poked into the enemy positions. On their right the 26th Infantry was up to the Exermont ravine where the Thirty-fifth Division had taken such a pounding and if nobody had gotten as far as orders said they were to go the first day, at least we were moving.

Next day they fought their way across the Exermont ravine in spite of German guns slamming at them from the heights on the far side, and went all the way to Arietal farm. From there, the orders said, a patrol had to push out all the way to Hill 269, because the Thirty-second Division was supposed to be there. The 26th Infantry didn't have the faintest idea where the Thirty-second Division was, but orders being orders, a sergeant took a patrol over to Hill 269. When he got there, he didn't find the Thirty-second, he didn't find Germans, he didn't find anything. Like the Remagen Bridge of the Second World War, we'd just gotten for free a position which should have cost a dirty fight. There were a few Germans on the eastern end of the hill and the Thirty-second was still far south, but the patrol took over their half of the hill and in due time the First scrounged for some men to support them. The infantry being otherwise engaged, a battalion of engineers—not really designed for this sort of work—was dug up and sent over to sit on the hill, a piece of high ground in the rear of the German line of resistance. During the next two days the Germans pulled back to handle the hole in their front and the American line ran straight from Fléville over to the Meuse.

Still the problem of the flanks: fire pouring down from across the Meuse and from the heights of the Argonne. Obviously, the attack had to be extended to the other side of the Meuse—and troops were brought up for the job—and the Argonne had to be pinched out. For the latter job the Eighty-second Division was brought up and slid in between the First and the Pennsylvanians of the Twenty-eighth who'd been making no headlines but doing such a job that their General Muir was going to wind up commanding a corps.

A strange outfit, this Eighty-second Division. It was really draft stuff—the All-American they called it; it had started with Alabama, Georgia, and Tennessee men and was then beefed up with draftees from all over the place. A lot of them couldn't read or write English.

Brought into the line, they'd pushed west from the First's bridge-head, across the Aire River, and straight for the Argonne heights. In getting over the water and up among the hills one outfit—G Company, 2d Battalion, 328th Infantry—had lost its commanding officer and as it tried to push into the hills around Châtel-Chéhery, it was being messed up by machine-gun fire from a hill to the left.

A patrol was put out to deal with the guns. It was run by an acting sergeant named Early and he had three corporals and 17 men with him. They went straight south to try to come up the hill from the other side. A few men went down from machine guns, then they ran into two Germans wearing Red Cross arm bands and took them in tow. Through the woods they went, and suddenly out into a clearing where some 75 Germans were waiting for their major to tell them to move. Spread out in a skirmish line, Early and his boys looked so for-midable that the Germans immediately threw up their hands and shouted "*Kamerad!*" Not so the machine gunners in the hills around the clearing. Formerly engaged in peppering the Eighty-second's men to the north, they slewed their guns around and sprayed the newcomers. Before they got through only eight Americans—Corporal Alvin Cullum York and seven privates—were on their feet.

The Germans shouldn't really have had to take on York. He was a six-foot, flame-haired mountain man from Pall Mall, Tennessee, and as a youngster he had been a big man for moonshine, rough-and-tumble fighting, and gambling. His mother had kept after him to join the church, though, and come 1915 he'd signed up with the Church of Christ in Christian Union. Not one to do things by halves, he went so thoroughly religious that he got to be second elder, and when the draft came along, the congregation agreed with him that the Lord had said, "Thou shalt not kill," and meant it. He ran through three draft-board appeals, had them denied, and then went down to camp in Georgia.

Alvin York was looking to get a noncombatant job where he could stay out of draft trouble and still keep the Lord's admonitions. We've had such conscientious objectors in every war—they make the bravest of hospital corpsmen—and York might have wound up there if a Captain Danforth hadn't observed that he was sure death with a rifle. Rather than let such a shooter get away, Danforth started arguing the Bible with him, quoting John and Ezekiel and Luke's "he that hath no sword, let him sell his garment and buy one," and "blessed are the peacemakers." York took it all in, then went home on leave, knelt down on the side of one of his Tennessee hills, and prayed. Somewhere during the prayer the Lord said it was all right.

Now he was in a hollow of ground in a French forest, his own men flat on their bellies to avoid the machine gunners and his prisoners on theirs for the same reason. York knelt down again, this time in the mud, raised his rifle, and went to work. Every time a machine gunner put his head up, the corporal drilled him. The gunners couldn't stop him; they were shooting a little warily for fear of hitting their own men.

Suddenly down the hill came some of the Germans, bayonets fixed, a lieutenant at the head, bent on doing with the cold steel what they couldn't do with bullets. York went right on shooting them down, then dropped his rifle as his last clip ran out. He said later that he didn't permit himself to cuss when the last bullet was expended. Instead, he took out his .45 automatic and went back at it.

He must have been a wonderful shot because the .45 is a weapon designed to shoot large holes in desperate men, but it's not worth a hoot for accuracy. York made it accurate; the Germans kept going down, the prisoner major got flighty and called on everyone to surrender. York lined them up, grouped the major and a couple of other men around him to keep the snipers from getting ideas, and started marching them out of the forest. On the way they picked up a few more prisoners, then ran into Americans who were about to shoot when York called on them to stop. Then they counted the prisoners— there were 132 of them and when they went back to the hollow there were 25 dead Germans to add to the bag.

Pershing called him "the greatest civilian soldier of the war," and Foch said, "What you did was the greatest thing accomplished by any private soldier in all the armies of Europe." They promoted him sergeant, gave him a Congressional Medal of Honor, and when he finally got back to the States without a scratch on him the members of the New York Stock Exchange carried him around the floor of their august institution on their shoulders. He could have traded on his reputation and gone into vaudeville, but he wouldn't. Instead, he went back to Pall Mall, back to farming, and back to a girl he'd known for years, and raised money for a school so the hill people wouldn't grow up as uneducated as he'd been. During the Second World War, the Army used him to talk to boys who thought the Lord didn't want them to fight. The fanciest statement he ever made about it all was, "I wanted to do the best I could."

On the same day as York was making himself a reputation, the move to get all that German artillery off the Meuse heights at the eastern end of the line started. The French, east of the river, attacked, and the American Thirty-third Division, which had been drawn up along the river since the start of the drive in September, was ordered to move across. For some reason the Illinois boys were talented with bridges. They had pushed little ones across Forges Swamp at the beginning of the offensive and now they got two big ones—one 120 feet long, the other 156 feet long—across the Meuse in spite of the fact that they had to be built under artillery fire. The infantry whipped across and by dark they'd cleared Consenvoie.

Unfortunately the results were not going to be very dramatic. The terrain so far had been bad enough—rolling hills and woods—but the whole front was now up to the main hill line and attacking was going to be slow and expensive. The line slipped forward enough for us to join up with the French at Grand-Pré in the gap of the Argonne Forest, but that was about it. In the opinion of the distinguished British historian Cyril Falls, who has no reason to argue the American case, we were fighting in the toughest terrain on the entire front, but Pershing was in no mood for excuses. On October 11 he exploded. Henceforth there would be two American armies—the First west of the Meuse commanded by Hunter Liggett, the Second east of the river under Robert Bullard. Other men moved up to take over the vacant corps they'd commanded and as a reminder of the price of failure, George Cameron, who'd had 5th Corps, was reassigned to take over the Fourth Division, for not going ahead faster. Since the AEF had been in France there'd been Blois—a general reassignment center for officers who failed to give satisfaction. From here on out, though, generals would be Bloised in profusion. With the British and French going much faster on the northern end of the front— it was ground the Germans were not quite so dead set to hold— Pershing, now army group commander, was going to have results or else.

For the rest of the month they chopped away at the line along the hills—to the north the so-called Kriemhilde Stellung—and although every division that got a crack at it claims to have broken it, none of them really did. They each took a bite and took their losses, and when October ran out, the last section of the line was still there. The commanders of the Third and Fifth divisions had been relieved; over in the Second Army General Clarence Edwards, who'd commanded the Yankee Division from the beginning, lost his job and there was wrath in Boston. Even Pershing was collecting a few lumps. On October 21 French Premier Clemenceau wrote Foch complaining that the American armies were moving too slowly and putting the blame on Pershing: ". . . thanks to his invincible obstinacy, he has won out against you as well as against your immediate subordinates. To go over all this again can only lead to useless regrets." It was Clemenceau's notion that the solution lay in asking Wilson for Pershing's relief. Foch ignored the suggestion and sent back an answer in which he excused the Americans on the ground of inexperienced staffs and "particularly difficult terrain." Excuses or no, it was only too true that we had very little to show for all the attrition of the past month. It was on the very edge of paying off, but none knew that—for the moment we looked bad.

One man who did come out of the month with a distinction of sorts was a Captain Frank Williams who, like York, was in the Eighty-second Division. In modern parlance, Williams might be called the fastest gun on Hill 182. Prewar, he'd been a sheriff in Wyoming and Montana and a performer with Buffalo Bill's Wild West Show. Come October 1918, and the captain was reconnoitering a hill north of St. Juvin. It was a foggy day and he didn't see the five Germans and their one American prisoner until they were close to him. In the grand manner of a sheriff coming down the main street after the bad man, Williams walked toward them, hands empty, pistol in its holster on his hip. The empty hands must have put the Germans off guard; at any rate, Williams got close, then drew fast to gun down four of them before the fifth surrendered.

Well enough, but the front as a whole was stalled. On the heights from Grand-Pré over to the Meuse, the tired divisions reorganized, brought up artillery, and got ready to attack again on November. 1.

A third German peace note reached Wilson on October 20 but

it didn't advance matters much. It said that the German Government hadn't really meant it was going to evacuate any territory, but simply wanted to sit down and talk about it. Moreover, it noted that there had been constitutional reforms and plans for an extension of the vote in Germany, so that now there was really a new German government of the most pacific nature.

In the States no one took a new government that still had the Kaiser at the head of it very seriously and, besides, there was something much more immediate to worry about. The influenza epidemic that had been creeping over from Europe since September had reached plague proportions.

By early October there were 1,695 new cases in New York City in one day alone and no one knew what was causing them. In desperation newspapers published the "3 C's for influenza—Clean Mouths, Clean Skins, and Clean Clothes"—but people kept right on getting sick. Some thought the disease spread in crowds—hence theater and working hours were staggered and shops closed early to cut down congestion. Then movie houses were closed altogether. The New York Telephone Company had so many employees out sick that it published ads apologizing for the deficiencies in its service. In Philadelphia the death toll ran so high that a coffin shortage developed. No one knew a cure, but Gude's Pepto-Mangan, "The Red Blood Builder," advertised that their stuff would fortify one against the ailment, while both Borden's Malted Milk and Phez "Pure Juice of the Loganberry" allowed that they could make the unfortunate more comfortable during the course of the illness. In all, there were nearly half a million Americans dead before the plague blew itself out in 1919.

Wilson had Secretary of State Lansing send the Germans an answer to their note that said no one had much faith in the new German Government and "feeling that the whole peace of the world depends now on plain speaking and straightforward action, the President deems it his duty to say, without any attempt to soften what may seem harsh words, that the nations of the world do not and cannot trust the word of those who have hitherto been the masters of German policy, and to point out once more that in concluding peace and attempting to undo the infinite injuries and injustices of this war the Government of the United States cannot deal with any but veritable representatives of the German people who have been assured of a genuine constitutional standing as the rulers of Germany."

In other words, the Kaiser had to go—but a lot of the other peace conditions were still up in the air and a great many people unhappy. At home the Republicans thought it was all too mild and, with Teddy Roosevelt making the loudest noises, were demanding something pretty close to unconditional surrender. In England the Admiralty wanted it clearly understood that the German Navy had to go. In France Clemenceau was concerned about the German Army's renewing the war after an armistice respite.

Curiously, the British and the French wanted the stiffest terms and at the same time were most concerned that Germany might break off negotiations and go on fighting. Actually, the politicians wanted stiff terms and the generals terms that would get the war over. When Foch, Haig, and Pershing met to discuss the matter, it was Pershing with the fresh, young army who laid down the hardest conditions. Across the line, in Berlin, the government of Liberal Chancellor Prince Max of Baden, which had been brought in to make peace, was getting tired of its generals. Ludendorff was let out, another note simply saying that the Germans awaited "proposals for an armistice" went to Washington, and then everyone sat around wondering how to tell the Kaiser that it was time for him to abdicate.

If the Kaiser remained dense about abdicating, it is hard to see that members of his last government were much less so. They knew that Wilhelm was through, they could even perceive that because of the supply situation they were in no shape to go on fighting the war, but the plain fact that the German Army was being whipped in battle does not really seem to have registered. The troops at the front knew it, infantry morale had been bad since midsummer, but in the German rear the old myth still held on: the army was unbeatable. If the war was being lost something else had to be the matter. Later Adolf Hitler would find the myth useful.

On the night of October 31 the men of the Seventy-eighth Division waited at the western end of the line and it was so quiet that a rumor came down that the war was over. "Yeah," said a rifleman, and pointed toward the German positions "Over there." Then another word came down—all seven American divisions were going over at five-thirty A.M.

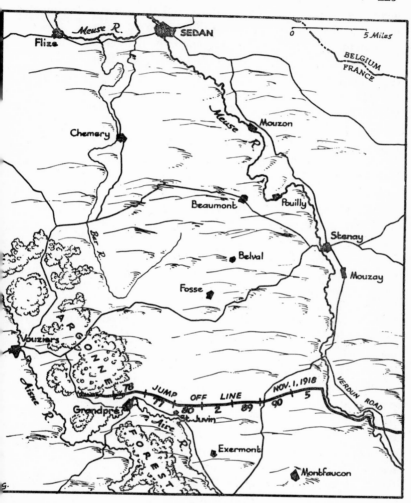

THE MEUSE-ARGONNE DRIVE, Part II: The battle line of November 1 and the ground over which the Americans traveled up to 11 A.M., November 11, 1918

It was cold and damp as they moved into the jump-off positions. At 3:30 A.M. the heartening sound of artillery pounding the lines across the way started. At five-thirty it was barely light, the men were stiff in the miserable weather, and there was a fog on the ground as they moved out. Seven divisions went forward.

From the start this was clearly going to be different. The machine guns were as bad as ever, but the enemy's artillery didn't come down quite so profusely as before. The pounding the Germans had taken through October was about to pay off. It went best in the center where the Second Division, which everyone knew would do well because it always did, had been put with the Eighty-ninth Division, Kansans and Missourians, to make up the 5th Corps. Charles Summerall, a brilliant artilleryman who'd commanded the First Division, had the corps, and when they moved out they romped. Over the hills and through the patches of wood they went, and by noon a veteran Marine noted that the enemy was in "full retreat." By dark they were five miles into the crumbling German lines.

On the flanks it was rougher, but per orders the Fifth Division managed to lunge forward, then turn to face the Meuse. On the left the Seventy-seventh and the Seventy-eighth barely got past their jump-off lines, but the enemy obviously couldn't hold long with the bulge in the middle of his front.

On November 2 the left flank and the center had pushed up toward Fosse. Only the right was stalled by a desperate German effort not to get peeled away from the Meuse, which was about the only defense line they had to fall back on.

When evening came the Second Division took note of the light opposition and remembered that old Stonewall Jackson's foot cavalry is part of the American military tradition. The men had been going for two days, they were tired, but General Lejeune figured they weren't through yet. He threw his two infantry regiments out on the road, moving them forward in marching order, long columns of twos, and they tramped off into the night. When stray machine gunners opened on them, the nearest company simply moved off the road, went into skirmish line, and cleaned them out. By midnight they were into Fosse.

On the third the front moved up again, and at dark the center of the line was facing the woods north of Belval. The Second Division simply called out its 9th Infantry and told them to get on the road and start marching again. Out they went through the cold rain, right through the woods they'd have had to fight for in daylight, and then captured a farm full of Germans who felt so secure so far in the rear that they had lights on. By daybreak the 9th had gone four miles and was nearly into Beaumont.

The American left kept moving, too—the Seventy-eighth Division came over a rise to see a French village hung with towels and sheets as white flags and thought the war was over, but it was only Frenchmen trying to keep the remains of their homes from being barraged. By the night of the fourth we were finally all the way north of the Argonne. From its top the line ran down to Pouilly, then along the west of the Meuse where the Germans were still holding. The whole axis of the attack was swinging: instead of driving north we were pushing east to get to the banks of the Meuse and then over.

Besides fighting a war and arranging a peace, there was also a national congressional election to be faced on November 4, and Wilson's political advisors were worried about it. The 1916 presidential victory had been a squeaker. Worse, it had been a victory for a very loose Democratic coalition of southerners, western farmers, and northern workers, and now that coalition showed signs of coming apart. The West thought the price of wheat was too low, the North had no enthusiasm for wartime prohibition. Then, too, off-year elections are usually hard on the party in power, and finally, a wartime government always has to do a lot of unpopular things such as drafting men and raising taxes.

Clearly the Democratic cause needed a boost, and from a cold-minded, vote-getting point of view, the best thing Wilson could have done would have been to out-Republican the Republicans. Had he wrapped himself in the American flag and shouted "On to Berlin" and "Hang the Kaiser," he might have carried the Congress for his party. Since nothing could have been more out of character, he went right ahead with his own sort of peace negotiations, based on the Fourteen Points, which were a deal too complicated to get the average voter stirred up.

Finally, on October 24, Wilson was persuaded to release a statement asking the country to vote in a Democratic Congress if it wanted a proper Wilsonian peace. Later, second guessers said that the statement so angered people that it lost the election all by itself. This is nonsense; the election was pretty well lost before Wilson ever opened his mouth. What the statement did do, though, was to make the Fourteen Points such a thoroughly partisan matter that when the League of Nations finally did come before Congress, the Republicans had almost no choice but to vote against it.

The people went to the polls and voted a Republican Congress, and the Democrats had to take what solace they could from the fact that a charmer named Al Smith had emerged on the national scene by eking out a win for the governorship of New York.

General John J. Pershing looked at his battle map on November 5 and could see that the First Army was almost up to the Meuse all along the line. Northernmost was the 1st Corps, and just left of its boundary lay Sedan. Through Sedan ran the last important lateral railway the Germans had; moreover, the city was a symbol, the site of the great German victory over the French in the Franco-Prussian War of 1870. Pershing wanted the First Army to capture the symbol. True, it lay within the territory of the French Fourth Army, but Pershing asked their General Maistre if he'd mind if the First nudged up his way a little and Maistre said he wouldn't.

Accordingly, the order went down to the 1st Corps—now the Rainbow and Seventy-seventh divisions:

"1. General Pershing desires that the honor of entering Sedan should fall to the First American Army. He has every confidence that the troops of the 1st Corps, assisted on their right by the 5th Corps, will enable him to realize this design.

"2. In transmitting the foregoing message, your attention is invited to the favorable opportunity now existing, for pressing our advantage throughout the night."

It was signed by Liggett, commanding the First Army, but before it went out it was amended. The First Army's chief of staff, Brigadier General Hugh Drum, took a look at it and had the First Army's operations officer, Colonel George Catlett Marshall, add at the end of the order, "Boundaries will not be considered binding."

Years later some people would try to make Marshall solely responsible for the change, but since he was a colonel and Drum a brigadier general, it would appear that Drum must take responsibility. Moreover, all he seems to have meant by it was that the French

Fourth Army had been alerted to Americans moving into their sector.

A good deal more could be read into it, though, and there is an old saying in the military that if an order *can* be misunderstood, it will be. When General Summerall at 5th Corps saw it, he decided that "assist" meant everything he could do. The divisions involved lay thus: on the north, the Rainbow and then the Seventy-seventh, then the First and the Second. Summerall promptly yanked the First Division out of line and told it to head straight north for Sedan.

The First, dead on its feet, exhausted, its men collapsing along the way, got out on five roads headed north and marched. The result was one of the most magnificent foul ups in the history of the American army. Straight across the Seventy-seventh Division's rear they tramped, disrupting supply lines and starting rumors that the Germans had somehow gotten in behind us. Then across the Rainbow's rear they went, tearing things up until an officer of the 168th Iowa got out on the road and told them to stop.

"Hell," said one of the First's battalion commanders, "this is the First Division, regular army. Forward, march!" And on they went to cap it all by capturing the Rainbow's General Douglas MacArthur, who somehow looked German to them because of his peculiarly floppy cap. There are those who claim that MacArthur never forgave George Marshall for the indignity.

All night they marched, and by morning they were closing Sedan and staggering with fatigue. By that time generals in profusion were flying about the front trying to bring some order out of the mess. The French, as Pershing should have realized, were damned if they were going to let anyone but the French recapture Sedan; the First and the Rainbow were pulled back to the old army boundary. Then the Rainbow was put in charge of all troops in its area—regardless of their division—until people could be put back where they belonged.

If the Germans had attacked during the confusion they might have smashed three divisions, but they didn't, and in the end Pershing wrote, "Under normal conditions the action of the officer or officers responsible for this movement of the First Division directly across the zones of action of two other divisions could not have been overlooked, but the splendid record of that unit and the approach of the end of hostilities suggested leniency."

Which may have been just as well for Pershing—after all, sending an American army into a French army's territory simply for the grandstand play of being first into Sedan had been his notion in the first place.

Through four years of war the German home front had held up magnificently. Later on Adolf Hitler would claim that it was the collapse of the civilians that did in the armed forces. The claim isn't true. The bad army morale had been common knowledge since midsummer of 1918. Now another branch of the armed forces was going to crack. Plans had been made in the German Fleet to steam out for one last, grand showdown battle with the British. The word got out and the sailors weren't having any. They didn't mutiny in the usual way, with officers taken hostage or killed, but simply refused to perform their duties in a cause that seemed to them lost. The revolt spread to the civilians only when sailors went ashore at Kiel, a city full of militant trade-unionists. There was a meeting in a city park, some 20,000 gathering to hear speeches. Even then the cry was not, "Stop the war," but "Long live the Republic," and "Down with the Kaiser."

To Prince Max in Berlin no words could have been more frightening. He was a liberal, but he was a prince. What was now in danger was not the war, but an entire system of government. The Kaiser might have to go, but possibly there was still time to avoid an outright German republic. Max already had a note from Lansing telling him that Foch had been empowered to receive German armistice representatives. To Foch went a message: "The German Government would be happy if, in the interest of humanity, the arrival of the German delegation before the Allied front might cause a provisional suspension of arms." The wireless message added that the leader of the peace delegation would be Mathias Erzberger, a Catholic leader of the Centrist Party. Foch sent back instructions for the rendezvous.

Erzberger, with his round, normally cheerful face, his pince-nez and his stand-up collar, looked more like a prosperous habitué of a Bavarian beer hall than a peace negotiator. He had scarcely started driving toward the French lines before his car skidded on a turn, smashed into a house, the car behind it piled up, and both vehicles were ruined. The convoy went on in the three remaining vehicles.

Lines of retreating German soldiers were moving back along the roads, and it was dark when they crossed into the French lines at La Capelle, forty-five miles east of Cambrai. There they were put onto a train, and with shades drawn traveled through the night to find themselves in the morning in the forest of Compiègne with Foch's train drawn up on an adjoining track. The Germans were escorted to the Allied commander's car.

Foch opened the discussion coldly, asking them why they were there, and Erzberger replied that he had to come to hear peace proposals. Foch replied that he had none to make. Erzberger said he understood that Foch was empowered to make known the armistice provisions. Foch said he could if they were asking for an armistice. Erzberger said they were, and they got down to business.

Now on November 7, Roy Howard of the United Press was in Brest to pick up transportation back to the States. Here he found Rear Admiral Wilson, in charge of the naval base, in possession of the red-hot dope that the war was over. The admiral said that it was official, that he had had it straight from the United States embassy in Paris, and he promptly published the news on the base. Over Howard came the giddy sense of having a beat, and after wrestling with the question of whether he should send a peace story on the admiral's word, he finally wrote out the cable. The censors on the base were out celebrating the peace, an ensign had the story sent out, and at one in the afternoon of November 7 the United States went wild.

Sirens and factory whistles blew, and church bells started to ring. Offices emptied as crowds piled into the streets until Fifth Avenue in New York was solid humanity curb to curb all the three-mile way from Washington Square to the Plaza Hotel. Those who stayed indoors showered the people below with ticker tape or any other paper ready to hand. At the Metropolitan Opera House a rehearsal of Verdi's *La Forza del Destino* was underway when the diva Geraldine Farrar burst in, trailing red, white, and blue streamers, to rush on stage and sing "The Star-Spangled Banner" accompanied by assorted singers, stagehands, and orchestra members. From a window overlooking Broadway and Forty-second Street a visiting French soprano not only intoned the American anthem, but threw in *La Marseillaise* for good measure. On a balcony of the Knickerbocker Hotel a mysterious gentleman appeared and spent the afternoon happily waving an Italian flag back and forth. Men in uniform ignored the restrictions on drinking, and a number of civilians found it particularly festive to smash their own derby hats and then wear them that way. Someone worked up an effigy of the Kaiser with a sign, "Bad Bill—Gone to Hell" and a shopkeeper left for the day with a sign on his door, "Closed for the Kaiser's Funeral."

By suppertime the Secretary of State had queried Paris and was announcing that there was definitely no peace yet, and the papers had the correction on the streets when they could find newsboys who weren't much happier selling the peace story. Howard had made a mistake—a honey—but the real blame must lie with an army press policy which had never seen fit to take reporters into its confidence.

Back in the railway car in the forest of Compiègne, Foch laid down the armistice terms and when he got through he was clearly demanding a military surrender. Five thousand pieces of German artillery were to be turned over to the Allies, and with them 25,000 machine guns and 1,700 planes. The Allies would occupy beachheads on the east bank of the Rhine, the Germans were to evacuate all occupied territory, trucks and railway equipment were to be surrendered. All submarines and 74 warships of various types were to be handed over.

Erzberger argued stoutly for lightening the sentence—though he had orders to sign whatever he had to if necessary—but behind him time was running out. The revolution was racing through Germany, a republic was clearly coming, whether the Kaiser wanted to get out or not, and Erzberger's orders were to get a settlement while there was still something left to save.

The American First Army was nosing across the Meuse all along its front and the Second Army was pushing north. From Switzerland to the Channel, nothing much more than a handful of German machine gunners and artillerymen—whose diligence must be admired —were holding back the sweep.

On the evening of November 8 Prince Max finally got up enough nerve to telephone the Kaiser, who was at Spa with the army headquarters, and tell him it was time to abdicate. Wilhelm heard him and then said he had every intention of staying where he was. He, in fact, wanted the army chief of staff, General Paul von Hindenburg, to turn his troops around and march on the revolution. Hindenburg turned the Kaiser down flatly and told him that the army could no longer guarantee his safety in Germany. On November 9 Wilhelm was on a train bound for Holland, gone from history except for periodic pictures of the old gentleman chopping wood for exercise which appeared in the newspapers during the twenties. Before the same day was out, Prince Max had resigned; out of the defeat and the revolution had come the ill-fated German Republic.

Poor Erzberger, his government collapsing behind him, was so anxious to get the thing settled that he asked for the last session of the Compiègne armistice discussions to start at 2:15 A.M. on November 11. At five-ten in the morning, the document was signed and Erzberger asked permission to read a singularly unrepentant telegram which he was sending on to Berlin. It concluded:

The German nation, which for fifty months has defied a world of enemies, will preserve in spite of every kind of violence, its liberty and unity.

A nation of seventy million suffers but does not die.

Foch muttered *"Très bien,"* and withdrew to radio his troops that all firing would cease at 11:00 A.M.

A captain in one of the Thirty-seventh Division's infantry regiments had bedded down on the night of November 10 in the second floor of a millinery shop in the thoroughly shot-up little town of Huyss. In spite of an occasional shell, he slept so well that when a messenger from the division woke him in the morning, he had a hard time understanding the man's message:

". . . I noticed a smile on the orderly's grimy face. There was considerable noise outside, coming from the streets of the little village. It sounded to my sleep-clouded brain rather remotely like singing or cheering. I reflected that it was surely out of place in a town so near the front."[2]

Then he read the cease-fire order, and when he finally realized that the shooting was going to stop—and it seemed to him that it must be just a temporary stoppage—he was conscious only of an overwhelming desire to go back to sleep.

At the Thirty-third Division they had attacked at dawn and runners were having trouble getting the peace word to the forward units. A bugler settled it by climbing to the top of a pile of dirt, raising his instrument to his lips, and blowing Recall over and over as hard as he could.

German artillery kept pouring it in all morning as though they didn't want to be caught with any ammunition left. Men died in the shelling, but the very last of all to go died because he wanted to. He was Private Henry Gunther of the Seventy-ninth Division's 313th Infantry. He'd been busted from sergeant and since had been taking chances to get his stripes back. At just one minute of eleven he went over the top all by himself and straight for a German machine gun across the way. They called him back, the machine-gun crew waved him off, but Gunther kept on until the machine gunners finally opened and riddled him. A few minutes later it was all over, and the Germans carried him back to his own lines on a stretcher.

The American guns kept on, too, and it got to be a matter of who was going to fire the last shot. In some batteries men stood in line for a turn at the firing lanyard. In the Yankee Division one ingenious outfit tied long ropes to the lanyards of each of its four guns, 200 men got on each of the lines, and just before eleven, they all got off the last shot together.

Then it stopped. The front was silent, and when the cheering did begin most of it came from the German side of the lines. From the doughboys there was a little shouting, but most of them just stood there thinking that they really had come through alive, or lay down in the cold mud and went to sleep. A Marine kept listening for shells coming in and noted in his diary that he couldn't get used to the fact that there weren't any. Some Germans came over to bum cigarettes, but they were sent back to their trenches and a picket line established.

The last German casualty in the American sector was a Lieutenant Thoma of the 19th Uhlans, and it happened more than an hour after the Armistice. He was going forward to see if a town that lay between the lines was required by the Americans for billeting when an Eighty-ninth Division outpost that didn't have the word opened fire and wounded him. Something must have snapped in Thoma; he drew his pistol and shot himself through the head.

That night there were lights and campfires and a veritable Fourth-of-July display from the Germans, who sent signal flares of all colors bursting into the sky around the skinny new moon.

It was 2:45 A.M. Washington time when the State Department announced to the nation: "The armistice has been signed." In New York, a searchlight on the Times Tower was turned on, a few bells and sirens started, and in Times Square an assemblage of milkmen, morning-paper deliverers, and similar early risers began to celebrate. Soon the citizens who kept more normal hours were on the streets, some coming out in overcoats thrown over pajamas to get the news. By midmorning the Department of Education decided there weren't enough kids in the schools to warrant keeping them open so the young merged with the grownups outside.

On Broadway an English girl climbed a small platform, asked the crowd for quiet, and sang the Doxology: "Praise God from whom all blessings flow . . ." and followed with "America" and the British and French national anthems as encores. R. H. Macy's department store promptly announced a Victory Sale, and a judge in General Sessions court spread the joy by freeing 13 men who had pleaded guilty to minor offenses during the day. In Magistrate Frothingham's Men's Night Court a crowd appeared with an effigy of the Kaiser and requested that he be sentenced to fifty years. Frothingham replied that the most severe sentence his court was permitted was six months in the workhouse, but that he'd be glad to oblige with that.

Having been awakened in the middle of the night to receive a telephone call announcing the Armistice, Wilson had gone back to sleep, then risen in the morning to prepare a message for the nation and another for Congress. To his secretary, Tumulty, he said that he felt a lot like a Confederate soldier General John Gordon used to tell about, who'd said during that war, "I love my country and I am fightin' for my country, but if this war ends, I'll be dad-burned if I ever love another country."

A few minutes before one o'clock the President went down the White House steps—just as he had done that April evening more than a year and a half before—and drove through the streets to address a joint session of Congress. Again the avenues were crowded, but the people were of one mind now, and they cheered him as he passed.

Wilson read the Senate and the House the Armistice terms and again it was Chief Justice White, who had led the cheering for the declaration of war, who cheered the loudest now. He sat with his hands poised in front of him, ready to clap on the slightest excuse.

La Follette, who hadn't cheered that earlier speech at all and who had voted against the war, sat silent again until Wilson came to "the war thus comes to an end," and then even that rock-faced man broke down and applauded. He was joined by others, then by the people in the galleries, and it built into the greatest acclamation Washington correspondents could ever recall.

The clapping and the shouting stopped and the world was quiet after a war that had lasted four years and three months. America had been in it for a little more than nineteen months. In the whole thing some thirteen million men had died in the fighting and at least the same number of people from attendant catastrophes and disease. Of men in service, America had lost 116,516 dead in all, 53,402 of them in battle, the rest by accident and sickness. There had been 205,690 wounded.

Wilson sailed for Europe in December and the man in the street hailed him as though a savior had come. George Creel had been spreading the Fourteen Points around the world, and if they didn't actually contain something for everybody, they were the only expression of peace aims that were a break with the past, that caught the imagination. On the face of it America had never been better off —we had turned the tide of war and now the man who wanted to do right was going to Paris to solve the world's problems.

How, then, did this war, before many years, become a war that was somehow embarrassing for Americans to talk about? How did it become a war in which what men had done at Belleau Wood and Soissons and in the Argonne get blurred into an image of old soldiers dropping water bombs from hotel windows at American Legion conventions?

In the first place, it was never a war that the average doughboy wanted to talk much about afterward. Never has America fought a war that was harder on the infantryman. A division going into battle was going to stay there until it lost roughly half of its infantry strength, and for the individual rifleman, that meant that either he or the man next to him was going to get it. Even though the Second World War casualties ran far higher on the total, the percentages weren't so consistently murderous.

Some later wanted to blame the heavy casualties on bad field officers or a bad high command, but the truth was that the defense simply had an enormous edge over the offense on the Western Front and the development of planes and tanks being what it was, there wasn't a great deal anyone could do about it. What had begun as the Great Adventure turned out to be quite something else for the men who did the fighting.

Now the French and the British took far heavier casualties than we did, and yet the war never fell into quite the disrepute in France or England that it did in America. There were cynical novels about it and the Oxford peace movement in England, but in England especially they remained proud of what England had done. The difference probably lies in the peace treaty.

The Treaty of Versailles had scarcely been signed before it became a matter of doctrine in this country that it was a failure and we'd fought for nothing because Wilson was too idealistic or he'd been outfoxed by wily Europeans, or bolshevism had confused the issue—or something. It was not, in fact, a bad peace, and by comparison with many previous peaces it was a pretty good one. It was simply an old-fashioned peace at a time when the world couldn't stand one.

The Frenchman Clemenceau is usually cast as the villain of the Paris Conference. He was not a villain, but he was an old, rather simply-motivated, and very tough man. He saw his task as one of making his nation secure against a Germany that was outdistancing France in both population and industrial resources. As he saw it, the answer was a hard peace—cripple Germany by making her pay reparations, cut her army to nothing, occupy ground east of the Rhine. He must have known that he couldn't cripple Germany forever, but it was the best answer he could think of.

Wilson sat at the peace table one down. He wanted the League of Nations and Clemenceau didn't give a damn about it. To get his League, Wilson gave in to Clemenceau on the hard peace—or, rather, he acted as though the League were more important than the Treaty itself. A genius such as the English economist John Maynard Keynes might see trouble ahead in the treaty and write *The Economic Consequences of the Peace,* but no one much listened to his closely reasoned argument that in reparations lay the seed of economic disaster, not only for Germany, but for the world.

Indeed, when the Republican Congress voted America out of the very League of Nations that Wilson had given away so much to create, no vast number of Americans thought any tremendous mistake had been made. Why, then, did the country feel that it was a bad peace?

For one thing, we'd been treated to the spectacle of European nations scrabbling for their own security, and it disgusted us because it never occurred to us that our own security was involved. France and Britain knew what they'd gone to war for—security. Their methods of achieving it at the peace table might be foolish, but they knew why they were there. We still didn't realize that we had gone to war wanting something—American security—and that all the money spent and the lives spent and the Wilsonian points had simply been steps in that direction. We could afford to be high toned about other nations bickering over unlikely bits of real estate such as Fiume, because they didn't mean anything to us, and Wilson never realized that they did mean a great deal to the nations involved. The people might be wrongheaded, but to be irritable because they had a problem pretty much precluded any chance of compromising it.

It would take another war before we realized that our security was permanently in danger, that we were a world power for keeps, and that keeping the peace was a day-by-day housekeeping chore and not something to be finished off at one conference. The young lady who sang "Praise God from whom all blessings flow" in Times Square on Armistice Day was simply repeating the old heresy that God is on someone's side in a war. The Germans, after all, had gone into battle in the belief that there was *"Gott mit uns."* It was time to say good-by to diplomacy by denunciation of problems-we-wish-weren't-there, but America was not quite ready for it.

We did much to be proud of in the First World War—Americans never fought better at Bunker Hill or Gettysburg or Omaha Beach—and save for some unworthy chivvying of people with German names or socialist leanings at home—very little to be ashamed of. But we would now have to behave like a grown-up world power permanently, and it would be another twenty years before the nation as a whole stopped being angry about the responsibility and faced up to the fact that problems, as God-from-whom-all-blessings-flow would be the first to admit, are permanent.

NOTES AND ACKNOWLEDGMENTS

The New York *Times* has been used as a basic day-to-day reference throughout. All newspaper quotations are from the *Times* unless otherwise specified.

Chapter I

I am much indebted, as anyone studying this period is bound to be, to Walter Millis' splendid *The Road to War* (Boston: Houghton Mifflin, 1935). It is a model of careful research and good writing. Volume V— *Over Here*— of Mark Sullivan's *Our Times* (New York: Charles Scribner's Sons, 1933) is also an invaluable reference.

[1] This press roundup is from an excellent little book, *Decision for War, 1917*, by Samuel Spencer, Jr. Rindge, New Hampshire: Richard Smith, Publisher, 1953.

[2] From *The Life and Times of Walter Hines Page*, by Burton J. Hendrick. New York: Doubleday, Page and Co., 1925.

[3] From Cobb of *The World*, compiled by John Heaten. New York: E. P. Dutton and Co., 1924.

[4] From *Eight Years with Wilson's Cabinet*, by David F. Houston. New York: Doubleday, Page and Co., 1926.

[5] From *The Life and Times of Walter Hines Page*, *op. cit.*

[6] From *Woodrow Wilson as I Know Him*, by Joseph P. Tumulty. New York: Doubleday, Page and Co., 1921.

[7] From *The Life and Times of Walter Hines Page*, *op. cit.*

[8] From Cobb of *The World*, *op. cit.*

[9] From *The Life and Times of Walter Hines Page*, *op. cit.*

[10] From *Woodrow Wilson as I Know Him*, *op. cit.*

[11] From *The Life and Times of Walter Hines Page*, *op. cit.*

Chapter II

[1] Quoted in *Newton D. Baker*, by Frederick Palmer. New York: Dodd, Mead & Co., Inc., 1931.

[2] From *How America Went to War*, by Benedict Crowell and Robert Wilson. New Haven, Connecticut: The Yale University Press, 1921.

3 From *The Battery Book—A History of Battery "A" 306 F. A.* New York: DeVinne Press, 1921.

4 *Ibid.*

5 From *History of the Twenty-ninth Division,* by John A. Cutchin and George Scott Stewart, Jr. Philadelphia, Pennsylvania: MacCalla & Co., 1921.

6 From *The History of the 306th Field Artillery.* New York: The Knickerbocker Press, 1920.

7 *Ibid.*

8 From *The Story of the 168th Infantry,* by John Taber. Iowa City, Iowa: The State Historical Society of Iowa, 1925.

9 From *Americans All—The Rainbow at War,* by Henry J. Reilly. Columbus, Ohio: The F. J. Heer Printing Co., 1936.

10 The story of Battery C is drawn from Captain Idus McLendon's own account, *The First Shot,* published in the *American Legion Monthly* in 1931.

Chapter III

1 From *How America Went to War, op. cit.*

2 From *Our Times* by Mark Sullivan.

3 From *The Life and Times of Walter Hines Page, op. cit.*

Chapter IV

Shipley Thomas' *The History of the A.E.F.* (New York: George H. Doran Company, 1920) was of the greatest assistance in this and subsequent military chapters.

1 From *Connecticut Fights—The History of the 102nd Regiment.* New Haven, Connecticut: The Quinnipiack Press, 1930.

2 From *Americans All, op. cit.*

3 *Ibid.*

4 *Ibid.*

5 *Ibid.*

6 Quoted in *With the Help of God and a Few Marines,* by General A. W. Catlin. New York: Doubleday, Page and Co. 1919. This book contains a fine description of the action.

[7] From *The Twenty-Eighth Division,* by Edward Martin. Pittsburgh, Pennsylvania: The Twenty-eighth Division Publishing Company, 1923.

[8] From *Americans All, op. cit.*

[9] *Ibid.*

Chapter V

[1] From *The Second Division, American Expeditionary Force in France, 1917–1919.* New York: The Historical Committee, Second Division Association, 1937.

[2] From *History of the First Division during the World War, 1917–1919.* Compiled and published by the Society of the First Division. Philadelphia, Pennsylvania: John C. Winston Co., 1931.

[3] From *The Twenty-eighth Division, op. cit.*

[4] From *Americans All, op. cit.*

[5] From *The Story of the 168th Infantry, op. cit.*

[6] From *Americans All, op. cit.*

[7] *Ibid.*

[8] From *Tales of the 32nd,* by G. W. Garlock. West Salem, Wisconsin: Badger Publishing Company, 1927.

[9] From *The Story of the 168th Infantry, op. cit.*

[10] From *Tales of the 32nd, op. cit.*

[11] From *The Fourth Division,* by Christian Bach and Henry Noble Hall. N.p., 1920.

[12] *Ibid.*

[13] From *My Experiences in the World War,* by John J. Pershing. New York: Frederick Stokes Company, 1931.

[14] From *History of the 89th Division, U.S.A.,* by George H. English, Jr. Published by the War Society of the 89th Division, 1920.

[15] *Ibid.*

Chapter VI

The Victory at Sea, by Rear Admiral William Sowden Sims in collaboration with Burton J. Hendrick (New York: Doubleday, Page and Company, 1921), and *A History of the Transport Service* by Rear Admiral Albert Gleaves (New York: George Doran, 1921), have been of the utmost importance to the entire chapter.

1 From *The Life and Times of Walter Hines Page*, op. cit.

2 From *The Victory at Sea*, op. cit.

3 The material for this episode is drawn from Captain J. K. Taussig's own account, "Destroyer Experiences During the Great War," in the United States Naval Institute *Proceedings*, December, 1922. Reprinted by permission.

4 From *The Victory at Sea*, op. cit.

5 From Taussig, op. cit.

6 From *The Fighting Fleets*, by Ralph Paine. Boston: Houghton Mifflin, 1918.

7 From *A History of the Transport Service*, op. cit.

8 From *The Fighting Fleets*, op. cit.

9 From *How America Went to War*, op. cit.

10 From *A History of the Transport Service*, op. cit.

11 This material and that following is from *The Yankee Mining Squadron*, by Captain Reginald Belknap. The United States Naval Institute, 1920.

Chapter VII

Quentin Reynold's *They Fought for The Sky*, (New York: Rinehart and Company, Inc., 1958) has been invaluable background on the entire air war.

1 Quoted in *The Lafayette Flying Corps*, by James Norman Hall and Charles Nordhoff. New York: Houghton Mifflin, 1921.

2 *Ibid.*

3 *Ibid.*

4 From *The Way of the Eagle*, by Charles Biddle. New York: Charles Scribner's Sons, 1919.

5 Quoted in *The Lafayette Flying Corps*, op. cit.

6 From *The Way of the Eagle*, op. cit.

7 *Ibid.*

8 From *History of the 20th Aero Squadron*, by C. G. Barth, Winona, Minnesota, 1924.

9 From *Up and At 'Em*, by H. E. Hartney. Harrisburg, Pennsylvania: Stackpole Sons, 1940.

10 Quoted in *The Lafayette Flying Corps*, op. cit.

Chapter VIII

The material on the Heber Springs, Arkansas, incident is from the files of the Arkansas *Gazette,* Little Rock's distinguished newspaper. I am much beholden to Miss Betty Jo Bittinger, the *Gazette's* librarian, for her help in digging the material out of their clips.

Chapter IX

1 For this and subsequent material on the Thirty-fifth Division I am indebted to Clair Kenamore's *From Vauquois Hill to Exermont* (St. Louis, Missouri: Guard Publishing Company, 1919.) If Mr. Kenamore is perhaps a shade on the National Guard side as against the regulars, his book is still a professional newspaperman's well-written, straightforward account of a complex situation.

2 From *The Thirty-Seventh Division in the World War,* by Ralph D. Cole and W. C. Howells, Columbus, Ohio: The Thirty-Seventh Division Veterans Association, 1929.

3 The *History of the Seventy-Seventh Division, August, 1917–November, 1918* (New York: Seventy-Seventh Division Association, 1919) has a good account of the Lost Battalion, but for much of the color and detail in the story of that unit I have relied on a wonderfully complete account by Fletcher Pratt and Thomas Johnson—*The Lost Battalion* (Indianapolis: The Bobbs-Merrill Company, 1938).

Chapter X

There are many excellent books on the armistice negotiations, but none better than *Armistice 1918* by Harry R. Rudin (New Haven, Connecticut: Yale University Press, 1944), and I have relied on it heavily.

1 From *America's Siberian Adventure,* by William S. Graves. New York: J. Cape and H. Smith, 1931.

2 From *The Thirty-seventh Division in the World War, op. cit.*

I am vastly indebted to Mr. William Mathews, now editor and publisher of the Arizona *Daily Star,* Tucson, Arizona, and formerly with the Second Division, for long letters and personal talks clarifying the actions his outfit was involved in. Mr. H. Wickliffe Rose was good enough to discuss the Navy's war with me. Mr. Charles Cushing, formerly of the *Stars and Stripes* staff, has been most kind and helpful. Finally, my gratitude to all the divisional and regimental historians—many of them anonymous—without whose efforts, good, bad, and indifferent, this book would have been completely impossible.

INDEX